THE GIFT OF
THOMAS JOSEPH WHITE
M.D., L.H.D., F.A.C.P.
TO THE LIBRARY OF
CABRINI COLLEGE
1981

THE STORY OF LOUIS McHENRY HOWE

☆

The Man Behind

ROOSEVELT

FDR Coll.

The Man Behind

ROOSEVELT

THE STORY OF
LOUIS McHENRY HOWE

by Lela Stiles

CLEVELAND   NEW YORK

THE WORLD PUBLISHING COMPANY

Library of Congress Catalog Card Number: 54-5340

FIRST EDITION

HC 454

To my beloved mother who passed away one
month after my book was accepted for publication

Contents

Illustrations

Foreword

THIS BIOGRAPHY of Louis Howe is delightfully written and has the advantage of giving a number of stories which I am sure would never have been printed unless someone close to the work Louis did had undertaken to write it. The sidelights on the relationship between my husband and Louis and what this relationship meant to my husband's public life in the early days and in the struggles of his future life will, I think, be a valuable contribution to history. There has seldom been a story of greater devotion to another man's success but at the same time one realizes that this was not due to any lack of ambition on the part of Louis McHenry Howe. He loved power, but he also recognized realities and he decided that in the end he would exercise more power through someone else and he prided himself on the judgment he used in choosing the individual with whom and for whom he was going to work.

Lela Stiles shows discrimination and powers of observation which mark her as a real reporter. I found her book delightful reading.

ELEANOR ROOSEVELT

Introduction

IT WAS A warm, hazy day in the late summer of 1928 when I first saw Louis McHenry Howe. With a little newspaper background I had gone to New York from my native Kentucky to write a column for southern and western papers. It was called "A Girl's Eye View of New York"—the viewpoint of a country girl seeing New York for the first time. Al Smith was running for President that year and in my quest for "names" to enliven my column I secured a temporary job with the Democratic National Committee in the General Motors Building just off Columbus Circle. By some quirk of fate I was assigned to the Division of Commerce and Industry in that industrious hive. Its chief was Franklin Roosevelt.

On my first day at work I looked into an inner office and saw, seated at a huge desk, a curious-looking little man with thinning hair, enormous eyes and a face as full of furrows as a plowed field. Sleeves rolled to the elbow revealed arms thin to the point of emaciation. Now and then a hacking cough racked his frail body as he crouched over a mass of papers on his desk. Startled, I inquired who he was. "That's Louis Howe, Mr. Roosevelt's right-hand man," I was told. "He runs this place."

I had never heard of Louis Howe and that such an insignificant-looking person could be clothed with such authority was a mystery to me. My feeling about him was equaled only by his impression of me. He couldn't see me for dust. He'd probably heard that I had come in to get data for a newspaper column, hence would be of little use to "Franklin"—which was the yardstick by which he measured everybody—and he took delight in giving me such menial tasks as running out for his newspapers or sending me off on quests for cigarettes and pencils. Gritting my teeth, I'd go, consoled with the thought that this was only temporary. I even made up speeches to say to him as I left the place for good, little dreaming that this was the beginning of an association that would last for eight interesting and dramatic years.

When Louis Howe died, as Franklin Roosevelt's first term was turning toward its close, and his funeral was held in the great East Room of the White House, the newspapers of the land paid him tribute and one editorialist exclaimed, "But the man deserves a book!" I knew, by then, that he did deserve a book and was so sure that whoever wrote it would interview all those who had worked for him that I sat down at my typewriter and painstakingly wrote all the things I remembered about him. I put the data away in my trunk and waited.

The years passed. Then Franklin Roosevelt died and thousands of words poured from the presses as the books about him multiplied. Associates of his wrote books and had books written about them. But there was nothing about Louis Howe. Friends, who knew my feeling that his story should be told, urged me to write it myself. I pulled my notes from my trunk, culled my diaries and read again all the letters I had written to my mother during the period I worked for Louis, for she had saved them all. I wrote a rough outline of the book and went to see Mrs. Roosevelt at Hyde Park. She gave me a whole day of her valuable time, urged me to go ahead and promised to help me in every way she could. I told her I believed, and intended to say, that Louis Howe did more than any other man to make Franklin Roosevelt President. She replied, "You can say that with my blessing."

Other friends of Louis came forward. Bernard M. Baruch gave of his time and sage counsel. Clarence Knapp, faithful boyhood friend; Mrs. Louis McHenry Howe; Mr. Frank C. Walker, long-time associate of Louis; Miss Fannie Hurst; Dr. Frank Freidel, Roosevelt historian; Mr. Herman Kahn, Director of the Roosevelt Library at Hyde Park, and his efficient staff; and many others, were generous with advice and encouragement. Davis Geiger, a Kentucky friend, urged me on toward publication. My grateful thanks to them all.

This is a simple story of Louis Howe as he was known to those who worked for him. It does not pretend to be a historical document. There is much more that should be said. My best hope is that the book may stir an interest in Louis Howe so that someday, perhaps, one of the country's historians will dedicate himself to the task of bringing before the world the full story of "the little boss" who, behind the scenes, played such an important part in shaping the destiny of the man who four times became President of the United States.

LELA STILES

Saratoga Days

ON THE platform in Madison Square Garden, on a blistering summer day in 1924, a tall man rose slowly to his feet. His son stepped forward to support him. A hush fell over the great hall.

"Mein Gawd!" muttered a small man high in the balcony, not as an oath but as a prayer, and those who knew Louis Howe very well sometimes believed that these were the first two words he ever uttered.

Lights were dimmed except for the brilliant ones above the platform. Louis Howe's deep introspective eyes pierced through the distance to that spot—through the haze of cigarette smoke, through the fluttering newspapers used as fans, past the shadowy figures of the politicians who always swarm over a political convention. He counted something more important than his own heartbeats. He counted steps—steps from the chair to the safety of the speaker's podium. Six steps—maybe eight. Like a hair, suspending the sword of Damocles, on that distance hung a long cherished dream.

Hesitant step by hesitant step the man came forward. "Spunky damn Dutchman," Howe muttered as his taut nerves slowly relaxed. Around him burst the cheers, swelling, swelling.

A sudden new fear seized Louis Howe. Suppose the crowd was swept away, forgot Al Smith and stampeded to Franklin Roose-

3

velt before he was ready for the nomination for the Presidency. Mein Gawd indeed!

He heard the voice of FDR—that strong, magnetic voice. He heard the words that named Al Smith "The Happy Warrior" for the pages of history. And he knew his dream was secure in the subtle way that only the mind of a Louis Howe could grasp. Dreams were like good trains. They had to run on schedule.

Louis wiped his forehead. Already he was thinking far beyond today, beyond Smith, to the convention when FDR *would* be the man. The mind through which Howe's dreams ran had only a single track. And those who wanted to know more about Franklin Roosevelt—where he was going and how he would get there— were wise if they obtained the confidence of the little man who sweated it out in the balcony that shimmering summer day.

Louis McHenry Howe, the man behind Roosevelt, was born on a cold, snowy morning in Indianapolis, Indiana. The date was January 14, 1871.

If anyone had told the proud parents that Louis would grow up to be a "President maker" they would have been indignant. "President or nothing!" they would have said. The youngster himself probably would have snorted and made a wry grimace. He always did when anyone tried to pin high-sounding titles on him.

Louis was a particularly cherished child since he was born late in his parents' life. His father was Captain Edward Porter Howe, son of Laura Porter and Elbridge Haynes Howe. The Porters were early settlers in Wethersfield, Connecticut. Soon after the Revolutionary War they moved to Thetford, Vermont, where Laura's father, Hezekiah, built a large brick house, still in use as an inn. The Howes were also early settlers, coming to Sudbury, Massachusetts, in the 1690's. The Howe line remained in Sudbury for several generations, then moved to Concord, Massachusetts; to Vermont, New Hampshire, and back to Massachusetts, settling in Westfield. To the town of Thetford came young Elbridge Howe selling buggy whips made in his home town of Westfield. Elbridge met, courted and married young Laura Porter and they lived in

Westfield for many years, where Edward Porter Howe was born. From there they moved to Cincinnati, Ohio, where young Edward went through high school. His excellence in mathematics won him a gold medal, which is still in the possession of the Howe family. The family next moved to Indianapolis, Indiana, where Edward, now a grown young man, joined the 101st Indiana Volunteers in the Army of the Cumberland. He rose to the rank of Captain.

Louis' mother was Eliza Blake Ray, daughter of Maria Rebecca Coe and James Mitchell Ray. The Coes were an old Puritan family which came to America in 1634, settling in Watertown, Massachusetts. After moving to Connecticut, where they became prosperous farmers and colony officials, one branch of the family went to Long Island, settling in the town of Hempstead. This branch intermarried with other families on the Island for several generations. Isaac Coe, Louis' great grandfather, was born in Hempstead, attended the public schools, then went to Rutgers University where he studied medicine. For a time he practised medicine with his brother in Berkeley County, Virginia, and in 1822 took his wife, Rebecca Cook, descendant of Francis Cook, Mayflower passenger, and his two daughters, Maria and Alma, to Indiana where he became one of the founders of the city of Indianapolis.

James Mitchell Ray, Louis' grandfather, was born in New Jersey, the son of a Scottish immigrant. The family migrated to Indiana when he was very young. He entered politics early in life and at the age of nineteen was deputy clerk of the Circuit Court at Lawrenceville, Indiana, before Indianapolis was founded. In April 1822, when he was a little over twenty-one years of age, he was elected County Clerk of Marion County. This election was the beginning of his public career in Indianapolis, where he met and married Maria Rebecca Coe. He rose rapidly in politics and later was appointed Deputy Commissioner of Internal Revenue, a post he held for many years in Washington. Louis Howe was startlingly like his grandfather Ray in manners and appearance. There is a marble bust of James M. Ray in Indianapolis, which one observer said "looks just like Louis Howe in one of his sour moments."

Eliza Blake Ray first married Henry Sharpe and had two daughters, Alma Marie and Cora. Eliza was a widow and the daughters were grown when she married Captain Howe, who had been appointed Adjutant General of the State by the Governor of Indiana, at the war's end. His chief duty was to pay off the Indiana troops when they returned home.

The Howe home was on North Pennsylvania Street, alongside the homes of such old, respected families as the Bradshaws, the Winters, the Hammonds, the Sharpes, and the Mayos. Down on Lockerbie Street lived a young man named James Whitcomb Riley, who was just beginning to write the poems which later made him beloved by all those who like homely, sentimental verse. A little further away lived a two-year-old toddler known as Booth Tarkington. In a nearby suburb a young man of five named George Ade romped and played.

From the very first Louis Howe was a delicate child, and every morning his fond parents took him to the home of Dr. Runnels, the family physician, for a checkup. They bought him a little pony and phaeton and, as they tenderly tucked him in, the other children gathered at the windows to watch, for the little phaeton represented the last word in elegance in those days and they believed little Louis and his equipage, and his daily visits to the doctor, lent their street an air of distinction.

Nearby was a large garden, where the children gathered to play in the afternoons and Louis went with his half sister, Cora, although he could not join in many of the games because of his delicate health. But he loved the excitement and the competition and sat in his carriage, taking part on the sidelines. Louis was a rather pathetic-looking little person with his emaciated figure and big, dark eyes and often he was carried by his devoted sister, so that they seemed a sort of Florence and Paul Dombey. And like Dickens' little Paul, Louis, too, in later years at least, "had a mind a deal too large for his frame."

At all seasons Louis' solicitous parents wrapped him in heavy garments, even red flannels in the wintertime. But later, when he became a national figure and one columnist wrote that "Howe always sleeps in his underwear," he was furious.

Some of the mothers in the neighborhood were critical of the way Louis' parents fussed over him. "That child would develop faster," they worried, "if he was not so pampered and not always under the eye of some anxious older person." But the doting parents, eager to shelter this beloved only son, gave no heed to these remarks. Captain Howe, even as the elder Dombey, doted on this delicate child and dreamed of the day when Louis would grow to manhood and follow in his footsteps.

When Louis was seven years old his parents moved to Saratoga Springs, New York, where Mrs. Howe's half sister Anna now lived. Anna was married to Dr. Sylvester Strong, who ran the well-known Dr. Strong's Sanitarium, which was partly a family hotel for those who came to drink the healing waters for which Saratoga was famous. Saratoga, then, was the mecca of the fashionable people of the day. An old woodcut shows a fastidious young belle and her young gentleman "taking the waters" by drinking daintily from a glass on one of the open porches of a fashionable hotel. "Many daughters," the caption read, "were in Saratoga with mammas seeking rich husbands for them."

It was in this atmosphere that Louis Howe grew up. He heard many fascinating tales of the famous people who had come there in the past. Joseph Bonaparte, brother of Napoleon, had been in Saratoga in the 1820's. Aaron Burr had first come in 1826, and returned for six years thereafter, with his mistress, Madame Jumel, who later became his wife. Edgar Allan Poe had lingered there in the 1830's, and many claimed that he wrote the first draft of "The Raven" in a Saratoga boardinghouse. Daniel Webster, John C. Calhoun, and Presidents Tyler, Van Buren, Buchanan and Fillmore had all registered at the luxurious hotel known as The United States. Ulysses S. Grant came to the Grand Union Hotel, first as a victorious general in 1865 and again in 1869 as President.

When little Louis Howe was not haunting the hotels to listen to tales about these great of bygone days, or to watch the current celebrities come and go, he might be found curled up in a corner, in his tight knee pants and high button shoes, reading a copy of "Pater's" paper (Louis always called Captain Howe "Pater"), as the Captain had become editor of the Saratoga *Sun*, "Official Paper of the Village." The *Sun* was patterned somewhat along the lines of the London *Times*. It had only four pages, the first taken up almost entirely with advertisements, but instead of the *Times'* famous "Agony Column" the *Sun* devoted the rest of the page to more prosaic items, such as reports of the Board of Education, a few fashion notes, and now and then, a poem. The price of the *Sun* was a dollar a year. "Do you take it? If not, why not? The *Sun* goes into the homes of the people and is read by every member of the family and, there being nothing objectionable in its columns, it can be safely read by all, with no fear of offending the purest taste."

Captain Howe's editorials were always interesting but extremely varied in content and made a great impression on the youthful Louis. In one issue—that of June 28, 1883—when Louis was twelve years old, they ranged from a hotly political "The Republican Party Must Go" to a patriotic "The Nation's Birthday" and a devout, full column on "Moses and the Pentateuch." The editorial about the Republicans was devoted entirely to the "scandals" of the Grant Administration, although Grant had not been President for seven years. Chester A. Arthur occupied the White House, but he had been a strong advocate for a third term for Grant and had been rewarded with second place on the ticket with James A. Garfield, taking over the Presidency when Garfield was assassinated. To Captain Howe, a vigorous Democrat, in spite of the fact that he had served in the Union Army, Republicans were all of the same stripe.

"The scandals of Grantism did not weaken the hold of the President on the party," the editorial said. "The Treasury ring, the Navy ring, the Army ring, the Post Office ring, the Land ring, the Pension ring, the Printing ring, the Whiskey ring, the Indian ring, the Washington ring—all flourished under Grant. The jobbers, the ringsters, the adventurers and thieves who infested the White House demanded a third term for Grant. The third term conspiracy failed because the party feared a crushing defeat if the experiment was tried."

Louis Howe was always blessed with a rare sense of humor and he must have chuckled at an item at the bottom of the editorial page, a curious admixture of news and propaganda, which the Captain had copied from the Cannelton, Indiana, *Enquirer*. "By a singular coincidence," the item said, "our fellow townsman Benjamin Board sprained his knee at the same time that Queen Victoria fell downstairs. Ben used the great pain cure St. Jacobs Oil and was all right the next day. If Vic had done the same thing she would have been all right in the morning."

In this same issue Captain Howe plugged vigorously for a fellow Indiana Democrat for Vice-President in the forthcoming elections of 1884—the Honorable William S. Holman, who had served several terms in Washington in the House of Representatives and, according to the Captain, "went through all those years of corruption with a spotless record and became known as 'The Great Objector.' "

When Louis was seventeen years of age his father, who had become active in politics and had been appointed postmaster at Saratoga by Grover Cleveland, made Louis his assistant editor. His father was also the Saratoga correspondent for the old New York *Herald* and supplemented his income by operating the Saratoga *Sun* Presses, which did a lively business in printing colored labels for tomato cans, as well as the advertising labels used so widely in those days on the handles of buggy whips. The *Sun* Presses were said to be the first in the country to do "three-color jobs" on tomato cans and business was so good that Louis spent considerable time covering the territory, taking care of the tomato can and buggy whip business.

Now and then, Louis assumed his father's chores as correspondent for the New York *Herald* and, in this capacity, met and interviewed many of the famed political figures who came to the "summer capital" to be boiled out and to plan schemes that later

were to come to fruition in Albany or Washington. Richard
Croker, Roscoe Conkling, Thomas "Me Too" Platt, Senator
David Hill, Big Tim Sullivan, and Joseph H. Choate were among
those Louis Howe came to know as the smell of big-time politics
began to tickle his nostrils.

Louis' parents planned for him to attend Yale University and
he attended Yates College to prepare himself for Yale. However,
his father decided his still delicate health would prohibit him
from spending long hours indoors at books, so in 1889, when
Louis was eighteen, Captain Howe took him on a long cruise to
the West Indies with the hope that it would benefit his health,
broaden his horizon, and make up, in part, for his lack of college
training. Even then Louis had a bad heart murmur, asthma, and
frequent spells of bronchitis which sapped his strength. On this
West Indian cruise the Captain reported their progress in amusing
letters to his wife, referring to himself as "Ancient Mariner" and
to Louis as "Awful Sailor." He also wrote reports of his trips to
his own and other papers to help defray expenses. In 1893, when
Louis was twenty-two, he and his father went on a cruise to the
Mediterranean, sailing on the S. S. *Augusta Victoria,* a most
luxurious ship. When they reached the Mediterranean Captain
Howe reported that they were served ice cream which actually
had been made back in New York!

While these trips helped to broaden Louis' outlook and seemed
to improve his health temporarily, he was still as frail and pallid
as he had been as a child. He tried to conceal the fact that he was
not so strong as other young men and took part in many strenuous
games for which he was not fitted. He bicycled, played tennis, rode
horseback and was one of the most agile dancers at the Saturday
night dances at the two big hotels.

Louis was not handsome. He was slightly built with nondescript
hair and features, but he had one redeeming feature that almost
offset all his other shortcomings—his brown eyes, which were
large and expressive and really beautiful. He knew he was not
handsome and even made remarks about his own appearance, but

one day, while riding his bicycle to the wedding rehearsal of his cousin Emma Strong, he had an accident which did something to his appearance that was to plague him for the rest of his life. As he rode down an incline his bicycle, which had no brakes, began to run wild and he stuck his foot into the spokes. The pointed toe of his shoe caught and he was thrown off the wheel into the gravel and badly hurt. Small particles of gravel were ground into his skin, leaving his face marked in places with small, dark scars, somewhat on the order of those borne by the victims of smallpox.

An old copy of the Saratoga *Sun,* dated 1895—when Louis was twenty-four years old—lists at its masthead, "E. P. Howe and Son, Proprietors" and "Edward P. Howe, Louis McH. Howe, Editors." This issue of the paper confirms the fact that Louis Howe was always a Democrat. Many people, after Louis emerged into the national spotlight, expressed the belief that he had no particular political leanings and only took part in Democratic campaigns and a Democratic Administration because of his admiration for Franklin D. Roosevelt. In 1895, however, when Grover Cleveland was President for the second time, Louis and his father, in the columns of the *Sun,* were castigating the Albany *Journal* for its "unfairness" in supporting a Republican Board of Supervisors in that county in a "gerrymander" which gave the Republicans three additional members in the Assembly. They devoted a column to "The Business Boom," pointing out signs of improvement in business conditions, and another column to "Increases in Wages," listing names of firms which had increased their employees' wages in all parts of the country.

Of Louis' skill as a reporter, W. Howard Moody, managing editor of the *Saratogian,* to whom Captain Howe's paper later was sold, said: "Louis Howe was a born newspaper man, and though he was a dangerous opponent on a paper he was also a generous one and was often known to sit down and dictate facts about a story which a cub might have missed, and slip them to him to save him from the editor's wrath. Louis Howe had a creed for newspaper work which all might well follow. It was this: 'To be a successful newspaper man you don't need to know the facts yourself, but you must know where to reach a man who does know and will give them to you.' "

One of Louis' most exciting assignments came from the *Herald* when President McKinley died and Theodore Roosevelt, then Vice-President, was vacationing in upstate New York. The *Herald* hastily dispatched Louis to meet and interview this young man who was so soon to become President. Louis rode by train to North Creek where the railroad ended, then hired a buckboard to head up into the mountains to meet "Teddy," coming from Mount Marcy in a similar equipage. They met at the "Tear of the Clouds" and here, in a wild and lonely setting, Louis Howe interviewed his first Roosevelt. "Teddy," he later said, "was so upset by the death of the President and by the immensity of the task which had fallen on his young shoulders that tears were rolling down his face when I first saw his buckboard come into view."

Another interesting assignment of Louis' was making a survey of political sentiment during election years, taking his own canvass of the election results, etc. Thus, he was one of the early "poll takers" and his predictions were so accurate that they were widely quoted, gradually adding to his stature in the newspaper field.

Louis Howe always had a flair for the dramatic and he loved theatricals almost as much as his newspaper work. He never missed a performance of the theatrical troupes which came to Saratoga to perform in the outdoor courts of the two big hotels, and it was here that he saw *Midsummer Night's Dream* and the *Merry Wives of Windsor* starring such great performers as Ada Rehan, Otis Skinner and DeWolf Hopper. He saw Victor Herbert, who, with his fifty-four-piece orchestra, gave nightly concerts on the porch of the Grand Union Hotel, and he saw Edgar Montillion Woolley, later known to millions as "Monty" Woolley of stage and screen, but then known as "Little Edgar," prance out on the stage, take the baton from Victor Herbert and swing it with youthful verve as he directed the huge orchestra. "Little Edgar's" father and a partner named Gerrans had leased the Grand Union in 1892 from the A. T. Stewart heirs, and Little Edgar had the run of the hotel and its environs.

Louis was active in the local theatrical life of Saratoga, beginning as director of the high school senior plays and later producing plays at Dr. Strong's Sanitarium for the entertainment of the guests.

Miss Elizabeth Gorman, one of his co-workers, remembers that even then Louis Howe was critical of the smallest thing that fell short of what he considered perfection.

"I remember," she said, "at one rehearsal of a high school play, I was sitting beside him in the darkened auditorium when he began to mutter, 'I'll have to back him out. I'll simply have to back him out, that's all.'

"What on earth are you talking about?" she asked.

" 'The lead!' he exploded. 'Mein Gawd, look at those feet! Why did they have to give me the biggest-footed boy in the class for the most important role in the play? When you get the furniture on stage he won't be able to turn around. I'll just have to back him off.'

"Why worry about that?" Miss Gorman asked. "You are not doing Shakespeare. You are doing low comedy."

" 'That's right,' Louis chuckled, 'It *is* low comedy, and that's my solution. I'll just make an asset of those feet.' "

That was Louis Howe. When he came up against something that stymied him momentarily, he turned it over and around, and if he couldn't get rid of it he made an asset of it.

"Mein Gawd," he'd say—and this was always his favorite expression whether used in exasperation or exhilaration—"don't ever admit you're licked."

One of Louis' collaborators in these theatrical ventures was Franklin Dowd, son of Dr. Charles Dowd, originator of our system of Standard Time, who also helped Louis put on plays at Temple Grove Seminary, a finishing school for young ladies in Saratoga. Louis coached and directed the plays in which the young ladies acted, and he and Franklin Dowd also wrote a play of their own, *The Madrigal,* which was repeated many times. Then Louis formed a sort of theatrical partnership with Clarence Knapp, later Mayor of Saratoga, and their plays delighted Saratoga audiences for years. *Pink Dominoes, Kleptomania,* Pinero's *The Magistrate,* and *Four-in-Hand* were some of their productions. *Pink Dominoes* was considered quite naughty and some of the strait-laced in the town uttered cries of dismay because the boys put on this production. This amused Louis Howe who always delighted in shocking a certain musty type of mind, and he only grinned when these pious wails reached his ears. "Such silly people give me a pain in the neck," he said, "and besides—you watch. I'll bet you my last dollar they all come to see the play, anyway." Most of them did.

Comedy was Louis' forte, and dramatic effects his specialty. In one of his productions he dressed himself as a prince of Siam and rode grandly across the stage in a chariot drawn by two billy goats!

In every production Louis directed, acted and even built the sets. An interior set which he built was used in amateur productions in Saratoga for the next fifteen years. "It was a common sight in those days," said Clarence Knapp, "to see Louis Howe sitting astride a 'jog' or 'flat' painting a set, cutting out paper flowers or even designing costumes, and his innovations in lighting and staging were so unique that they even surpassed those in the New York theaters of the day."

Louis' co-workers had the greatest admiration for his talents and took their cues from him without question.

"I always felt as if I'd been decorated," said Elizabeth Gorman, "when Louis patted me on the back and said 'Good work.' "

Strangely, considering his later career, the first play in which Louis Howe himself starred in Saratoga was called *The Private Secretary.*

Louis also liked to sing and had a fair tenor voice. He sang in the Bethesda Episcopal Choir in Saratoga and also in the choir of the Second Presbyterian Church. Out of this Bethesda association grew a little singing group that met twice a week for several years. After rehearsals for these songfests the group would adjourn to the old Worden Café, then presided over by the popular and beloved John Bennett, a leader in the Masonic fraternity and, in one of the little stalls along the Broadway side of the café, they discussed over mugs of coffee and ale the theater, art and the ever-absorbing topic, politics of the day.

Louis was quite a beau in those days. In spite of his lack of good looks, his engaging manner and a puckish sense of humor made him very popular with the younger set. He was even described as a "gay blade" by one of his contemporaries. He often led the "germans" at the Saturday night dances at the two big hotels, and was the first to date new belles who came with their mammas to Dr. Strong's to "take the waters." Bridge was just coming into popular favor then and Louis gave lessons for pay to the wealthy ladies at the hotels.

Louis played the field as far as the girls were concerned until the summer of 1896, when he was twenty-five years old. It was then that Miss Grace Hartley of Fall River, Massachusetts, came to Dr. Strong's with her mother. Grace's father was Dr. James W. Hartley, born in Darwin, England, who came to America when he was nineteen and married Mary Jane Borden of Massachusetts. Grace was one of four children.

Young Grace Hartley, a Vassar student, had no need to "take the waters" for she was the picture of health and good looks, but her mother brought her along, partly for company and partly to get her away from a young gentleman from Ireland who had come to this country on business and had lingered to court Grace. Mrs. Hartley did not relish the thought of her daughter moving to a distant land and was trying, in discreet ways, to break up the romance.

When Louis Howe heard of this new, good-looking girl at Dr. Strong's he lost no time in meeting her. Miss Hartley, according to her own statement, "was not a bit impressed with Louis Howe at that first meeting." But soon they were seeing each other more frequently, were whirling around the floor at the Grand Union on Saturday nights, or walking along the tree-shaded streets of the town, deep in earnest conversation. Mrs. Hartley was not displeased, since this new interest was taking her daughter's mind off the absent Irishman. What she didn't know was that, while her daughter had not been impressed at that first meeting, Louis Howe certainly was laying serious siege to the young woman's heart. When Grace returned to Fall River in the autumn bulky letters came from Saratoga regularly, and by the next summer when Grace and her mother returned to Saratoga, the young man from Ireland had receded into the background. Louis continued his ardent courtship all through the summer, began to make trips to Fall River when Miss Hartley returned, and, by the fall of 1898, when Grace came back to Saratoga to visit friends, they were engaged. The Spanish-American War had started and Louis was trying to get an assignment to go to the Philippines as a war correspondent. On the evening of November 9 Grace went home to Fall River. Louis asked if he might ride part of the way with her and on the train began the first big campaign of his life. They were in love, engaged, were planning to be married the following spring, but he might be snatched to far-off lands at any moment. Why not get married right now? "Right now?" said the astonished young woman. "I don't understand." The ardent young man had this all planned. Soon they would reach North Adams, Massachusetts, which was a junction. He knew of a little village across the Vermont line, only a short ride from the junction, where there was a justice of the peace. Almost before Grace Hartley knew what she was doing she was being hustled off the train and across the Vermont line. The marriage vows were said in a sleepy little village by a justice of the peace as oil lamps sputtered on the table, and two witnesses, hastily summoned by the justice, affixed their signatures to the wedding document. Louis also knew of an attractive old inn in the village where they served marvelous food, and there they had a pheasant dinner by candlelight, before the young bride took a later train to Fall River, leaving the groom the lonely ride back to Saratoga. November 9 was also the bride's birthday and ever afterward, on this birthday-wedding anniversary, Louis insisted on a pheasant dinner with all the trimmings in celebration of the double event.

"I had a hard time explaining to my mother why I was so late getting home that night," Mrs. Howe says, with a smile, recalling those days. "We did not tell her or anybody else we were married. I think she found it out though, maybe by reading one of Louis' letters. However, she gave no sign, so I was never sure."

There was good reason for Mrs. Hartley to give no sign. She had planned a big church wedding for this only daughter, born rather late in her parents' lives (the youngest of her three brothers was fifteen years old when she was born). This premature wedding might have upset Mrs. Hartley's plans if she had let Grace know she was in on the secret. As it was, she went ahead with plans for the ceremony, and on May 6, Louis Howe, who had missed out on his assignment to the Philippines, came to Fall River to take part in a big wedding, with the bride in white satin and six lovely bridesmaids. After a brief honeymoon they returned to Saratoga where Louis settled down with his wife in a home which Mrs. Hartley, now a widow, generously gave them as a wedding present.

On the fourth day of June the following year one of the grand events of Louis Howe's life took place. Mrs. Howe, who had gone to Fall River to await this event, notified him that on that day a little daughter, Mary Howe, had been born, and a shower of cigars fell on Louis' surprised newspaper, theatrical and singing cronies.

There was just one flaw in the young couple's happiness. Louis' health, which had always worried his mother and father, now became the deep concern of his wife. He kept doggedly on with his work at the *Sun,* however, and as correspondent for the New York *Herald,* a job he had taken over completely from a father in failing health. Louis was also supplementing his income by various free-lance enterprises, and in April 1901, he won the prize offered by the *Journal Saturday Review* for the best short book review.

"Thousands upon thousands of reviews poured in from all parts of the country," the *Review* reported, "and the task of reading them all was Herculean." Louis Howe's review was finally judged the best of the lot, and while the prize was only twenty dollars, the prestige of winning against such competition gave him immense satisfaction.

"The first edition of 'The Helmet of Navarre,' " Louis said in his review, "is 100,000 copies. Let that fact silence the pessimistic cry that the spirit of chivalry is dead! Still deep in the dullest hearts lurks the buccaneer's love for the ripple beneath the keel and the taut rigging's hum. Still through the coldest veins runs the warm blood that leaps at the crash of steel on a stricken field.

"Only we may no longer don armor and away through mysterious woods where dreadful dragons and distressed damsels await our sword. For is not every forest path, even in the uttermost parts of the earth, neatly marked down in various colored inks that he who wheels may read?

"Yet may the old lust for danger be somewhat slaked, as beside the evening lamp we follow the virile author's soul out of the printed page, beyond the narrow study walls, through the magic land of Nowhere to see great deeds that might have been. This is the charm of 'The Helmet of Navarre.'

"Crude it may be, improbable it must be, for the probable is always uninteresting and the people we know invariably dull. But we have wept over Mary Wilkins' homely death beds, have taken 'Robert Elsmere' as a literary cod liver oil for our moral systems, and now we would be knights-errant and breathe the fresh air once more!

"Therefore will the hundred thousand copies go, and more to follow. The book will not live forever; with Weyman's and Hope's, the dust will gather on its covers. Yet will our lives be a little brighter, yea, our aims a little nobler, even for the brief journey from the dull, sordid, money-making of today."

When little Mary Howe was about a year old, Mrs. Howe persuaded Louis to go with her on a cruise to the West Indies. Louis could not afford the cruise, so he went to his papers and also to the McClure syndicate with a suggested list of articles he wanted to write.

The assignment was arranged and he wrote illuminating stories on such items as "Strangest Shipyard in the World—How the Dutch Colonists of Saba build boats in the crater of a volcano and lower them three hundred feet to the sea"; "Pirates of the Spanish Main—Among the smugglers' caves of St. Eustatius linger the last descendants of the famous Buccaneers"; and "An Interview with the High Priestess of the Voodoo Worshippers—On the Island of St. Vincent lived the head of the most horrible religion in the world. Votaries will kill with the scratch of a poison fingernail."

Louis' name was becoming well known in the newspaper and political circles of the state, as his astute and timely observations left their impression on the readers of the day. He was now spending several weeks of the year in New York City in his work on the *Herald,* and in December 1905 became an active member of the New York Pen Club. Ill health and the infirmities of age had forced Captain Howe to give up the Saratoga *Sun,* which was later merged with the *Saratogian.* In the winter of 1907 the New York *Herald* made Louis the Albany correspondent for its evening counterpart, the New York *Telegram.* As "second-string man" for the *Herald* in Albany he would continue to send special dispatches to that paper, also.

Louis and Grace rented an apartment in Albany for the legislative session in one of the old "brownstone fronts," and it was here, in the state capital, that the political training Louis had acquired in the "summer capital" at Saratoga, was to serve him well. It was here, too, that for the first time his path crossed that of Franklin Roosevelt—a meeting that was to point the stars of destiny for both.

[2]

Meeting FDR

W HEN Louis Howe arrived in Albany to cover the Legislature, Charles Evans Hughes, the newly elected Governor, was making his dramatic fight to wrest the public service corporations of the state from the grasp of private interests. The political machines and big corporations had gained such a tight hold on the state's service and regulatory bodies, that newspapermen met regularly and cynically to estimate how many senators were controlled by each of the big corporations.

"There are six grand divisions in Albany to fight the Governor's reforms," Louis wrote to his paper, "the Standard Oil Interests, the Pulp and Water Power Companies, the Railroads, the Insurance Companies, the Gas Companies, and the New York Traction Interests." Then with keen reportorial acumen he gave the number of senators controlled by each division and called them by name!

"No legislative correspondent in forecasting the vote on a measure of public interest asks 'How will this Senator vote?'" he wrote, "but how does Senator so and so's boss stand on the matter? To find this out he then ascertains how the particular group of corporations, which in turn control the boss, regard the measure. Then he knows.

"Nothing so amuses the experienced corporation lobbyist," he said, "as to see a well meaning but inexperienced citizen, anxious for the fate of some reform bill, pore over the roll call of the upper

20

house and gravely speculate upon what this or that Senator thinks about it; for the lobbyist knows that the Senators, with the exception of possibly a dozen 'free-lances,' are the male chessmen of the great financial interests that move them at will upon the board in the game of legislation.

"Across the table sits the public moving aimlessly and often wrongly under the confusing counsels of inexperienced reformers who seldom have agreed upon a united course of action. Is it any wonder that in the long run the corporations cry 'checkmate' and the senatorial pawns are put away for another year's game?"

A bitter battle developed as Governor Hughes, determined to end the evil, took his fight to the people of the state. They rallied to his call, and after long weeks of intensive struggle, the fight was won. No one was more pleased than Louis Howe, and although he had not met him, he was seeing eye to eye with young Franklin Roosevelt, who also admired the Hughes' campaign pledge of reform so much that he had even voted for him.

"How come," Louis Howe asked, "that the corporations have this year met defeat? The answer is plain. It is because the public has this year placed the direction of the game in the hands of one man, Charles Evans Hughes."

Merlo J. Pusey, in his biography of Hughes, named Louis Howe as one of the "keen observers of public affairs" who became enthusiastic exponents of the Hughes policies. "Many people at the time," Pusey said, "believed that the brilliant Frank H. Simonds of the New York *Evening Post,* because of his 'facile stories about the new regime,' was closer to Hughes than any other newspaperman in Albany, but actually he was no more intimate with the Governor than were Louis Howe, John Palmer Gavit, Louis Seibold, and several others."[1]

Many of Louis' contemporaries acknowledged him as an outstanding member of their craft and admired him, sometimes grudgingly, for his ability to scent a story and to dig until he had uncovered every minute facet of the case.

[1] Merlo J. Pusey, *Charles Evans Hughes* (New York: The Macmillan Company, 1951).

"Louis Howe was the bane of every newspaperman in Albany," said Edward R. Anker, who was with the Associated Press at the State Capitol at the time. "He could smell a story a mile off and he kept us all digging to keep up with him. He never slept. He spent hours on hours in the musty old basement at the Capitol, going through old records for background material for practically every story he wrote. His news sense was terrific. One reporter, irritated by this thoroughness of Louis' and his habit of spending so much time in the basement among the old records, dubbed him 'the water rat' of the Capitol Building and the name stuck as long as he was in Albany."

Mrs. Howe readily would have agreed with Mr. Anker's estimate of the amount of time Louis spent chasing a story. She speaks of those days and even of their honeymoon days in Saratoga as full of "constant doorbell ringings" by telegraph boys with messages from the paper to run down this or that story. "Why look for him here?" she would ask. "You should know better. He is downtown, at the Capitol, at the Press Club, anywhere else but home for there are no stories here. Go and look for him somewhere else."

Occasionally the *Telegram* would snatch Louis off the Albany beat to chase a story elsewhere. In July 1908 they sent him to Troy to cover a murder case. Apparently he applied his Albany methods there, running down clues, getting background, etc., but this was not fast enough for his paper, which was being scooped by the other New York dailies. "Send something new for each edition," the paper wired him. "This is *not* a political convention."

Louis loved to read murder stories, but covering them was not his specialty and he was glad when the paper finally realized this and let him stick to the political beat.

Louis had a free hand when the legislature was not in session, however, and his paper let him take on other assignments. The Commission of the State Reservation at Saratoga Springs was created by an act of the Legislature in 1909 for the purpose of restoring and perpetually preserving the Saratoga mineral springs and wells "on or under lands of the Reservation of the State of New York." The first chairman of the Commission was Mr. Spencer Trask, who lived on a large estate known as "Yaddo," and who was greatly interested in Saratoga as a health center. He also was keenly interested in Louis Howe as a reporter and writer and suggested him as the one to go to Europe to make a study of the methods of foreign governments and municipalities in the operation and control of their mineral water springs. So in January 1910, Louis, with Mrs. Howe, sailed for Europe to visit the best known cures in England, France and Germany—Harrogate, Aix-les-Bains, Vichy, Nauheim, and Carlsbad. Louis made his preliminary reports in the form of letters from the various spas and they proved to be so interesting that they were printed in full in the Saratoga *Sun.*

In Louis' final survey, upon his return, he emphasized that mineral water springs were universally recognized by the governments in Europe as natural resources of great importance from a standpoint of health to the public and as a material source of revenue to the state. His comprehensive report was highly commended by the members of the Commission, and less than three years after his trip the State of New York took over one hundred and sixty-three mineral springs at Saratoga, with a large acreage for bathhouses, drink halls, and recreation centers.

After Louis' return from the strenuous trip to Europe he suffered an almost complete physical breakdown, and one doctor who attended him told him that his heart was so bad he probably would not live more than six months. He rejected this theory vigorously and so did Mrs. Howe, who set off at once for Massachusetts to find a place where Louis could have complete rest and quiet for the summer. She found an isolated cottage near Westport Point on "Horseneck" Beach, and rented it for the season. Here Louis rested, slept, sunned, lost his pallor and gained some weight. Though 1910 was an election year, he did not attempt to write his *Herald* canvasses that fall: he was saving his strength for the more strenuous duties of the winter covering the 1911 session of the legislature.

When the session opened he and Mrs. Howe again went to Albany and rented an apartment for themselves and Mary, now ten years old. When people asked why they didn't have another child to keep the little girl company Louis would always beam, "Why have another child when Mary Howe is so perfect? We could never repeat that performance!"

Louis was now forty years old. He was still not lovely to look at with the exception of his fine and luminous eyes. His hair had thinned, his face was lined, not so much from the years as from the suffering, which was his almost constant companion. The way he dressed added little to his appearance, for his suits, though bought from excellent tailors, immediately took on the appearance of gunny sacks after he had worn them twice. He was a chain smoker and never smoked any brand but Sweet Caporals. The ashes of these Sweet Caps adorned every suit he wore like a trademark.

His hats were nondescript and he wore an atrocious type of high collar that looked as if it might swallow his head at any moment. These collars later became the subject of good-natured teasing when he entered the national spotlight. "Why do you wear such an old-fashioned collar?" people would ask.

His reply was always the same.

"Because," he said, "God gave me the neck of a swan, and a swan's neck is beautiful—but only on a swan!"

Louis liked his job but at times it seemed dull unless enlivened by such dramatic episodes as the Hughes fight in the legislature against the corporations. If the legislators were Democrats from New York City they took orders from Tammany Hall; if they were upstate Democrats, most of them also took orders from Tammany Hall. The Republicans almost controlled the state outside of New York City, and Louis didn't expect much of them at any time with the exception of a rebel like Hughes. So he took immediate notice when he heard that Dutchess County, always Republican, was sending a Democrat named Roosevelt to the Senate this session. "But that's Lou Payne's bailiwick," Louis Howe said,

Louis Howe
at the age of eight.

Howe and his daughter Mary
when she was one year old.

Howe and his son Hartley at
Horseneck Beach, Mass.

NEW YORK STATE WILSON CONFERENCE
31 NASSAU STREET
NEW YORK

HON. FRANKLIN D. ROOSEVELT
Chairman Executive Committee

LAWRENCE B. DUNHAM
Secretary

ROOM 1409
Telephone Connection

Beloved and Revered Future President:
This is a line to remind you that you
have a date with me to go in swimming. Also that your young hopefuls (I
rather like that spelling and am going to let it stand) have a date to come
down and dig in the sand. My wife writes me that the miserable shack we
had to take this year is "horrid" and that she expects to live on the piazza
There is,however, I am informed a stove that is adequate to the occassion
and I will have you understand that I am some cook I trust therefore that
"en route" You and yours will moter down early in the morning to
Westport Point NOT Westport Harbor, and spend the day,Bring bathing suits
for the grown ups and sand pails for the kids . Please punctuate this to
suit yourself. There is a man at my ear telling me the story of his life
and why he is for Wilson- I am glad he is for Wilson,but must confess that
Idoubt if Wilson would be for him.
When you reach Westport Point ask at either of the two stores where the
Howe's live down on Horse neck It is only half a mile straigt ahead- Dont
try to get down on to the beach in the car. They get rich down there
pulling out cars from the sand. You can go,however down to where the
road leads straight to the water, about three hundred feet from the surf,
Stop by the barn and foot it the rest of the way, You turn to the right
and keep right on walking until you getthere
You will note that I have not mentioned particularly that I hope
your better half will come along, This is not an oversight,but I fear that
in adding this to my invitation I may make the invitation to her so warm
and cordial as to arouse the green eyed monster in your breast. I will
therefor hide my real feelings behind the "safe and Sane" statement that
Mrs Howe Hopes to see Mrs Roosevelt at the same time.
You might telegraph me the day before you are coming, addressing
the wire to L.Howe Horseneck Beach, Westport Point, Mass. The telegraph
station being Westport point. Or you can telephone to the post office and
Store at Westport point and they will send a boy out with the message.
Every time I duck under the cool water this week I will think of
you at Baltimore and regret(?) that I am not along.
Yours,

Howe

Courtesy Director Franklin D. Roosevelt Library, Hyde Park

A letter written in 1912 to Franklin D. Roosevelt.

disbelievingly. Lou Payne was the chief lieutenant of the Honorable Thomas C. Platt, master of the Republican party not only in
Dutchess County but in the whole state of New York. This particular district was so hopelessly Republican that the Democratic
nomination within it became a "mere friendly compliment for a
nice young man." But who thought the young man would win?
"A perfectly hopeless fight," Louis said in wonder. "Yet Roosevelt
won it." Louis pondered that name, Roosevelt, a long time. A
great name. Louis, though a Democrat, had always admired
Teddy. But this new Roosevelt—he shook his head. Must have
been elected by some kind of fluke. Only son of rich parents. Educated at Groton and Harvard. "Spoiled silk-pants sort of guy,"
was the way Louis had him ticketed, in spite of a grudging admiration for anyone who could outwit Lou Payne.

Louis was scratching idly away on his copy paper on the opening day of the session, waiting for the clerk to call the roll, when
he heard a rustle go through the Senate chamber. He peered down
the rows of seats. Striding down the aisle, head back, glasses
agleam on his patrician nose, came Franklin Roosevelt. He flashed
a grin as his eyes swept the room, and lifted to the press gallery,
before he dropped into the big leather chair behind the desk
marked "26," which was the seat always occupied by the Senator
from Dutchess County. Louis Howe rubbed his chin. The young
blood had spirit. Personality, too. He decided to watch.

Young Roosevelt had the old-timers in the legislative halls
shaking their heads, too. They couldn't type him. How could a
fellow named Roosevelt be a Democrat? He further confounded
them by his openly expressed admiration for his distant cousin,
Theodore Roosevelt, Republican President of the United States,
who had given his niece, Anna Eleanor, in marriage to Franklin
D. on St. Patrick's Day just six years before. Teddy, a Republican;
Franklin, a Democrat. They didn't understand it.

Big Tim Sullivan, a Tammany stalwart from New York City,
when he read Roosevelt's name on the list of newly elected legislators, must have been seized with prophetic powers, for he ex-

claimed: "If we've caught a Roosevelt we'd better take him down and drop him off the dock right now."

This premonition of Sullivan's foretold trouble for the regulars and that trouble was not long in coming.

Events went smoothly enough, however, until Tammany Hall put forward its candidate for the United States Senate. In those days, before United States Senators were elected by direct vote of the people, they were elected by the legislatures of the various states. Tammany's candidate was William F. Sheehan, who had been a Democratic leader in Buffalo, Democratic National Committeeman from New York, practising lawyer in New York City, and was known as the political agent of the utility companies and other powerful corporations. Little, if any, opposition was expected from the Democrats, for when Charles F. Murphy, powerful Tammany boss, cracked the whip they climbed on the bandwagon.

Louis Howe looked on with a resigned and weary air. He had seen it so often. He and everyone else knew that a Democrat with the nerve to oppose Tammany would be committing political suicide. That's why he could hardly believe his keen, reportorial nose when he sniffed the first scent of revolt from the young man from Dutchess, who had decided that Sheehan—dubbed "Blue-eyed Billy" because of his bland blue eyes—wouldn't do. Franklin Roosevelt had nothing against Sheehan personally. He simply thought that a man with all those public connections should not be placed in a position where he might be tempted to use his power for private instead of public good.

Wild rumors flew around the halls that Roosevelt, with twenty other "young Turks," would refuse to attend the caucus on Sheehan and that he and his group would issue a statement of their own. Louis, who would not have hesitated to steal the statement if he could have gotten his hands on it in advance, fumed because there was no leak from this secret meeting. He was the first to grab a copy of their manifesto, and to retire to a corner to gloat as he read:

"The votes of those who represent the people should not be

smothered in caucus; the people should know just how their representatives vote, untrammeled by any caucus action; and any majority secured for any candidate should be credited to the representatives in the Legislature and not someone outside the body," and so on.

This was mutiny! Louis Howe took another long look at this youngster who was challenging the Tammany tiger. He knew this crafty animal's power so well, had watched its claws curl cruelly about its victims. He shook his head incredulously. Could this young aristocrat really do anything about it? He didn't know but a strange and heady excitement stirred within him. "Mein Gawd! The boy's got courage!" he muttered into his high, priest-like collar.

When the Sheehan fight entered its second day Louis took his first note in print of the "silk-pants" member from Dutchess although, in that first story, he did not call him by name.

"Twenty-one men," he said, "so little reckoned within politics that their very names, until yesterday, were practically unknown outside the limits of their home districts, these men successfully defying the weight of Tammany Hall, blocking the progress of one of the most carefully planned political moves in recent years, standing unterrified by threats and unmoved by the most cunning politicians, such is the amazing feature of the struggle at Albany today. All night and again today every known form of coercion and persuasion has been used to win these twenty-one novices over to the Sheehan camp in vain.

"It is impossible to talk to one of them without feeling that they are terribly in earnest, that they have conceived something of the spirit of the old martyrs and are convinced that they must stand firm, even though the heavens fall. Led by a 'new Senator' without experience in the game, who looks like a boy, they have proved an ability to meet cunning with determination rarely shown by older men. Never in the history of Albany have twenty-one men threatened such total ruin of machine plans. It is the most humanly interesting political fight of many years."

As the days passed and the fight grew hotter, Louis reported that Tammany was having the insurgents "shadowed" and that reprisals were being practised on them in every conceivable form. One member, whose home was mortgaged for $10,000, found the mortgage suddenly foreclosed by the banker who had asked him to join the Murphy ranks, but who had been met with a firm refusal.

A clerk of one of the senate committees, whose brother was an insurgent Assemblyman, suddenly found himself without a job. Roosevelt himself, who was head of one of the senate committees, had his own clerk jerked from him and, when he sprang to his feet and demanded the man's reinstatement, he was sneeringly told that there was no way to get a clerk reinstated "who had not satisfactorily performed the duties of his office."

As the days raced into weeks, with no end to the struggle, tempers grew so short that one hardly dared mention the Sheehan fight unless he wanted to get into one himself. One visitor from New York, wandering around the halls, asked in all innocence, "For pity's sake, when are you all going to end this deadlock up here?" He was surprised to find himself picked up bodily by the seat of his pants and thrown violently down the Capitol steps.

"Well," said Franklin Roosevelt, "if the Sheehan people want to make it a long session we can accommodate them. The responsibility for the deadlock rests squarely on them and nothing they can say or do can shift it to us."

"And," said Louis Howe, who was enjoying the whole show to the hilt, "all the per diem clerks and attendants are going around with cheerful faces and asking if it is pleasant in Albany in July!"

Louis' paper ran a three-column cartoon on its front page, in which the Capitol building was pictured with a huge Tiger hovering over it, its paws holding the doors of the building closed. The caption read: "The Deadlock. This is costing the taxpayers $2,500 per day!"

Murphy admitted that pressure was being brought on him from Democrats all over the United States to end the deadlock, in the interest of party harmony, but he said defiantly, "Mr. Sheehan is the candidate of the majority and *must* be elected."

"Right in the middle of the battle," Louis said, "one of the insurgents who lived in an upstate county went home for the week-end and when he picked up the papers on Sunday he blanched with horror at the front-page streamer headline, 'Eight insurgents killed.' He was wondering whether to flee the country until the whole thing blew over when he noticed that the dateline was a town in Mexico where a revolution was taking place!"

Louis told gleefully of a trick pulled on the handsome young insurgent from Dutchess County, which eased the tension for a few hours, at least. For some years it had been the unwritten rule of the Senate that the senator who occupied the seat on the extreme right of the speaker's rostrum had to furnish a red carnation, every morning during the session, to each senator in the back row of seats on that side of the chamber. Just how this custom originated was unknown, but the name "carnation row" had become firmly fixed in that section of the Senate, and Senator Roosevelt, who occupied the seat of honor for the session, faithfully brought in red carnations for his colleagues every morning.

Albany was full of women suffragettes in those days, and their bill to give women the vote was to have a hearing on a certain Wednesday. It was then that an envious senator, who sat outside the favored "carnation row," saw a chance to make trouble. When the "votes for women" contingent arrived on the scene he was observed whispering to them, and pointing to the red flower in Senator Roosevelt's buttonhole.

Later, Roosevelt and Senator Wainwright, who also wore the badge of "carnation row," strolled over to the Assembly side, which by this time was filled with "votes for women" ladies, waiting for the hearings to begin. Both Roosevelt and Wainwright were handsome men and usually managed to catch the ladies' eyes wherever they went. This time, however, the women looked coldly through them, or past them. Much mystified, the two joined another group of ladies but their attempts to start a conversation came to nothing. Each group as they approached melted away from them with glances of scorn until at last one woman launched, from force of habit, into an argument for her cause. Suddenly, however, she stopped and turned haughtily away.

"But I forgot," she said. "Of course it is no use to talk to either of you as you choose to show your dislike of our work so plainly."

Senator Roosevelt asked her what on earth she was talking about.

"Why," she said, "Senator ———— told us this morning that you had formed a horrid club of some kind with the motto, 'Woman's place is at the fireside, not the polls,' and that all members wore red carnations to show that they had signed a solemn pledge never to give women the vote."

"And in spite of all their protestations," Louis reported, "the victims of the joke were unable to set themselves straight, although they labored to that end all the rest of the afternoon."

Finally, as the repercussions of the Sheehan fight jarred the city rooms in New York, Louis' editor told him to interview this young hellcat Roosevelt and see what made him that way. Louis accepted the assignment eagerly and made an engagement for the next evening to see Roosevelt at his home. As Louis Howe walked along the quiet Albany streets his pulses stirred and some strange awareness stole over him as the twinkling lights of the Roosevelt home came into view. A servant met him at the door and took his hat, leaving him alone in the large, old-fashioned library in the rather elegantly furnished home which the young Roosevelts had rented for the session. As Louis' keen eyes roamed around the room his attention was suddenly caught by a coat of arms over the fireplace, with a hand holding firmly to an impressive-looking club. Louis grinned. "Teddy's big stick," he thought. "If this young man keeps on the way he's going, he'll be using one, too, whamming tiger heads."

As Louis heard quick footsteps coming along the corridor he rose, stood still and listened. In a moment, Franklin Roosevelt, his step so buoyant that he almost seemed to spring into the room, was there holding out his hands in welcome to Louis Howe. Louis

looked at him a long moment, measuring him. Then to open the
conversation, he pointed to the coat of arms, remarking that it
seemed appropriate that FDR have a club handy just in case.
Franklin Roosevelt immediately grew serious. He strode up and
down the room as he began to talk of the struggle for power waged
by Tammany Hall, and of the unalterable determination of the
insurgents to see the battle through. He struck his clenched fist
into his hand as he emphasized his points, his young face grim
with determination.

"Nothing will change us, nothing," he said as the firelight
played across his finely chiseled features. "We will stand against
him, and we will not falter. We have the votes to defeat him with
no matter what they say. Oh, I know they say we are doing this
to attract attention, that we want to get our names on the front
pages of the papers. How little they know us! We are doing it as
a matter of party principle, solely. They speak of getting some of
our men to desert the cause. They have ways of trying to bring
this about—I know that. But we have no deserters from our ranks
and we will have none. If the election of Sheehan depends upon
the breaking up of our lines he will never be elected! Never!"

Louis Howe sat in a huge armchair that almost engulfed his
slight form as Roosevelt talked, taking in every detail of the
scene—the handsome, striding figure, the flickering firelight, the
coat of arms. His senses stirred with a mounting admiration, and
he scarcely moved as the rich voice went on.

"Oh, I know," Roosevelt said, as he shrugged his shoulders in
an impatient gesture, "we are reading ourselves out of the party.
They say so. What party? The Tammany party? We are Democrats. We believe in this fight with all our hearts and souls. They
say the only way we can get back is to surrender. We certainly do
not share *that* view, I can tell you that. If we went back, then
what? They would simply take us over their knees and spank us
and keep on spanking us. Are we children?" Suddenly his face
broke into a smile. "Well, that's that," he said. "You can tell your
paper that we are in this fight to a finish and we are in it to win!"

Louis told his paper all this and more. One thing he did not tell, but filed it away in his heart, and many years passed before he revealed his own personal feelings on that momentous night.

"I was so impressed with Franklin Roosevelt," he said, "his seriousness, his earnestness, his firm dedication to his cause, that from that moment we became friends—and almost at that very first meeting I made up my mind that he was Presidential timber and that nothing but an accident could keep him from becoming President of the United States."

Here, in Louis Howe's own words, is the answer to that oft repeated question, "When did Louis Howe first decide that Franklin Roosevelt would someday be President?"

Mrs. Howe is one who could have answered it then, if anyone had asked her, for on the Sunday following the interview, as she and Louis were about to enter church in Albany he suddenly gripped her arm. "See that tall young fellow in front of us?" he asked. "That's Franklin D. Roosevelt. Some day that young man will be President of the United States. You wait and see!"

So, from that first meeting the historic friendship grew, and from that moment on there was no greater advocate of the cause of Franklin Roosevelt than Louis Howe. He had espoused the cause for which Roosevelt was fighting; now he was espousing the fighter himself. He became one of the young insurgent's advisers, conferred with him and his little band of rebels, and sat in on many of their councils, in the room where he had listened to the Roosevelt declaration of independence, the room where the symbolic hand held aloft the symbolic, insurgent club.

The Sheehan fight raged on until finally the situation grew so tense that Roosevelt and his crowd had to hold their meetings in secret places.

"If that nice, innocent young man," raged old Tim Sullivan who had wanted to drop the young man off the dock and now wished he had, "is trying to make us a minority party, that is exactly what that nice, innocent young man is going to do if he is not careful."

But to all this young Roosevelt just grinned, and the more they slammed him the harder he fought. "The donkey's got his ears back," said Louis Howe in gleeful admiration.

The fledgling first-term Senator now had the mighty Tiger backed against the wall and its jaws were beginning to drip the blood of defeat. Here was something! Newspaper dispatches rustled between Albany and New York City like blown leaves in a gale. The battle raged for eleven long weeks and might have gone on longer if a fire hadn't broken out in the Capitol building. "The fight was so hot it set the whole damned building ablaze," Louis said. The place was gutted, slime dripped from the walls, black, bilgy-looking water was everywhere. The members had to meet in makeshift rooms and gradually their ardor began to fade. The party leaders had reached the point where everything in Albany made them mad—especially Franklin D. Roosevelt. They decided to get out. But the insurgents had sworn not to leave Albany until Tammany gave up Sheehan, and the Tammanyites finally collapsed. They named another man.

Their compromise candidate was James A. O'Gorman, but if any member of the Tammany crowd was happy about the outcome he was hard to find as they trooped from Albany with muttered threats of revenge.

"A new Senator in Albany is of importance somewhere between that of a janitor and a committee clerk," Louis chortled, summing up the fight, "yet this perfectly impossible young man, objecting to the Tammany choice for a United States Senator, proceeded to gather 'round him a group of minor and unknown legislators from both houses sufficient to block Tammany's choice. This absurd and quixotic performance, mind you, was against Tammany, the absolute master of the Democratic party in the entire state; no upstate leader of any consequence would dare disregard an order to come down to New York and see the Chief and hat in hand stand humbly at the Wigwam door and get explicit instructions as to what he is to do about this or that. It was obvious that this was a hopeless proposition. By no possibility could such a curiously assorted group hang together under any leadership, but as the deadlock continued for days, for weeks, for months without a desertion from the Roosevelt standard, Tammany's chuckles turned to growls and in spite of the fact that this was a perfectly hopeless fight Roosevelt won it!"

But back in its lair, licking its wounds, the Tiger planned revenge. Another year was coming. Election year! Wait till those rebels stuck their heads up again and looked for the voters. It was freely predicted that none of the twenty-one insurgents would ever return to Albany, least of all that upstart, that political mistake, that Roosevelt.

"I was one of those," Louis said, "who was just damfool enough to believe that he would. Anyway, I bet a hundred dollars on the strength of it."

In the spring of 1912 Thomas Mott Osborne, mayor of Auburn, New York, organized the New York State Wilson Conference, an organization in which independent Democrats could function in support of Woodrow Wilson for President. Franklin Roosevelt became chairman of the Executive Committee and asked Louis to do publicity. Louis took leave from his paper and began at once turning out reams of letters and newspaper articles. "As masterpieces of the English language you better have them framed," he wrote to FDR. It was in June of this year that Louis Howe wrote a letter to Franklin Roosevelt, addressing him as "Beloved and Revered Future President," little dreaming that the letter would one day be reproduced in a story of his life to prove, without question, that he was the original "Roosevelt for President" man.

After Woodrow Wilson was nominated, the New York State Wilson Conference disbanded and the Empire State Democracy took its place with Osborne, Roosevelt and Louis in the new organization. However, in August, Mr. Osborne who was "angeling" the venture ran out of funds, and Franklin Roosevelt came down with typhoid fever. Louis, who had given up his place on the *Herald* canvass in this election year, suddenly found himself out of a job.

"I notified the Herald as soon as Wilson was nominated," he wrote to FDR, "and it made my boss very angry, as it upset his schedule. Now I am in a hole because there are five long months before Albany and the price of living has not gone down any. If you can connect me with a job during the campaign, for heaven's sake help me out, for this mess is a bad business for me. To my mind, now is the time to put that Young Men's Wilson Clubs idea through, using it as a blind to build up an anti-Murphy organization."

As predicted, dark days had come upon those who had opposed the Tammany machine in the Sheehan fight. One of the insurgents, who ran a little country newspaper which depended for revenue largely on printing from the state, was punished by losing his contract, and his paper went to the wall. So the sordid story ran. They could not ruin Franklin Roosevelt financially but they could attack him in other ways.

Roosevelt wasn't worried, though, until he came down with typhoid fever and the doctors forbade him to leave his bed, much less make a campaign. Things looked pretty hopeless. But as he thought about Louis' letter, and how to help him, he suddenly remembered how they had often talked about the importance of contact with voters who lived away from the centers of voting population, and how they both had some good ideas about how to reach this untapped source of votes. With the exception of Poughkeepsie and a few other towns, FDR's district was largely rural. Louis knew the reactions of these rural voters well from his work with the *Herald* canvass, and FDR remembered how accurate these canvasses had been. He reached for the telephone.

"Louis," he said, "you have so many ideas on how to run a campaign I'm going to give you a chance to put them into practice. I'm flat on my back and the doctors say I have to stay here. You run the campaign. You'll have a checkbook and a free hand. Now, go to it."

Louis went into this fight with the knowledge that it was far more important than merely the re-election of a member of the Senate of the State of New York. This young man was on his way, but a setback now might forever ruin his chances of higher things. Louis' plans were elaborate and thorough. He established his headquarters in the old Morgan House in Poughkeepsie and brought Mrs. Howe down from Saratoga with their year-old son, Hartley Howe, who had been born the previous November. Eleven years had elapsed since the birth of Mary and Hartley came as a welcome surprise to the Howe home. From that time on Louis Howe divided his devotion between Mary and this wonderful son whom he never wanted out of his sight. He took Mrs. Howe and the baby with him on his trips over the district, chugging along in one of those high-wheeled automobiles of the time, Mrs. Howe swathed in a duster and hat, with thick veil to keep out the dust, a costume essential to any kind of motoring in those days. Louis wore a wide-billed canvas cap.

One of the first things Louis did was to go to his friend, William Church Osborn, chairman of the Market Committee of the State Food Commission, to see what could be done for the farmers who were plagued by having to deal through "commission merchants." Osborn outlined some proposed legislation to protect the farmers in this situation, and Louis had copies of the proposed bill printed and attached to the "personal" letters which he sent out over Roosevelt's name to the farmers in the district. These letters were all multigraphed, but had the names and addresses typed in so skillfully that the recipients didn't doubt that they were being personally addressed by the candidate himself. Louis cannily asked the farmers what they thought of this proposed legislation, what they thought should be included in the bill, and asked that they thresh the matter out at their Grange meetings. "This matter so directly affects the farmers and is so important as to be above partisan politics," Louis ghosted, obviously with tongue in cheek, considering the partisan politics he was playing.

He also sent scores of these "personal letters" from FDR to the shad fishermen along the Hudson River, telling them that the conservation commission had promised to rescind the new high license fees, which had them all worried. He "rolled out the barrel" for the apple growers, by promising them that he (FDR) would back legislation to standardize the size of apple barrels so that they would not be cheated by having their apples measured in oversize barrels, as had been done in the past.

Mr. Roosevelt's Republican opponent was Jacob Southard, banker and president of a light and power company. Louis hit at him with some more "personal letters" to the voters, accusing him of not making personal visits to them and taking the interest in their problems that he should. Of course, they understood that FDR, although flat on his back, was thinking of their problems all the time, between doctor's visits and doses of medicine!

Louis didn't miss a trick. He committed FDR to the support of woman suffrage and other progressive measures, then put all these statements together and ran them in the form of full-page newspaper ads in the county papers. He thoughtfully sent FDR copies of the ad before he ran it, saying he could cut out, by telegram, any items he didn't like. "As I have pledged you in all this," he wrote, "I thought you might like to know, casually, what kind of a mess I was getting you into!"

He sent daily reports of his activities to FDR, as well as items he thought good for a laugh. "I am jollying White, one of our workers," he said, "to wear a chauffeur's cap and leggings as we tour the district, so as to throw all the style we can. We are toting the Archbishop up from Fishkill tomorrow," and so on. He also made one or two quick trips down to New York to make his cheerful reports to the invalid in person.

"Keep that temperature down," he warned in one message, "so you can get on the job. I am having more fun than a goat. They will know they have been to a horse race before we are done! Your slave and servant, Louis Howe."

Louis almost lost the fun, though, when two things happened near the end of the campaign: The Republicans tried to register men who were working temporarily in Putnam County on the New York City aqueduct, and the opposition spread the word that Roosevelt's fight on "Blue-eyed Billy" Sheehan was motivated by anti-Catholicism. This stratagem was a last-minute thrust and, in spite of all Louis could do, it cost FDR votes. However, Roosevelt won by a narrow margin and ran ahead of Sulzer, the candidate for Governor, and Woodrow Wilson.

FDR had fun with Louis about the checkbook he had turned over to him for use in the campaign. Now and then he'd ask Louis if he needed more money and Louis always said, No, he had plenty in the bank. One day the bank notified FDR that this account was overdrawn. Louis still insisted that he hadn't spent all the money until FDR looked at the checkbook. Louis had absent-mindedly added the balance instead of deducting it. FDR always loved to tell this story on Louis; then he'd add only half-jokingly, "Of course, Louis knows nothing about economics."

It was during this period that Mrs. Roosevelt received her first real taste of politics and she didn't like it. When Louis came to the house she looked upon his visits with no enthusiasm whatsoever and received him with cool politeness. She knew him only as one of the newspapermen who was in and out of the house during the Sheehan fight and she definitely did not approve of him. She thought he smoked too many cigarettes and he was careless about clothes. Mostly, though, she admitted, it was the cigarettes. He filled the house with smoke every time he came.

"I certainly made a nuisance of myself in those days," she later said, with a smile. "I had no sense of values whatsoever. I often wonder how the men put up with me at all." It was a relief to her when the campaign was over and Louis called Roosevelt on the phone on election night. "Well, Mr. Senator," he said cheerfully, "you're elected. Also, you got a lot bigger majority than you did the first time."

All of FDR's friends were enthusiastic about Louis' work in the campaign. "Howe did gallant work under very adverse circumstances," William Church Osborn said. "He was about as loyal and wholehearted as a man could be." What amazed the politicians most, however, was the small amount of money Louis spent. He ran the campaign for something less than $2,500, took a salary of only $300 for himself and filed a meager expense account of a little over a hundred and twenty dollars.

And so, with this initial campaign began Louis Howe's political enlistment with Franklin Roosevelt. Many historians will speculate on what it was that caused Louis Howe to look deep and see what others missed in FDR, for there were other astute observers in those early days who could not visualize him as a coming political figure. Frances Perkins, who knew him well in Albany and became not only a close friend in later years, but a member of his Cabinet, admits that she could not "see" FDR in those early years. She thought him very opinionated and high-handed.

Thomas Mott Osborne, later the famed warden of Sing Sing prison, who had joined with FDR in the Sheehan fight and worked with him in the New York State Wilson Conference and Empire State Democracy, developed a great admiration for him. "From that time on," said Rudolph W. Chamberlain, Osborne's biographer, "Osborne watched over the political career of Franklin D. Roosevelt with an almost paternal solicitude. It is too much to ask, however, that he should discern in his boyish ally those qualities which twenty years later were to make Roosevelt President of the United States."[2]

It is not likely that Louis, in that historic first meeting with Franklin Roosevelt, when he envisioned him as a future President, thought of himself—the little newspaperman on an errand for his paper—as a "king maker." Just when *this* idea first took shape in his mind is something no one really knows, for Louis never said. But it is certain that it was not too long after the Sheehan fight that he began to see himself, perhaps a shadowy figure at first, in this picture of the future. His first admiration for Roosevelt grew to a warm liking, then, finally, to a love almost comparable to that of a father for a son.

Louis was small, ugly and insignificant looking. Roosevelt was big, handsome and dramatic. Louis Howe closed his eyes and saw these two divergent personalities merge into a political entity and the picture fascinated him.

[2] Rudolph W. Chamberlain, *There Is No Truce* (New York: The Macmillan Company, 1935).

He knew that his principal service to his brilliant young friend would lie in balancing his older years and broader experience against the eager enthusiasm of the young aristocrat in the days that lay ahead.

"To provide the toe weights" was the way he always put it.

Navy Days

T HE NAVY," one reporter cried. "I have it! Louis is bound to be exposed to water. Let us give him a dozen cakes of soap and maybe he'll finally come clean!"

The pressroom boys at Albany had just heard that Franklin D. Roosevelt, the new Assistant Secretary of the Navy in the Wilson administration, was taking Louis Howe to Washington.

The newsman's remark about Louis' "coming clean," of course, had reference to the dark scars Louis bore on his face from his bicycle accident. In addition, he had stayed in the blazing sun too long on a side trip into Egypt with his father, on their Mediterranean cruise, causing his skin to darken permanently in the exposed places. His colleagues were always bantering him, wanting to know why he didn't wash his face. He took this in fair humor but they could always get a scowl from him by calling him "Lewis." He insisted that since his name had the French spelling—Louis—it should get the French pronunciation "Louie." He was quite insistent about this.

Two days after Woodrow Wilson was inaugurated on March 4, 1913, Josephus Daniels, whom he had selected as his Secretary of the Navy, asked him, provided he had no one else in mind, to appoint Franklin Roosevelt as Assistant Secretary. Mr. Daniels had admired the young man's grit in the Sheehan fight, had come to know him well during the Democratic Convention in Baltimore and elsewhere, and liked the cut of his jib. So Franklin D. Roosevelt became Assistant Secretary of the Navy, thus carrying on a tradition, since "Teddy" had served in that same capacity under Secretary of the Navy Long in the early part of the McKinley administration.

Roosevelt inherited as his personal secretary Charles H. McCarthy, an efficient, loyal young man who had served under several of his predecessors; but FDR also felt the need of his own Man Friday in this new job, so he dispatched an invitation to Louis to join him as his private secretary. Louis, who wouldn't have missed the experience for the world, gave up his beloved newspaper job with hardly a backward glance, and sent a typical wire: "I am game," he said, "but it's going to break me!" In Washington he installed Mrs. Howe, Mary and little Hartley in a boardinghouse on M Street until they could find suitable quarters. Then he began a job which at first was as bewildering to him as it would have been to a Zulu chieftain. "I can still see us as we entered that office for the first time," he laughed. "Though a newspaperman I had never learned what the duties of a secretary to the Assistant Secretary of the Navy were. So, standing beside Franklin's desk, I blotted his signature as he signed official papers for several days!"

Louis caught on fast, but it was not all easy sailing. Pretty soon he and McCarthy began to get in each other's way and there were several clashes between them. Each was efficient in his own field, but often there were disagreements as to the areas of these fields. McCarthy thought Louis encroached on his territory and Louis was sure McCarthy was trying to encroach on his. Roosevelt, who needed both but each in his own spot, managed somehow to keep these clashes from breaking into open warfare. Once, after he had been in the Navy Department for some time, he wrote to Mrs. Roosevelt who was away from Washington, "Louis goes to Newfoundland tomorrow and I shall try to clean up his back work for him! He is so wonderful on the big things that he lets the routine slide. I need a thoroughgoing hack without brilliancy like the faithful McCarthy to keep things running."[1]

[1] Elliott Roosevelt, editor, *F.D.R., His Personal Letters* (3 vols., New York: Duell, Sloan & Pearce, Inc., 1948, 1950).

Louis began to annoy the Admirals, too. With their passion for neatness, they shuddered when they saw him sitting serenely behind his desk in Roosevelt's outer office, his shirt sleeves rolled up, ashes from his Sweet Caps floating across his desk, his stringy tie drooping beneath his impossible collar. One thing they could have given him credit for: while he was never in uniform, as long as he was in the Navy Department that tie was always the right shade of Navy blue, and never any other color.

While Louis Howe's appearance, according to one authority, "repelled most officers and some labor leaders," the officers were cautious about mentioning this fact to Franklin Roosevelt. However, on one occasion when FDR told a captain he was sending Louis down to inspect his ship, the captain, unable to restrain himself, blurted out, "Well, Mr. Secretary, if you do I can tell you what will happen. As soon as he comes aboard they will take him up on the foc'sle, strip him and scrub him down with sand and canvas." FDR howled.

The labor leaders, however, quickly came to respect and admire Louis Howe when they realized that he was the one who was leading the young and enthusiastic socialite Roosevelt away from the exclusive Metropolitan Club and other fashionable places, and down to the Navy Yards to check personally on what was going on. The Assistant Secretary of the Navy had supervision of the shore establishments which employed thousands of civilians, and Louis hammered home to FDR the importance of taking a personal interest in their problems. Louis was the one who insisted that Roosevelt personally attend the hearings on labor problems affecting these men and not delegate the job to an assistant, as had been done before. Many times labor leaders, who came to the office with problems which might well have been settled by others, were ushered instead into FDR's office, and Louis persuaded "the Boss" to spend hours listening to them and getting their viewpoint.

That Louis was motivated by political considerations there is little doubt. He said years later that the friends Franklin made among the labor people during his Navy days stayed with him the

rest of his life, and his sympathy for their problems made him
popular with labor all over the country. Louis was the one who
hurried to the Navy Yards when strikes threatened, and he often
had to take drastic and hasty action which might have placed
FDR in trouble if his judgment proved wrong, for of course he
always acted in the Assistant Secretary's name. He nearly always
sided with the labor leaders in the various disputes and this did
not improve his standing with the officers, many of whom took out
whatever antilabor feelings they had on Louis. If you had asked
him why he sided with the laborers against the officers he might
have answered mockingly, that it was because there were more
labor votes than officers' votes, although he did have a real sympathy for the workers and their problems.

FDR always insisted that politics be kept out of the Navy Yards,
and maintained that the best way to produce votes for the Democrats was to manage the yards efficiently. Just the same, maybe
behind FDR's back, Louis Howe was blithely clearing promotions
in at least one Navy Yard with the Democratic Congressman in
the district where the yard was located.

Congressmen were always calling on Mr. Roosevelt for routine
favors, such as using his influence to get young men into the
Annapolis Naval Academy, and much of this work fell on Louis'
shoulders. The way he handled some of them is illustrated by the
letter he wrote to Congressman Lathrop Brown, who had roomed
with Mr. Roosevelt at Harvard:

> Now, about your young friend . . . who appears to be one of
> nature's noblemen and to have nothing against him except that
> he has broken most of the Ten Commandments. I am willing to
> admit that if we bar from the Navy every gent who has become
> mixed up with a beautiful female we would have to put most of
> our ships out of commission and I am afraid we might lose an
> admiral or two, but in this case the young man was unfortunately
> caught with the goods. You have run against one of the Secre-
> tary's strongest antipathies. And while I know Mr. Roosevelt
> will speak to Mr. Daniels about the case again, I honestly do not

think he has a chance on earth. Do you want one of those "we are doing everything on earth to get this done because of the affection for the Congressman" letters or not? Will send you a masterpiece that will convince your friends that Mr. Roosevelt is sitting on Mr. Daniels' doorstep every night waiting for a chance to make one more plea when he comes home to supper, if that will ease the strain any.[2]

In another field Louis was able to garner some patronage which might be of future use to Franklin politically, but it was a rather slow and maddening process and involved so much connivance and paperwork that, at times, it hardly seemed worth the gamble. The appointment of postmasters was then, as now, patronage for members of Congress who guarded it jealously, but where districts sent Republican Representatives to Washington during a Democratic Administration, or vice versa, the post office patronage in those districts was usually taken over by whoever was best able to grab it. Upstate New York during the Wilson Administration sent many Republican Congressmen to Washington, and Roosevelt and Howe moved into this vacuum and tried to get postmasters friendly to FDR appointed. Often, however, they ran afoul of local Democratic leaders, who were sending their own recommendations to Democratic Senator James A. O'Gorman, or clearing them with Tammany Hall.

Postmaster General Albert Burleson cooperated with FDR to the extent of sending him lists of the post office vacancies in New York State, but he did it somewhat warily, not being a great admirer of the youthful Assistant Secretary for some reason. And he didn't always accept FDR's recommendations. Louis kept a fat file on all these appointments and used every avenue he could think of to get FDR's men placed in the jobs. He was lucky to have a cooperative ally in the Post Office Department in the person of the First Assistant Postmaster General, Daniel C. Roper. Louis conferred with him frequently, all the while keeping FDR posted on the way he handled each case.

[2] September 21, 1915.

In April 1914 he wrote FDR, then absent from Washington:

> I saw Mr. Roper again today. We are getting what you might
> call chummy. Postoffice matters are going nicely and I think
> Ketcham is sure to win out in Orange County after my talk. Mr.
> Burleson had his talk with the President and came back, accord-
> ing to Mr. Roper, undecided. Mr. Roper says he argued with him
> some more and that Mr. Burleson finally concluded to put it
> through and that he was going to break the news to O'Gorman
> in a few days. If you hear of that portion of the Postoffice Depart-
> ment roof sailing off into space accompanied by a violent ex-
> plosion you will understand that the interview took place.

Roosevelt inaugurated a rigid system of economy as soon as he
took office, which meant going over every contract, to see that the
Navy was getting its money's worth. He delegated to Louis the
task of going over these contracts and Louis wore pencils to stubs,
checking and rechecking every item, always with the thought in
mind that Franklin would receive the credit for any economies
they managed to effect. When a rush order came through for
foundry equipment, just before the end of the fiscal year in 1913,
there was a request with it that bidding be waived in favor of one
firm. This annoyed Secretary Daniels who insisted that bids be
submitted. The favored firm was, as usual, among the high bidders
and the request was made that the low bids not be considered.
Mr. Daniels stood firm and told them they must consider the low
bidder. "Whereupon," said Louis Howe, "there appears to have
been some fancy figuring done and today a man who was low is
haunting Mr. Daniels' office with a complaint of some kind."

The hassle over this was mild, however, compared to the furor
over awarding the Navy's contracts for coal. At that time the
Navy would not buy coal from mines or jobbers that did not meet
the rigid specifications which the Navy enforced. This situation
meant that the few mine owners able to meet these requirements
had a monopoly, and FDR and Louis set out to smash the "combination." Louis raised a row in the summer of 1913, when FDR
was away, because the Navy Paymaster's office had awarded a
coal contract to a firm whose bid was five cents higher than an-

other's. Secretary Daniels, who was backing Roosevelt and Howe to the limit, took the coal contracts out of the Paymaster's office and put them in the office of the Assistant Secretary. Louis sent a memo to FDR about the ruckus "for his personal eyes only," and hinted that the high bids seemed to have a "fatal fascination" for a certain man in the Paymaster's office, who claimed he let the award to the high bidder because he thought the other man probably would furnish inferior coal. "The Department is not justified," Louis said, "when a man bids in good faith, in assuming that he is going to cheat us. If we can't trust a man's word why not bar him from bidding?"

It was Louis who drafted new Navy specifications which were not "so all-fired rigid," making it possible for the coal brokers to submit lower figures than the big coal interests, who were in many cases tied up with the railroads. When, under these new specifications, the bids were opened, it was found that in the first two contracts awarded there had been a saving of about $27,500. The Pocahontas Fuel Company, which was closely tied with the Norfolk and Western Railway System, had its contract shaved from 170,000 to 12,000 tons, and so on. Louis was gleeful about these savings but he had not reckoned on Capitol Hill. Senator William E. Chilton of West Virginia objected, and claimed that the Navy was cutting coal orders from his state at a time when the mines were suffering from a slump in the iron and steel industry. Louis wrote him a letter over FDR's signature. "If business is so good with the West Virginia mines," he said crisply, "as to make them feel that they can afford to keep up with the combination price, even at the loss of the Navy's 600,000 tons, I do not see that they can be really suffering."

Louis tipped over a hornet's nest. The new coal did not come up to the Navy standards, ship commanders insisted. The complaints raised wide echoes on the Hill. Eventually, spurred by the commanders, the House Naval Affairs Committee instituted an investigation. Louis prepared the statement which Secretary Daniels was to use before the Committee and bore down heavily on the machinations of the wicked "coal trust," coining encomiums for the gallant fight the Navy Department was making to "restore free enterprise." However, the new Paymaster General to whom Louis' report had to be submitted first, cut Louis' eloquence down to the bare essentials—poetic justice, in a way, as it was Louis who caused the Paymaster's office to lose the coal contracts in the first place. Secretary Daniels decided there were not enough plain facts in the report to back him up, and that he would let FDR handle the whole matter. This delighted Louis, who already had submitted his flowery report to FDR, as he felt sure Franklin had the eloquence to put it over before the Committee.

FDR, appearing before the Committee the following week to talk about coal, talked instead about defense. Always enthusiastic about a bigger navy, he made such an excellent presentation for his cause that the Congressmen were greatly taken with him, especially those Congressmen who advocated a big navy. Congressman Roberts from West Virginia, where unrest over the new coal contracts was high, watched his chance, however, and brought up the coal subject. FDR had Louis' statement with him and, without hesitation, he boldly presented it exactly as Louis had written it. Unfortunately, he had not checked Louis' figures thoroughly and the Committee immediately questioned him about them, while Louis sat back and suffered.

Louis also worried about the unfavorable publicity Franklin would probably receive in next day's papers, but in this instance, he had a rare stroke of luck, even though it meant bad luck and tragedy elsewhere. World War I was on in Europe by this time. The next day the papers recorded a severe blow to British naval prestige. Three English towns had been shelled by German cruisers. Shocked and horrified over this incident, the people remembered with gratitude FDR's plugging for a stronger navy, and this tragedy convinced many Americans that we needed one. The newspapers played up FDR's testimony on defense, and relegated the coal subject to a minor place in the news. Louis Howe sat back, mopped his brow, and heaved a deep sigh of relief over Franklin's escape.

Louis also had his problems with the Russians, who began

"walking out" long before the days of the United Nations. Soon after the United States entered the war the Carnegie Steel Company, which had sixty-two plants in war work, notified the Navy Department that a large number of their Russian employees were leaving to go back to Russia, that the Russian Consul was encouraging them and giving financial aid to cover transportation. Louis, investigating the matter, found that there was nothing the Navy could do, but wrote a long letter about how sorry he felt. "Why anybody gainfully employed by such a generous and philanthropic company would want to go back to Russia now," he wrote gracefully, "is beyond me." Whether this "buttery" reply compensated the Carnegie people for the loss of their Russians history does not say.

In spite of Louis' carelessness on his coal figures, more and more contracts were turned over to him for scrutiny, and Admiral Leahy, who was detail officer in the Bureau of Navigation from 1913 to 1915, groaned at the way Louis slowly and meticulously went over each and every one, often delaying important contracts for days. "He subjected them to close and suspicious scrutiny," the Admiral said, "as though he suspected graft in every one. In time, however, he came to have confidence in the Naval officers who drew them up and he became a strong asset in the Department."

There were a few other Naval officers who grudgingly admitted Louis' capabilities, but none questioned his loyalty to Franklin Roosevelt. Admiral Emory S. Land, then a member of Admiral Sims's staff, called Louis the "Number One squid" and often said Louis Howe drove him to sea duty. Ultimately, however, he came to admire and respect Louis' dogged qualities. "He was a damned smart able man," the Admiral said, "and the best adviser Roosevelt ever had, because he always had the guts to say 'no.' "

John Hancock, an officer in the Bureau of Supplies and Accounts, was sure Louis let political considerations sway him and said he often "gummed the works" because of this. He granted, however, that Louis was useful at times because he provided prodding and served as a "good irritant, a gadfly."

Some officers felt that Roosevelt, too, let political considerations sway him in many things, especially in the field of awarding contracts, and that he leaned toward anyone "who had been a classmate or was a member of the Newport crowd," as they put it. "One particular promoter, Arthur P. Homer," said Frank Freidel in his book, *Franklin D. Roosevelt: The Apprenticeship,* "although not of this background, was so thoroughly in the good graces of Roosevelt and Howe that the supply officers thought they saw many signs of his influence. When the Bureau of Engineering recommended that a contract for engines go to a certain manufacturer the proposal came back from Howe with Homer's firm, Sterling Motors, substituted. Since the first manufacturer had known of the Bureau of Engineering's decision in his favor this caused considerable embarrassment."

"Franklin was always right," was Louis' motto, except when he disagreed with him himself, and he sided vigorously with him on one project to which even Secretary Daniels, as well as most of the Naval officers, were in opposition. In the early days of the war, FDR advocated building 50-foot harbor patrol launches, convinced that they would be useful in running down "rumors of secret enemy wireless stations, gun-running depots, submarine fuel or repair bases, or even submarines taking shelter in secluded waters," etc. When Secretary Daniels failed to order the boats built FDR went ahead on his own, and arranged, tentatively, for a number of them to be built anyway, hoping he could bring the Secretary around to his point of view. Most of the officers felt that the 50-foot boats would not be of any value, unless used in smooth waters inside the harbors, and that this would limit their usefulness. They felt that the 110-foot patrol boats, already in use, would do almost everything the 50-foot boats would do.

Louis was using every trick he could think of to bring the officers around to Franklin's point of view. There is a story that he went to Admiral Hugh Rodman, who was waiting for sea duty, and hinted to him that it would be to his advantage to drop his opposition to the 50-foot boats, and that the salty Kentuckian cursed him roundly.

Louis was also criticized by the *Army and Navy Register* when he changed regulations so that sailors could buy some other kind of tobacco besides Bull Durham, which was all they had been able to get on shipboard. Louis also arranged for them to buy various brands of toothpaste and other items. The *Register* charged that he was forcing sailors to buy unknown brands and "driving worthy bidders away from the Navy Department." Fearing that their attack might hurt Franklin, Louis took full blame and sent a memo to FDR: "The attack concerns only the wicked performance of my wicked self," he said, "and will leave the Assistant Secretary unscathed." Louis was not too worried about the outcries of the Naval officers and the *Army and Navy Register* as long as Secretary Daniels was pleased, and the Secretary was delighted with Louis' and Franklin's work and proclaimed, in his first annual report, that "through better and fuller competition" the Navy had already saved $150,000.

Louis not only turned the credit for every saving he effected toward Franklin, but also saw that Franklin received all the favorable publicity. In 1915, when FDR and Mrs. Roosevelt went to the Panama Pacific Exposition in San Francisco with Vice-President Marshall, the Vice-President naturally was the one to whom the newspapers paid attention. Louis took note of it and only half in jest wired FDR that he'd better fire whatever press agent was handling him on the Coast. "Try," he said, "to get at least a line in amongst the patent medicine advertisements!"

Louis was pretty happy when Franklin escaped some unfavorable publicity about a much publicized incident in the Navy Department, because he was on the West Coast when the incident broke in the papers. Secretary Daniels, an ardent Prohibitionist, had issued an order drying up the officers' wine mess, thus bringing the ridicule and fury of the officers down on his head. When the order appeared and the storm broke, FDR received a hasty, tongue-in-cheek message from Louis:

"You will doubtless be given an opportunity to sustain this program," he said, "certainly by private argument with the officers you meet on the Coast and possibly at some formal occasion.

I know how greatly you regret not being here at the time to share in some of the glory. As it is, of course, I can tell the newspapermen nothing except that you are away and know nothing about it."

Louis had now moved his family from the boardinghouse on M Street into an unfurnished apartment on P Street and had the best of their furniture moved down so they could have a semblance of a home in Washington. With the furniture came Louis' books, which delighted Mary Howe who had just started high school at Miss Madeira's, the fashionable girls' school in Washington. "The sight of our beloved books again," she said, "was a demoralizing joy to me, for I much preferred reading Kipling and Dumas rather than the dull story of Julius Caesar's Gallic Wars! Usually we had Thanksgiving or Christmas dinner with the Roosevelts," she added, recalling those youthful days, "and all in all, Washington was a fascinating place for a girl who, with Albany in the winter, Saratoga or Fall River in the spring and fall, often attended three schools in one year."

Washington was a fascinating place for little Hartley, too. He loved to go down to see his dad in the Navy Department; the messengers would lead him around to the room where the ship models were and explain them to him, while he listened round-eyed and full of awe at the wonderful things he saw.

Louis had joined the choir at St. Thomas Church, and when word went around that he had been an amateur actor he was called upon to take part in amateur plays. He had little time to give to this activity now, however, though, for a while, he was a member of the Drama League Players. He played the part of the clerk who was "typical of the grumbler over war conditions, high prices and the like" in Shaw's lampoon on conditions in England during the earlier stages of the war. The play, which had only three characters, was put on at famed Poli's Theater in Washington, and, according to one reviewer, "The Drama League Players found the three-act fancy to their liking as did the audience, which was enthusiastic over the reading of the Shavian dialogue." Louis also helped Mrs. Albert Sidney Burleson, wife of the Postmaster General, adapt several plays for production in The Little Theater in the Post Office Department building. He played a little golf at the Washington Country Club, still trying half-heartedly to be physically active; but he soon gave it up as his frail physique would not permit much outdoors activity.

FDR often sent Louis on trips for him with complete confidence that he would represent the Navy Department almost as well as FDR could himself. In 1916 when he sent Louis to visit the New Orleans Navy Yard, the naval constructor there wrote to FDR, "It is a source of wonder to me how a man not connected with the Naval service can have obtained in three years the detailed knowledge of the situation that is possessed by Mr. Howe."

The Navy Department had under consideration the building of one or more bases in the Caribbean, and FDR sent Louis to Cuba to inspect the base at Guantánamo. FDR came down with a bad throat infection before Louis sailed and the doctor forbade him to see anybody, but he did see Louis for last-minute instructions. The next day, when Louis was on the high seas, FDR's fever shot up alarmingly and Mrs. Roosevelt and Mrs. Howe held a conference about whether to notify Louis. Mrs. Roosevelt thought they should, but Mrs. Howe, who knew better than anyone else of Louis' fanatical devotion to Franklin, shook her head. "You'd better not let him know Franklin is worse," she said firmly, "that is, unless you want him to jump right off that ship and swim ashore and rush back here to him." They didn't cable Louis until he reached Cuba and by that time FDR was much improved.

When illness struck FDR on another occasion, however, Louis was right there. One night in the summer of 1915, when Mrs. Roosevelt was at Campobello, FDR phoned Louis to come over at once, saying he had a terrible pain in his stomach. Louis, who thought the attack was simple indigestion, stalled a bit, even though the families only lived a few blocks apart. "Oh, take a pill," he said. "It's nothing but that cherry pie and glass of milk you had for lunch. I told you not to eat it." When he realized that FDR was really ill, however, he hastily went over, rushed him to the hospital and the Roosevelt appendix was removed in the early hours of the morning. FDR was preparing to take a trip to Europe and this changed all his plans, so Louis used his spare time thinking up ways to cheer the restless invalid. He wrote an illustrated poem and sent it to FDR with a card, wrapped in seven yards of Government red tape. "This is all bound round and round and round and round AND round with red tape," Louis wrote, "because that's the way things are done in the Navy Department."

The team of Roosevelt and Howe was fast developing a reputation for speeding up procurement, Louis himself being credited with speeding the construction of the battleship *New Mexico*—a special assignment given to him by FDR—and the two are remembered still for some of their daring exploits.

During the early days of the war when our government was feverishly building destroyers, a certain type of motor generator was needed and none could be found. General Electric, which had been building them, did not have any and could not begin one in less than six months. Louis told Secretary Daniels that he had a hot tip that a generator, just the type needed, had been shipped somewhere, but no one knew where. He asked for a blank commandeering order and a "bright young man" to scout around and find the thing. The order was issued and the young man went off on his mission. After a few days he found, in a long train of cars in a Philadelphia railroad yard, something big and impressive enough to be the generator. It was consigned simply to "General Electric." When he found that it was really what he wanted, he slapped on the commandeering order, had the car yanked out of the train of cars and headed for the shipbuilding yard within two hours.

It was not until months later that Roosevelt and Howe found out that the motor generator they had "stolen" had been on its way to a big hotel then under construction in New York City. They wouldn't have known it then if the Statler Hotel Company hadn't sent a plaintive but good-humored letter to the Navy Department, telling them they had delayed the opening of the new Pennsylvania Hotel for three months.

On another occasion Louis pushed aside a few bales of red tape and waded into the diplomatic field. Secretary Daniels had been bothered by the fact that all the much needed high-grade sodium nitrate, which met the Navy's specifications, was under the control of one company. Couldn't the office of the Assistant Secretary do something? Louis at once started investigating, and found that the Chilean government had some very fine reserves of high-grade nitrate which it was drawing on for its own use. But he didn't go to the State Department and start long and involved negotiations. He just hitched up his trousers, put on his battered hat and set out for the Chilean Embassy. Since the nitrate belonged to the Chilean government, he told the surprised official in charge, and was needed by the American government, why was it necessary to deal with a commercial intermediary? The United States Navy needed five million pounds of nitrate. Didn't the Chilean government, as a friendly power, sympathize with the predicament of the United States Navy? Louis then made the proposition that if the Chilean government would deliver the five million pounds at Antofagasta, a seaport off the Chilean coast, the United States Navy would send its colliers down to bring it to the United States. The official promised to look into the matter.

In a few days the official sent for Louis and told him that the Chilean government would be pleased to furnish the nitrate.

"But," he said nervously, "your specifications are so elaborate—we cannot guarantee—"

Louis, on this occasion extremely gallant, rose to his full height and bowed so low he almost jackknifed.

"We will waive all specifications," he said. "This is not a matter for specifications, but of honor between two friendly governments. Just provide us with what you consider good nitrate. I feel sure it will meet the Navy's specifications."[3]

The days that passed while the colliers steamed south to Antofagasta, loaded the nitrate and steamed back to Norfolk, were anxious ones for Louis Howe, who "had stuck his neck out

[3] Ernest K. Lindley, *Franklin D. Roosevelt: A Career in Progressive Democracy* (Indianapolis: The Bobbs-Merrill Company, 1931).

aplenty," as he put it. Naval experts were predicting daily that the nitrate might blow the power plants to kingdom come—or else not be fit to set off a firecracker.

Louis didn't go to Norfolk for the test, but made arrangements for the results to be phoned to him at his office in the Navy Department. Sitting with the phone gripped in his hand, he waited for what seemed endless hours. When the phone jangled he grabbed it grimly, then settled back and listened with a tense expression that gradually changed to a triumphant smile. He replaced the phone and stepped into the inner office where Roosevelt sat, signing papers.

"Louis," said FDR, "I can see from your face that the test went off all right. Give me the story."

"Oh," said Louis, trying to look nonchalant, "it was all right. All that the test proved was that it was just about the finest nitrate ever shipped into this country. That's all."

Roosevelt leaped to his feet and there was a quiet backslapping match between the Assistant Secretary of the Navy and his pint-sized Man Friday in the high-ceilinged office across the shady street from the White House.

For all these behind-the-scenes maneuverings which, years later, Louis Howe said it gave him chills to recall, he earned the title of "Daniels' Spy," a title which pleased his love of mystery and intrigue.

He had other titles, however. "They have made a brand new job for me. It is called Assistant to the Assistant Secretary," he wrote to his old friend, Howard Moody, two months after the war began. "As I am also a member of the Munitions Board, a special committee of the Council of National Defense on Transportation, and am about to become a member of the Precedence Committee, which has to determine what the manufacturers of the country shall make first, I rarely have any complaints for lack of things to do."

Secretary Daniels was well aware that Louis Howe, in his unswerving loyalty to Franklin Roosevelt, never made a move without the thought uppermost in his mind, "Will this help or hurt

Howe sketching on Horseneck Beach, 1912.

Howe in his office in the Navy Department (1913-1921).

A "watermelon feast" in the Navy Department. Howe at the extreme left; FDR, right center.

Howe with his secretary, Margaret Durand ("Rabbit").

Franklin's chances?" "Louis Howe would have sidetracked both
President Wilson and myself," he once said ruefully, "to get
Franklin Roosevelt to the White House."

In his book *The Wilson Era,* however, Mr. Daniels paid a great
tribute to this little man whom, he once confided to a friend, he
considered the strangest person he had ever met.

"Always fertile in resources and suggestions and with a keen
sense of public opinion," Mr. Daniels said, "Howe had boldness
in as large measure as his chief. And he could write, having a
style that was luminous and convincing. Roosevelt leaned upon
Howe whose devotion made him sensitive to every wind that
might affect Franklin in his public career.

"Always keeping himself in the background, he knew all the
tides and eddies in the Navy Department, in the administration
and in the political life of the country. . . . Even in 1913 he expected to see 'Franklin' occupy the White House, and to further
that ambition he devoted his every effort. His one and only ambition was to steer 'Franklin's' course so that he could take the tide
at the full."[4]

[4] Josephus Daniels, *The Wilson Era* (Chapel Hill: University of North Carolina Press, 1944).

[4]

Undaunted by Defeat

SHORTLY after Roosevelt took his oath of office in the Navy Department, he and Louis found themselves in the middle of an intra-party fight in New York State. Governor Sulzer and Tammany Hall attacked each other early in the game. Snarling charges flew between the Tiger's lair and the Capitol in Albany which Sulzer called "The People's House" to indicate that he was the man of the people. FDR, who had had his own troubles with Tammany, sided with Sulzer but did not come out openly for him; he and Louis both felt that Sulzer did not have the stamina to buck Tammany in earnest. Tammany instituted impeachment proceedings against Sulzer, with the charge that he had used campaign funds to speculate in the stock market, and Sulzer, in turn, accused Tammany of stealing millions of dollars which had been allocated for repairing the Capitol and the state highways.

From time to time Sulzer sent urgent appeals to Roosevelt for help, but Louis, urging FDR to stay clear of the "whole mess," was busy drafting neat "pussy-footed answers," as he called them, to the Governor's cries. Sulzer was impeached in October, less than a month before the election, the Democrats were roundly defeated in the state, and Tammany, in spite of its victory over Sulzer, also went down in a blistering defeat.

The state was practically leaderless now, so far as the Democrats were concerned, and it seemed an opportune time for some-

58

body to step in and start rebuilding the shattered fences. Into this void FDR, with Woodrow Wilson's blessing, made his move to pull the various forces together in an effort to unify them for the fight in the gubernatorial and senate races. Soon signs began to appear that Roosevelt himself might try for the nomination for governor, or for the United States Senate. The Constitutional amendment, by which United States Senators were elected by direct vote of the people, had just become the law of the land and many people credited FDR's fight against Sheehan for bringing to a head this much needed reform. On December 10 the New York *Sun* ran a flattering article about Roosevelt which many, in the know, thought was inspired by Louis Howe. The article said that if the new governor, Martin H. Glynn, did not break loose from Tammany entirely, Woodrow Wilson would favor Franklin Roosevelt for the nomination for governor. Democrats were all for this move on FDR's part and insisted that he either declare for governor or for the senate, but he issued strenuous denials from time to time that he had any interest in either post. He kept on with these denials through the spring and early summer of 1914, but on August 13 he suddenly wired Louis, who was at the beach, that "an important political development" had compelled him to enter the race. "My senses have not yet left me," he added, somewhat ambiguously.

There is a difference of opinion among historians as to what the "important political development" was that caused FDR to change his mind so quickly, for on that same day, he had said he would like nothing better than to get into the fight were it not for "his work in the Navy Department." Many believed that Woodrow Wilson was behind Roosevelt but he never said so openly, although William Gibbs McAdoo, Wilson's Secretary of the Treasury, was backing him.

Whether Louis was in sympathy with this sudden decision is not clear, but judging by the fact that FDR wired Louis as he did, one may assume that Louis was not. However, as soon as Franklin's decision was made, Louis went to work. He hastened back to

Washington and started conferring with McAdoo and thinking about money.

"I think you had better start a campaign fund," he wired FDR, who was in Campobello where Mrs. Roosevelt was expecting the advent of a new baby, "and suggest a check for $50.00 to be accounted for on your return. I will keep the other $50.00 intact, as from the looks of things I will have to jump over to New York and get things really going."

"You will have all the three hundred and eighty letters to sign in a few days," he wrote a little later, "as I am having them written on your best paper and I want you to sign them personally."

Franklin D. Roosevelt, Jr., was born on August 17, and Louis blamed this important event for FDR's failure to answer his letters promptly.

"For the love of Mike," he needled, "stop seeing if the kid has cut a tooth and drop me a post card." Getting no reply to this he fired back, "I suppose the baby talks quite fluently by this time. Are you waiting for your son to be old enough to act as your stenographer before writing me?"

Both Louis and FDR, of course, expected Tammany to put up a candidate against Roosevelt, and when the rumor spread that it would be William Randolph Hearst, Louis wired FDR that he "had been offering up prayers that the report that Hearst would run was true."

As time went on, however, and Tammany hesitated, Louis was jubilant.

"They have only made a petition and no way settled for getting them out," he wrote to FDR. "Also, other things are at loose ends and now is our time to get busy before any other candidate is trotted out."

"The truth is," he said optimistically, "that they haven't anything to say against you and no one is very anxious to bell the cat. Particularly when they have the idea that the President occasionally pats him on the back and calls him 'pretty pussy' and gives him a nice saucer of warm patronage milk to drink." Louis probably referred to Navy jobs which had gone to "deserving Democrats," blithely skittering over the fact that many of these saucers of patronage milk had been set before the cat by Man Friday himself.

Louis kept this stream of advice and gossip running in a steady flow to FDR whether he received answers to his letters or not. "Get me a copy of the Saratoga platform of the Republicans," he wrote. "I can't very well shoot holes in it without a copy. I had a long talk with McAdoo tonight, the results of which you will probably get by telegraph tomorrow." In a somewhat conciliatory mood he added, "I think this is the right time to show you don't hate all Tammany."

"I am sending you seventy-five letters," he wrote a few days later, "which please sign and send at once. I am playing the game the same way I did in the State Senate campaign, letting Tammany look after its strongholds in the cities and letting John Hennessy [candidate for governor] look after the cities while I go gunning in the rural districts, which Tammany has never thought worthwhile looking after. I have used some of your nice stationery and have had each letter written separately because I want to impress the rural mind. It is important that they all be mailed at once. We don't want one paper getting it ahead of another."

Louis received a jolt amid all this optimistic activity when Tammany, after weeks of vacillation, suddenly came up with the name of James W. Gerard, the popular wartime Ambassador to Germany, as their candidate for the Senate.

Louis and FDR spent some time in wishful thinking that Gerard would not run. Their hopes rose when Gerard said he might not be able to make a long campaign, or even any campaign at all, because he could not leave his duties in Berlin. He let his name be used as a candidate, however, much to Louis' distress, though he was comforted by the fact that Gerard did not have the open backing of the Administration. But then, he had to admit, neither did Franklin.

Louis was now busily writing to every Democrat he knew personally in the state of New York. "Let me know," he urged, "what you find right under your noses. This will give us an insight into what the silent voters are thinking, the ones not organized."

"I shall, of course, look daily for a statement from you to the press," he wrote a prominent state official, "to the effect that Mr. Roosevelt is the *only* proper man to be elected to the Senate."

"Don't forget to wear your plug hat in the big parade," he admonished FDR, shortly before Labor Day. "I am sending you two letters," he added, "one to be sent to each of the twenty-seven Democratic papers and one to the one hundred and eighty-nine independent papers, asking for their advertising rates and saying how valuable you find newspaper advertising. Some will fall for it and others will print it because your letter praises newspaper advertising."

Louis even whipped up his own "news plate" for the papers with an attractive, smiling photograph of Mr. Roosevelt. He was trying to offset the effect of earlier photographs which had been used and which made FDR look like a haughty, arrogant individual. Louis even sent the editors a ready-made headline which asserted that "Wilson's Assistant Secretary of the Navy has the backing of the Administration." A cautious old newspaperman, however, Louis did not link his news story to this headline, since Wilson had never come out openly for Roosevelt.

Another part of Louis' strategy was to have thousands of handbills printed which contained resolutions adopted by a state labor organization favoring FDR's candidacy. He sent these to political henchmen in the manufacturing centers for distribution to the various factories. He also tried to get endorsements from Navy Yard labor leaders, but this backfired when he was informed that the circulars he had written did not bear the union label.

He also struck a snag when he sent ten thousand of his labor leaflets to Richard Drummond, one of the Democratic leaders in Auburn, New York, and asked him to see that they were distributed to factory workers there. Drummond declined, saying that the factories were running short time, with greatly reduced forces, and that distribution of the leaflets would not help the campaign. Louis was considerably annoyed but he dropped the subject as far as the factories were concerned. He just went ahead and ordered twenty thousand handbills and had them scattered all over the town just before election day.

In spite of this intense mail and publicity campaign on Louis' part, and Roosevelt's whirlwind three weeks' speaking tour in the state, the popular Gerard, who had not even come home but had let his friends run the campaign for him, was gaining fast, and Louis looked around for a scapegoat in case Franklin didn't make it. He settled on John Hennessy, the candidate for governor, described by one newspaper as a "reform gubernatorial candidate," and "a flamboyant Irish reporter." When Gerard defeated FDR by almost two to one "it was all Hennessy's fault," of course. "He ruined us," Louis still was fuming a year later, "and he will sink any ship on which he is a passenger."

Roosevelt took his defeat more philosophically, announced that he would support Gerard in the general election, and was even jaunty about the whole thing as he departed for Washington, waving his hat to supporters who gathered at the station. "Never mind," he called gaily, "never mind, we paved the way!"

This good-sport attitude brought a shower of bouquets from the New York *Times*. "He is a regular, blown-in-the-bottle, antiseptic, non-corroding, dyed-in-the-wool Democrat!" the newspaper exclaimed editorially.

By the fall of 1915 FDR was beginning to show signs that he was in agreement with Louis on "Now is the time to show you don't hate all Tammany." He spoke at a meeting in New York's Greenwich Village, where he gave eloquent praise to Tammany's choice for sheriff, Alfred E. Smith, with whom he had served in the legislature in Albany, and whom he considered a liberal in spite of his Tammany connections. The following summer he left his duties in the Navy Department long enough to journey to the State Democratic Convention in Saratoga Springs to bring a message from the President, which said the Administration would keep a "hands off" attitude in New York City affairs in return for the nomination of Judge Samuel Seabury for governor. Tammany Hall even favored FDR himself against Seabury, but he was wholly wrapped up in his work in the Navy Department and did not rise to the bait.

By the summer of 1917, however, FDR was being photographed with his old foe, Charles F. Murphy, at the annual big Fourth of July celebration staged by Tammany Hall. As a result, by the spring of 1918 Roosevelt was seriously sought by independent Democrats as their candidate for governor and by Tammany Hall, too. Murphy felt that Roosevelt was the only man who could defeat former Governor Charles Whitman, pushed in many quarters for a third term. FDR insisted he was not a candidate and even wrote a letter to his old friend John E. Mack, Dutchess County Democratic leader, taking himself out of the race and recommending William Church Osborn instead. He was planning a trip abroad for the Navy Department, and before he sailed, he worked hard on getting everybody to agree on a candidate other than himself; in spite of his letter endorsing Osborn, he plumped hard for Al Smith, now president of the Board of Aldermen of New York City. Before FDR sailed in July he had lined up what support he could for Smith in New York City, and had given Louis the job of working on upstate leaders to demand Al's nomination. Louis and FDR did such a good job that when the convention met Al was almost the unanimous choice of the delegates. This must have placed Louis in an anomalous position, for he and Osborn had worked closely together in FDR's race for the Senate in 1912, and Osborn was considered a close friend of Mr. Roosevelt. However, when Osborn wrote to FDR asking for his support, his letter was answered by Louis who told him that of course Franklin could do nothing because he would "be away a long time." Louis then went to Mrs. Roosevelt and suggested that she hint to FDR that the President and Secretary Daniels thought it best for him not to return until after the New York primaries were over, since FDR would be in an embarrassing position if he had to repudiate Mr. Osborn after writing the letter. Of course, Louis pointed out, Franklin could come home after the primary and endorse the man who had been selected, after the others had had "a few days to cool down." This worked out fine as far as Mr. Roosevelt was concerned, but Osborn, who had been turned down flat by Tammany, was so mad he announced he would not support Al Smith in the primaries.

Louis was highly pleased with the results of all this maneuvering, for Franklin's candidate, Al Smith, was elected in November, and Franklin, by his refusal to run in the middle of a war, and with all the good publicity, had become a figure Louis was sure the politicians would have to reckon with when the war was over.

FDR grew steadily in political stature, and by the summer of 1920 he was one of the elected delegates to the Democratic National Convention in San Francisco. The war was over and anything could happen, but probably neither Louis Howe nor FDR was prepared for the dramatic turn of events at the convention. FDR, enthusiastic about Al Smith's record as Governor of New York, went out prepared to work for him for President, with little hope that he would be nominated, but with the hope that Al's name would be better known in the country, leading to the nomination at a later date. FDR left Louis behind to run "the shop," as Louis always called their office in the Navy Department, and Louis settled down happily to watch the daily papers and the Navy pressroom ticker for everything pertaining to Franklin's doings at the big show. He chortled gleefully when the news came in that FDR, after Al Smith's name had been put in nomination by Bourke Cochran, was in such a hurry to second the nomination that he leaped nimbly over a row of seats in his hurry to reach the platform. "Just like Franklin," he said, when, as a large photograph of Woodrow Wilson was unveiled, FDR angrily grabbed the New York banner from a Tammany leader and charged down the aisle with it while the New York delegation sat glued to its seats. Every other delegation had risen in tribute to the wartime President, now ill and stricken in Washington. Louis was still hanging over the news ticker late at night when the thrilling news came in that James M. Cox, who was finally nominated for President, had told his campaign manager immediately that he wanted Franklin D. Roosevelt as his running mate.

Louis could hardly wait for the next day, and hung on every word when Roosevelt's name was put in nomination by Judge Timothy T. Ansberry of the District of Columbia, when Josephus Daniels graciously made a speech in praise of his young assistant, and when Al Smith, in the true spirit of *quid pro quo,* also seconded his nomination. When the rules were suspended as state after state fell into line, and Franklin Roosevelt was nominated by acclamation, back in Washington, hunched over the ticker, a weary and wizened little man took a closer look at the jigsaw plans he had been formulating for years and quietly began to fit them into their proper places.

He sent FDR a wire immediately, telling him he should make "efficient government" his keynote, and also told him he should ask Cox to announce publicly that the Vice-President would sit in on Cabinet meetings. Cox refused, however. He was afraid, he told FDR, that the Senators might think their presiding officer was a spy for the Administration.

The publicity about FDR's nomination was in the main extremely good, and Louis Howe collected every item that appeared, to be hoarded for use in the campaign. He gloated when the New York *Globe,* a Republican paper, said that if the Democrats won even the Republicans would be glad to have a Roosevelt in Washington, and he grinned when Oswald Villard of *The Nation,* comparing FDR to Teddy, said any comparison was in FDR's favor as he was of a "distinctly finer quality and truer independence." He ground his cigarette out angrily when Robert McCormick of the Chicago *Tribune* called Franklin the "one-half of one per cent Roosevelt," and declared that "If Franklin was Theodore, then Elihu Root was Gene Debs and William Jennings Bryan a brewer!"

At the request of President Wilson FDR stayed on in the Navy Department until shortly before the formal notification ceremonies, which took place at Hyde Park. When he resigned from the Navy Department, Louis looked on proudly as two thousand employees cheered wildly and Secretary Daniels presented FDR with a loving cup. The workers at the Navy Gun Factory marched in a body to the Navy building to present FDR with a gavel made from the President's yacht, the *Mayflower,* and to thank him for the cooperation he always had given them. This was added proof to Louis that the workers were solidly for Franklin.

In spite of Louis' advice to make more economy in government the slogan, FDR and Cox were in agreement that the League of Nations was the most important matter facing the country and the world, and that they would concentrate on it in the campaign, win or lose. When FDR set out on his first speaking trip through the West, which took him to Seattle, Louis, who had many things to wind up for FDR in the Navy Department, stayed behind. He was also in the throes of helping his family settle in a new apartment on Twentieth Street in Washington, which Mary Howe, then a student at Vassar, remembers looked down into the garden of the house on S Street where Woodrow Wilson spent his last days after leaving the Presidency.

Mr. Roosevelt took with him on this first trip Renah H. Camalier, who had succeeded Charles McCarthy as his secretary when McCarthy resigned to become a member of the Emergency Fleet Corporation. He also took Marvin McIntyre, lovable and affable former newspaperman from Kentucky who had covered the Navy Department as head of the Navy Press Bureau, and was in the confidence of both Roosevelt and Howe. Stephen T. Early, brilliant and brittle newspaperman who had covered the Navy Department for the Associated Press, went ahead as Roosevelt's advance agent, with instructions from Louis to keep him informed on how he found things along the way for Franklin. From Chicago Steve wired that as he saw it so far the educated classes favored the League, hence were sympathetic to FDR, but that these classes were in the minority and that the majority were opposed to the League or indifferent because they did not understand it. But the smile came back to Louis' face when Steve wired from Minneapolis that he had gone through the crowd while FDR was speaking, getting the comments from the spectators. "Without exception they are excellent for the boss," he said. "He is speaking easier, going good, and will be a finished product before we see New York again."

In Steve's opinion, however, FDR was making an uphill fight, in spite of the enthusiasm for him personally. While there was a great sentiment for the League in many places, the Wilson administration was very unpopular. "The bitterness toward Wilson is evident everywhere and deeply rooted," Steve wired Louis from South Dakota. "He hasn't a friend."

At the end of August FDR returned to his New York headquarters well pleased with his trip. Louis was pleased, too, for there was no doubt that the vigorous campaign Franklin was waging was having its impact on the country. However, neither had any illusions about this personal popularity having enough pull to affect the eventual outcome. FDR had told Louis at the very beginning of the campaign, "The votes will be cast for Harding and not for Coolidge, for Cox and not for me." "That's obvious, isn't it?" Louis agreed.

Louis was probably the one who urged FDR to needle Harding for his "front porch campaign." Harding was receiving delegations at Marion, Ohio, but doing very little speaking.

"We will drag him off the front porch," FDR declared. "It is just as important for the candidates to get in touch with the United States as it is for the voters to have a chance to hear them. No man having the viewpoint merely of Ohio or Massachusetts or New York is fitted to be President or Vice-President. He must know the nation."

FDR was hewing to Louis' line to make "efficient government" his program when he said, "The golden rule of the true public servant is to give to his work the same or even higher interest and efficiency than he would give to his private affairs." To Harding's cry of "normalcy" FDR said, "We can never go back. The good old days are gone forever; we have no regrets. For our eyes are trained ahead—forward to better new days. . . ."

When Roosevelt left on his next trip early in September, Louis Howe went with him. McIntyre and Early were along, as were

Camalier and James Sullivan (another stenographer), Tom Lynch—an old Albany friend, and Stanley Prenosil, the only newspaperman assigned continuously to cover the Vice-Presidential candidate.

The Associated Press, which had not bothered to have a staff man on the train on FDR's first trip, assigned Prenosil because of an incident that had occurred in Butte, Montana. An AP man had reported that FDR left the text of his prepared speech to boast, "I wrote Haiti's constitution myself and, if I do say it, I think it is a pretty good constitution." This brought a terrific barrage from the Republicans, with Harding asserting that if he was elected President he would "not empower an Assistant Secretary of the Navy to draft a constitution for a helpless neighbor in the West Indies and jam it down their throats at the point of bayonets borne by United States Marines." FDR hotly denied that he made the remark about Haiti, other newspapermen claimed that he did, and the AP decided it was better to keep a man on FDR's coattails at all times than to depend on reports from the various stops.

Louis knew the value of having this sharp young reporter aboard and made haste to establish cordial relations with him. Each night he would get the early morning editions of the papers and sit down with Prenosil—FDR often sitting in—and prepare a rough draft of the high points of the speeches to be made next day. This enabled Prenosil to write some "background" stories in advance, and it assured Louis that any comments made by Franklin "off the cuff" would be accurately quoted in the future, at least by the Associated Press.

The first foray on this September trip was into New England and upstate New York, although Steve Early had reported both as "hopelessly lost territory." FDR barged in gaily anyway, but the farmers and others in upstate New York were so apathetic that along the Erie Railroad on which the campaign car, attached to the regular train, traveled, they often found only thirty or forty people at the stops.

"At Binghamton," FDR said, "the local people had difficulty

in filling the comparatively small hall. That difficulty may have been due to the fact, however, that Babe Ruth and Madame Galli-Curci were in town at the same time!"

Things were so dull during this phase of the trip that Louis dreamed up a little stunt to have some fun. He had the men aboard the train place bets on where they would find the smallest crowds during the day. The loser had to wear an enormous bow tie of a horrible hue which Louis had scrounged from somewhere, and go out on the station platform and stroll up and down while the natives gaped in astonishment.

In October, however, FDR headed west again at such a lively clip that he often made ten or more speeches in a single day. The schedule was so strenuous that tempers grew short and one day the cold war which had been going on between Louis and Camalier suddenly warmed up, to such an extent that Louis challenged Camalier to a fist fight. Camalier weighed some two hundred pounds and Louis about a hundred and thirty, but he was ready to try to cut Camalier down to his size anyway. Camalier was a hard-working young man and was devoted to FDR, but for some reason Louis didn't care for him and the feeling became mutual as time went on. It took FDR himself to quiet Louis down.

As for FDR, he was in high good humor all the time and enjoyed the whole experience.

"We really had trouble holding Franklin down on that trip," Louis said. "His enthusiasm was so great that we were after him constantly to keep him from wearing himself down to his bones. He wanted to speak every time the train slowed down and when I'd remonstrate with him he'd say enthusiastically, 'Why not? These people will be my bosses if I'm elected. I think they've got a right to know what they're hiring.' "

At one station Mr. Roosevelt, speaking from the back platform of the train, ran over his time and the members of the party began to look at each other nervously. The engineer, who had stepped to the platform to listen, settled everything. "You just take all the extra time you need, Mr. Roosevelt," he said, "and I'll make it up between here and the next station."

"He did, too," Louis said, "almost jerking our back teeth out going around curves!"

One of the funniest incidents of the trip involved Louis. The members of the party spent most of their time in the private car with little opportunity to stay in hotels except for a weekend now and then. On these rare occasions they raced for a hotel, a hot bath, and change of clothes. Once when the Roosevelt train traveling west and that of Governor Cox traveling east were to meet at Terre Haute, Indiana, FDR arranged to board the Cox train and ride to Indianapolis. He took Louis, Tom Lynch and Stanley Prenosil. As soon as the Cox train pulled out they all ran for a hotel and a bath. As they passed a newsstand, however, Louis grabbed all the papers, made for the parlor of the suite, took off his coat, shirt and shoes, sank down in a big chair, and began to pore over the papers, marking certain items for future use. The others took their baths, and then FDR started prodding Louis to hurry and get his bath as time was growing short. "Okay, okay," said Louis, busily slashing away with his pencil. He kept marking and stalling until FDR, with twinkling eyes, called Prenosil and Lynch into the next room. "Louis'll keep his nose stuck in those papers till we miss the train," he said. "Let's just give him a bath." Prenosil drew the tub of water, FDR motioned to Lynch, and the three of them grabbed Louis, removed his trousers, and threw him in the tub. Louis came up fighting but FDR, strong and youthful, and Lynch and Prenosil, also no weaklings, grabbed soap and towels and literally gave Louis a bath as he swore to kill them all if he could only lay hands on a gun. They had to dry his under-things on a radiator and, during this drying process Louis calmly wrapped himself in a blanket, went back to his arm chair, and buried his nose in the papers until time to run for the train.

Mrs. Roosevelt was the only woman aboard on this trip and it was here that she grew to know and like Louis Howe. Although she and Mrs. Howe were friends and saw each other frequently in Washington, she had not seen much of Louis and had resented his close association with her husband, feeling that his interests clashed with hers at times. And she *still* didn't like his clothes!

She was a somewhat timid person and was quite bewildered by all the goings on aboard the train and by the things she had to do as the wife of a candidate: listen to much the same speeches day after day, and look pleased and thrilled when she met the local celebrities. It was a strange experience for her. Louis, wise in campaigning ways, took her under his wing and thus began what she always termed "the start of her political education."

Mrs. Roosevelt had not traveled a great deal in the West and Louis made a point of sitting with her in the observation car and talking about the history of the places through which they were passing. She was a little embarrassed about being the only woman on the train and confused by the activities of the newspapermen and others who gathered in FDR's stateroom in the evenings for a good game of poker. She thought all this card playing, smoking and late hours were bad, and interfered with her husband's rest. She fretted about it and Louis, anxious to change her viewpoint, would leave FDR scowling over a losing hand or gloating over a winning one, and go to her stateroom for a chat. Often he took with him the draft of Mr. Roosevelt's speech for the next day and went over it with her, asking her advice and comments. Before long he had her discussing many subjects in which she had not been much interested. When he could, Louis also slipped in a good word for his newspaper pals. Hearing their colorful language, seeing them at the poker table, Mrs. Roosevelt was positive that they were all pretty hellish fellows, but Louis finally convinced her that at heart they were pretty good. She admitted that because of Louis' interpretation she came to look with interest on the writing fraternity and gained a liking for it that she never lost. But it was her new understanding of Louis Howe that was important to both of them.

"The fact that Louis had rather extraordinary eyes and a fine mind I was not to discover," she said, "and it was by the externals alone that I had judged him prior to this trip."[1]

It is hard to believe, seeing Mrs. Roosevelt so poised and confident today, that she suffered so with shyness, but we have her

[1] Eleanor Roosevelt, *This Is My Story* (New York: Harper & Brothers, 1937).

word for that and also for the fact that it was through the long and patient efforts of Louis Howe that she finally overcame it.

"One night Louis took me out to dinner," Mrs. Roosevelt recalled, "and sat all evening at a table he didn't like, eating food he didn't like, simply because he knew it would embarrass me and make me uncomfortable by getting up and moving to another table."[2]

FDR's enthusiasm, and that of Governor Cox, reached such proportions near the end of the campaign, as their crowds grew bigger and more receptive, that they were sending optimistic telegrams to each other, but it was becoming clear to Louis Howe and other realists that the ticket was going down to defeat. However, even they were not prepared for the landslide that swept Harding into the Presidency with sixty-one per cent of the popular vote.

FDR took his defeat the same way he had taken his defeat for the United States Senate six years before—with a lighthearted insouciance that was puzzling to many Democrats who felt the party lay in ruin.

He gave each member of the party who traveled with him a pair of cuff links as a memento of the campaign. These members became known as the "Cuff Links Club" and they met with FDR on his birthday each year thereafter as long as he lived. Their "Cuff Links dinners" became famous in Washington.

But Louis Howe was not downhearted because he knew how FDR had grown in stature. He and FDR at once began writing letters to the Democratic leaders over the country, with optimistic suggestions on how to reorganize the party for the Congressional elections two years hence. Louis happily basked in the knowledge that FDR, who had made over eight hundred speeches during the campaign, had taken strong hold on the country's imagination and would ever after have to be reckoned with in national politics. He thought the feeling about FDR in the country was expressed pretty well by a letter from the director of publicity of the Democratic State Central Committee in Seattle, Washington, which had been the focal point of FDR's first campaign swing:

[2] *Ibid.*

"Notwithstanding the results of November 2nd," he wrote to FDR, "I want you to know that you made a great host of friends on your trip through the west. To be quite candid about it, the western folks liked your 'style' and progressivism immensely . . . the ultra-progressive west has high hopes for aid from you and cooperation in the future."

That Louis Howe was undaunted by both these setbacks in FDR's career—his defeat in 1914 and again in 1920—is evidenced by the confident forecast he made to three of his friends, not long after the election. Looking out the window of his office in the Navy Department at the white façade of the building across the street, with Samuel McGowan, Rear Admiral Christian Peoples and Lieutenant Commander S. R. Fuller, Jr., Louis put one hand on McGowan's shoulder and the other on the shoulder of Admiral Peoples.

"Boys," he said, nodding toward the White House, "do you see that building over there? That's where Franklin is going someday." He paused a moment, then smiled.

"Franklin," he added, "and I!"

[5]

Campobello

TWO telegrams sent almost simultaneously in the summer of 1921 played their part in an event which was to change the course of Louis Howe's entire life. One was a message from his wife on Campobello Island telling him to come at once, that Franklin Roosevelt had been stricken with a strange malady. The other was dispatched to an oil company in New England which had offered Louis a job with an attractive salary, and which he had prepared to take until the day when he would be with Franklin again in some political capacity. The Roosevelts with their children, Mrs. Howe, and young Hartley, had gone to the Roosevelt summer home at Campobello Island and Louis was to come later, if he could get away. He had stayed in the Navy Department for some weeks to conclude some work on contracts and to help another Roosevelt start in the job. Colonel Theodore Roosevelt, Jr., son of "Teddy," still carrying on the tradition of a Roosevelt in the Navy Department, was now Assistant Secretary of the Navy in the administration of Warren G. Harding.

The story of how Franklin Roosevelt was struck down by infantile paralysis has often been told but will be retold briefly here to bring into focus the part that Louis Howe played in this tragic drama. One hot afternoon in August Franklin Roosevelt took his boys out sailing, and on the way home they saw a forest fire raging not far inland. They immediately made for shore to help fight the fire. When they returned FDR, who had complained of feeling tired for several days, decided a good swim was what he needed

75

and plunged into the icy Bay of Fundy. The mail had arrived when he came in and he sat for a time in his wet bathing suit, going through the letters. Still feeling tired and chilly, he skipped supper and went to bed.

A big camping trip had been planned for next day and the Roosevelts, Mrs. Howe and the children were to leave early in the morning and stay three days. The children were in a whoop of excitement. The next morning, however, Mr. Roosevelt was running a temperature but insisted that they go without him. Mrs. Roosevelt stayed behind, however, unwilling to leave him when he was not feeling well, and sent the children on with Mrs. Howe and another friend. Then she sent for Dr. Bennett, the old family physician from Lubec, Maine, just across the bay. The doctor thought at first that FDR had just an ordinary cold brought on by overheating in the fire fighting, followed by the cold swim. He'd probably be all right if he stayed in bed and was careful. But Mrs. Roosevelt was not wholly reassured, and by the time the camping trip was over it was plain that the strong and vigorous Roosevelt legs were becoming badly paralyzed.

Then Louis Howe took over. He had come as swiftly as he could travel after receiving Mrs. Howe's wire. Hartley, who had been counting the minutes till his dad arrived, remembers that, grim of countenance, with scarcely a glance at any of them, Louis went immediately to Franklin Roosevelt's bedroom. All day he sat at the foot of the bed rubbing FDR's feet, or stood over him rubbing his aching back, while FDR said over and over, "I don't know what is the matter with me, Louis. I just don't know."

Dr. Keen of Bar Harbor had been called for consultation and Louis went to meet him when he arrived. When Dr. Keen and Dr. Bennett decided that FDR's malady might be infantile paralysis, Mrs. Roosevelt, in addition to her anxiety over her husband, was in a state of near panic about the children until the doctors assured her that there was little danger that they would be affected.

Whatever Louis Howe felt as he looked down at that inert form and at that handsome face etched in lines of pain was carefully guarded. He assumed an air of optimism for the benefit of the others. If he asked himself, "Is this the end of the dream?" it is plain that he answered the question in the negative, by the plans he began to make as soon as it was realized that Franklin Roosevelt had infantile paralysis. It was then that he sent the telegram. He could not come, he told the company which had offered him the job. His duty was here—here with Franklin Roosevelt.

The words "infantile paralysis" had dire implications in those days. So little was known about it that Louis Howe knew all kinds of rumors would fly if the public became aware that Franklin Roosevelt had it, so he took the most elaborate pains to keep this knowledge from the outside world. He let it be known through the medium of the press that Mr. Roosevelt had a heavy cold and was confined to his bed for a time. "There is even a possibility," Louis explained to Mrs. Roosevelt, "that if the public heard the words 'infantile paralysis' it might think that Franklin's mind had been affected. There will be confusion in the public mind with meningitis, too. It's a thing that will plague him the rest of his life, but later he will be better able to meet it. The public must not see him again until they can see him cheerful and smiling. The wrong thing at this time might wreck his political career."

The words "political career" fell with queer emphasis on Eleanor Roosevelt's ears. Wifelike, her thoughts at that moment strayed no further than how to allay the purely physical suffering of her stricken helpmate. She looked at Louis Howe strangely.

"Do you really believe that Franklin still has a political future?" she asked.

"I believe," said Louis Howe, "that someday Franklin will be President."

"There were many people who did not like Louis Howe," said Gerald W. Johnson in his book, *Roosevelt: Dictator or Democrat?*. "He had his faults, without a doubt, but there was a touch of genuine greatness in Louis Howe. Plenty of men are only too willing to attach their fortunes to a star that is rising in the political firmament; but it takes a great man to attach himself to a leader at the moment of that leader's apparent ruin. . . . Louis Howe's enlisting for the duration was very nearly the only gleam of light in a prospect so gloomy that death itself could hardly have made it much darker."[1]

Eleanor Roosevelt put it more simply, but with great feeling. "From that time on," she said, "Louis Howe put his whole heart into working for my husband's future."

And so, as Franklin Roosevelt lay white and still during those long summer days, Louis Howe sat by his side with words of encouragement and cheer. And when Roosevelt read till his eyes stung from so much reading, Louis gently took the book from his hands and read to him. He read everything in the Roosevelt library he thought would interest the invalid; then he combed the libraries of friends on the island for books and read those. He read the daily papers to Franklin, to keep him abreast of national and world events and, as the slow days dragged on, Louis Howe made Roosevelt feel that though he lay there ill and stricken he was still, in a sense, a part of the stream of events flowing with the times.

Then fall came and it was no longer possible to keep the invalid at Campobello, nor to keep the curious world outside. And Roosevelt himself was anxious to get away now, for this idyllic place where he had come every summer since he was a boy, where he had roamed and romped and laughed and fished and played, this place had become to him a sort of silent enemy, a place of hurt instead of joy. That this feeling stayed on in his heart, though he never talked of it, is evidenced by the fact that he never went to Campobello again in all the long years from the summer of 1921 until the summer of 1933. He was President of the United States when he joyfully sailed the *Amberjack II* along Campobello's shores, and waved his battered old sea hat again toward its green, remembered hills.

Mrs. Howe and Hartley had long since gone home but Louis stayed on at Campobello, his days now spent in planning how to

[1] Gerald W. Johnson, *Roosevelt: Dictator or Democrat?* (New York: Harper and Brothers, Inc., 1941).

break the news of Franklin's illness to the country. So secretive was he about it that when his daughter Mary, who had been in Europe with a group of college students, arrived home, he met her at the boat, told her about it, but warned her not to repeat one word to a single soul.

Mr. Roosevelt was to be taken from the island to the Presbyterian Hospital in New York City and Louis planned each step with the greatest care. He made known that on September 14 Mr. Roosevelt would cross the bay from the island to Eastport, Maine, where a special railroad car, secured by FDR's uncle Frederic Delano, and which could be switched in Boston without change, waited on a siding. A crowd of townspeople and reporters waited at the Eastport dock.

Louis arranged for a stretcher to be brought to the house, and Mr. Roosevelt was placed on it with great gentleness and carried down to the Roosevelt private dock. There Captain Calder, a faithful family friend, waited in his motorboat. They laid Mr. Roosevelt on the floor boards, in the bottom of the boat; then, with Louis at his side, the boat chugged slowly across the bay. But, as Louis had carefully planned in advance, they did not land at the dock where the crowd waited, but on the opposite side of the harbor where there were no spectators. They put FDR on a baggage dray and Louis and a few others walked alongside the dray, shielding FDR from view until they reached the place where the private car waited. It was necessary to take out a window of the car and slide the stretcher through the opening. Only when they had FDR safely aboard and propped up by an open window did Louis send word to the dock. Reporters and townspeople streamed over to the car and there they saw Franklin D. Roosevelt by the window, his cigarette tilted at a jaunty angle, smiling and calling greetings. He kept smiling and shouted greetings until the train gathered speed and slowly faded from view. Louis Howe sat back in the car, mopped his brow and heaved a long sigh of relief.

"The sweat," he later said, "rolled down my back as we crossed that bay, like old man river rolling to the sea."

But another test was ahead: the arrival at the station in New York. The train was rolled in on a siding and there were no reporters. Louis had kept the time of arrival secret from all but a few close friends who waited on the platform.

"And do you know," he said, "all Franklin seemed to think about as we came into the station was how to keep his friends from feeling too badly when they saw him." As the stretcher slowly slid through the window and his massive body, now prone and still, came into view, FDR's eyes searched the platform for familiar faces, and he called out to them, waving his cigarette holder cheerily as he greeted each one by name.

"Come along with me to the hospital," he called gaily, "so we can have a good visit, and catch up. I've been 'out of it' for some weeks you know. Bring me up to date."

"I remember tough, old Tom Lynch," Louis said. "He mumbled that he had to get back down in town right away and then he turned away, so Franklin couldn't see the tears that were streaming down his cheeks."

A stabbing thought comes to me as I write these lines. Once I too saw Franklin D. Roosevelt lifted through the windows of a railroad car. It was the night of April 14, 1945. He had been brought from Warm Springs, Georgia, where he had passed away two days before. The great funeral at the White House was over and he was going home to the Hyde Park he had always loved so well. Grace Tully, his secretary, had come by in the White House car to take me and two other friends down to the funeral train where we planned to get aboard before the sad cortege arrived. So many thousands of people jammed the station and the plaza that we were delayed for many minutes before we could push our way through the vast throng. When we started through the lines an officer waved us back beyond the ropes stretched around the funeral train. A Secret Service man stepped forward.

"It's all right," he said. "It is Miss Tully, the President's secretary, and her friends. Let them go through."

Just then a shaft of light shot from somewhere behind us and quivered for a moment on a sight I shall never forget. The flag-draped casket containing the last mortal remains of our beloved "Boss" was being gently lifted in stalwart arms through the windows of the funeral car. Miss Tully, who had seen this same sad sight twice in the past two days—once at Warm Springs when the car left there and again when it arrived in Washington, broke into quiet weeping. John Boettiger, the President's son-in-law, stepped swiftly from the shadows at this moment and escorted us down the side of the train until we could get aboard and find our car.

As we passed down the long, darkened corridors of the train, suddenly, without warning, we stepped into a small sitting room dignified, warm and softly lighted. There, sitting on a couch with his wife and lovely blonde daughter, was the new President of the United States, Harry S. Truman. With them was James F. Byrnes, soon to become the new Secretary of State. The President arose swiftly and shook hands with us, introduced us to Mrs. Truman and Margaret and graciously asked us to stay. But Miss Tully murmured her thanks, and we moved on down the corridors as the darkened train slid slowly into the night.

But back to those September days in the fall of 1921, in New York, where Franklin Roosevelt, who had left New York in the full vigor of young manhood a few months before, returned a stricken, and many thought a defeated, man. So many adjustments had to be made. What to do—where to begin? Again this problem descended on the narrow shoulders of Louis Howe. He knew he had to tell the newspapers something, so on September 16 the papers carried his carefully prepared story that Franklin D. Roosevelt had been stricken with infantile paralysis at Campobello.

Louis was the one who had to ask Dr. Lovett, the eminent specialist who had been called in, just what Mr. Roosevelt's chances were of ever recovering the use of his lower limbs. Louis was to ask the questions, with the idea that the doctor would be more brutally frank with him than with a member of the family.

The doctor told Louis frankly that though Mr. Roosevelt's condition would grow no worse his improvement would be very slight unless he had the most extraordinary will and patience—and that hours, days, weeks, months and years of constant effort would be needed to bring the muscles back. "My experience has been," he said, "that few people possess the courage and determination to make the fight, but if Mr. Roosevelt's interest in resuming active life is great enough, his will to recover strong enough, there is undoubtedly a chance."

When Louis told this to the Roosevelt family, Eleanor Roosevelt agreed with his suggestion that under no circumstances should they ever treat Mr. Roosevelt as an invalid. They would treat him instead as a normal human being, temporarily unable to get about. The decision about the treatments would be left up to him.

Mr. Roosevelt's mother, however, did not go along too readily with this program. She had made up her mind that her son never would lead an active life again. Why couldn't he come to Hyde Park to live—there was much he could do. He could study, he could write, he could manage the estate—life could be full in spite of this misfortune. But a political future? That was just a wild dream.

"You have good common sense, Louis," she said. "Can't you see that a political future is now out of the question for my son?"

Louis Howe looked at her long and steadily. "I expect him to be President," he said quietly. "Anyway he is going to have his chance."

Then Louis flung his challenge to FDR: "Either you can retire and become a country squire, or gather up your courage and plunge forward as though nothing had happened. You are a man of destiny," he said firmly, "and I will go along with you every inch of the hard way, if that is the way you choose. Besides," he said, partly in earnest and partly to bring a smile to the tired face, "this makes it certain that you'll be President. My reason? You'll get the sympathy of the public and you will be spared the handshaking, the platform stumping, the bazaar openings—in short all the political nonsense that ruins so many men."

"As far as I was concerned though," Louis Howe said later, "I was betting on a sure thing. I knew my man would win because I knew my man. He accepted the challenge too, and his courage through those black years was so magnificent I decided that the greatest adventure of which a man could dream would be to put him in the White House.

"And there are times," Louis Howe told me in his office, many years later, "when I doubt if Franklin might ever have been President if he had not been stricken, tragic though it was. You see, he had a thousand interests. You couldn't pin him down. He rode, he swam, he played golf, tennis, he sailed, he collected stamps, he politicked, he did about every damn thing under the sun a man could think of doing. Then suddenly there he was flat on his back, with nothing to do but think. He began to read, he began to think, he talked, he gathered people around him—his thoughts expanded, his horizon widened. He began to see the other fellow's point of view. He thought of others who were ill and afflicted and in want. He dwelt on many things which had not bothered him much before. Lying there, he grew bigger day by day.

"I am not at all sure," Louis said, half seriously and half in jest, "but that, were it the possible thing to do, a year or two in bed should be prescribed for all our statesmen to enable them to study and learn the complexities of our modern life!"

In his challenge to FDR to go ahead with his life, however, Louis Howe did not fail to show him both sides of the question. He pointed out that FDR could, if he wished, lead a useful life engaged in literary work, and other things that required no personal agility. He also laid stress on the uncertainty of hope and the certainty of years of painful effort which must follow a real determination to recover, of the long and grueling regime of massage and exercise. He told him of the doctor's warning that even with all this there might be no results at all.

Franklin Roosevelt listened to him quietly, and with careful attention. When Louis had finished he flashed him a smile.

"Well," he said cheerfully, "when do we begin?"

"I knew then," said Louis Howe, "that you could never lick Franklin!"

[6]

With the Strength of Louis Howe

AND SO, aided and encouraged by Louis Howe and Eleanor Roosevelt, Franklin Roosevelt began his battle to live a normal life. Louis now became a full-fledged member of the Roosevelt household, an arrangement that continued to the day of his death and took him from the Roosevelt town house in New York City to the family estate at Hyde Park, the Governor's mansion in Albany, and finally to the White House.

Franklin Roosevelt sent for Mrs. Howe after the decision was made that Louis would stay at his side.

"Grace," he said, "I don't want you to come to New York to live. Louis will stay with us as a member of the family during the week, but on weekends should have a place where he can rest and be free. If you and he live here in the city the temptation would be great for me to call on him at all hours, but if he gets away I won't have the nerve to bother him. I'll see to it that he gets away on Friday nights and leads his own private life a couple of days."

Many adjustments had to be made at the Roosevelt home, since doubling up became necessary to make room for Louis and Mr. Roosevelt's nurse, who was in daily attendance. Anna, then a teen-age girl in a private school in New York which she didn't like, surrendered her room to Louis and she didn't like this either. Mrs. Roosevelt speaks of those days as trying ones indeed. The

85

little boys slept in their grandmother's house next door while Mrs. Roosevelt slept on a couch, or wherever she could.

Mrs. Howe rented a house on Church Street in Poughkeepsie where Mary was a senior at Vassar, and Louis went up for weekends. Mary always looked forward to these visits and she and her friends still talk about the outdoor picnic Louis gave for them after the Senior prom. He rented cars and took seven or eight couples out into the back country near Fishkill, where he cooked and served, at the end of long sticks, succulent steaks three inches thick.

As a graduation gift Louis arranged for Mary to christen a submarine. The whole family went to Portsmouth Navy Yard for the event, and Louis proudly watched when his daughter broke a bottle of champagne across the nose of the *S-13* and received a gold watch, which she still has, as a memento of the occasion.

The following year Mary went to California to take a job with the Lick Observatory and Mrs. Howe rented a house in Fall River to be near her mother. Louis never owned a home in Fall River and the only people he really knew there were friends of Mrs. Howe's. Fall River was just a weekend refuge in the wintertime. His real love was the cottage at Horseneck Beach, seventeen miles away, which the Howes had bought two years after Mrs. Howe rented it in 1910, and where they now spent their summers.

Louis could really "get away from it all" at the cottage. It could be reached only by a narrow road running so close to the water that when the tide was in you couldn't travel it at all, and the family and visitors always had to time their arrival or departure by the ebb and flow of the tide! The beach was an exciting place for ten-year-old Hartley who played in the sand, or swam and sailed his model boats as the lazy summer days drifted by. But the real time began for Hartley on Saturday morning when his father was due from New York. "I'd run down at least a hundred times during the morning," he said, "to look through Dad's field glasses to see if he was on his way. He never failed to bring me something, which he gave to me, first thing, then he'd go off and sleep for hours."

On Sundays, though, the two of them had wonderful times in the wood-working shop which Louis had made from an old barn on the place. Here he and Hartley worked on ship models, wooden figurines, and other fascinating items, and Louis even turned out some furniture for the cottage, which Mrs. Howe describes as not exactly things of beauty, but well made and fine for use in the cottage where living was extremely simple, even to the use of lamps and candles.

FDR enjoyed a good laugh as a result of one of Louis' weekend trips. It was in the late fall and there were only a few more weekends at the beach. Mrs. Howe was to meet Louis at the train upon his arrival and she wired him confirming the train time, then ended with the usual "Love." When she read the telegram over and found she had room for two more words she thought she'd let him know how the weather was at the beach, so she added "growing colder." This made the message read: "Love growing colder." Louis was in the room with FDR when the message was delivered. He read it, then passed it over to FDR who chortled when he reached the ending. "Louis," FDR said, "get up there right away. When your wife wires that her love is growing colder it's time for you to get a move on!"

FDR, an avid collector, missed not being able to attend the various auctions to look for rare stamps, old prints, ship models and the like, so Louis took over this chore, brought catalogues to the bedside, pored over them with FDR, then spent hours in the various auction rooms until he found just the thing that would gladden Franklin's heart. One day, in an old out-of-the-way shop, he saw a picture which looked familiar though covered with grime and dirt. The shopkeeper wiped off the dirt, and Louis offered him $25.00 for the picture, which the man was glad to accept. Louis rushed to Franklin with an authentic portrait of the great Naval hero, John Paul Jones, one of the very few, it is said, for which Jones posed in person. FDR was delighted.[1]

Louis was not a collector but he loved cats and, while on one of these excursions for FDR, picked up a carved wooden cat

[1] Grace Tully, *F.D.R., My Boss* (New York: Charles Scribner's Sons, 1949).

which had been made in Egypt. After that he was always on the lookout for rare stones and other trinkets to set off his cat to advantage. To while away the time as he sat with FDR he'd group these stones about his feline treasure, changing and shifting them until the lights caught the beauty of the stones in just the color combination he wanted. This "cat activity" amused FDR, who declared that it bore out what he had always suspected—Louis was a born old maid!

"I believe I'll play with my stamps awhile, Louis," he'd say, getting out his big stamp book and settling back with it, "and you can play with your 'cat's nest.'"

When FDR grew restless for the outdoors at Hyde Park, Louis would sit with him on the side porch or on the great shaded lawn that overlooked the Hudson River, and here they'd work on models of sailboats. When the models were completed Louis, and one of the men who worked on the estate, would help FDR into a rowboat, and they'd row slowly along the smooth surface of the river as the little sailboats, like bright butterflies, skipped along in the water beside them.

Fortunately Mr. Roosevelt's general health was good, and by February of the next year he was out of his wheelchair and up on crutches. He kept on with many of his former activities, one of which was the vice-presidency of the Fidelity and Deposit Company of Baltimore, and by autumn he was making daily trips to his office downtown.

Louis was wrestling daily with a problem which loomed large in his mind—how to get Franklin actively interested in politics again. He was already using the old trick of turning a major weakness into a source of strength. FDR could not go out to see the people but people could be brought to him through letters, and Louis exploited this medium to the utmost. He saw that FDR wrote to practically everybody he knew in the country, and that incoming letters received careful, individual replies.

Louis decided that one of the best things he could do was to have Mrs. Roosevelt also interested in politics and thus bring a political atmosphere right into FDR's bedroom. But this was a problem, too. Mrs. Roosevelt was a homebody, with five growing children on her hands. What could she possibly do, she asked. Louis finally convinced her that it was important that her husband become actively interested in the political world again as mental therapy, so reluctantly she agreed to try whatever Louis wished her to do. Soon Louis was steering her to people he thought would start her in her new role—Miss Marian Dickerman, an instructor at the Todhunter School in New York City, Mrs. James Laidlaw of the Women's Trade Union League, and Miss Nancy Cook, who was with the Democratic State Committee. Miss Cook persuaded Mrs. Roosevelt to preside over a meeting of the Democratic State Committee during a fund-raising campaign. Mrs. Roosevelt admitted that she knew so little about what the Committee was trying to do that when she rose to her feet she had no idea what she would say. She struggled through this ordeal somehow and grew a little more confident, with Louis' encouragement. Louis would go with her when she made a talk in public, sit in the back of the room, and then tell her later all the things she shouldn't have done!

Once he asked her why she laughed at a certain point in her speech. "Why, I didn't know I laughed," she said. "There wasn't any reason to laugh."

"I know there wasn't," said Louis dryly, "so why did you give that silly little giggle?"

However, it wasn't too hard to follow Louis' instructions on speechmaking: "Have something to say, say it and then sit down!"

Louis soon had evidence that the political spark was not really dead in FDR's mind, for by March 1922 he was writing about the political situation to old friends in Washington. He wrote to James M. Cox, his running mate of 1920, that he was thinking, even then, in terms of how to prevent the seeds of isolationism being sown in this country.

"What I am basically convinced of, and I know you are, after your trip abroad," FDR said, "is that the country is beginning to recognize that national isolation on our part will not allow further disintegration in the Near East, Europe, etc., but from our own selfish point of view will bring hard times, cut off exports. . . .

How far the Democratic party should go just now is a thing which the leaders should talk over in the near future."

FDR was even mentioned that fall as a candidate for governor to offset William Randolph Hearst who was trying to get the nomination, but Louis shook his head vigorously, and so did FDR, who finally prevailed on Al Smith to come back into public life and stop Hearst. Smith took the challenge and wanted FDR to run on the ticket with him as a candidate for the United States Senate, but again FDR and Louis Howe said no. While Louis was anxious for Franklin to enter the national political arena he knew it was too soon and laid down an iron rule: Franklin must never be carried in public and he must never run for national office until he could go before the country without his crutches.

In the spring of 1922 FDR went to Florida to cruise on a houseboat, which he and a friend named John Lawrence had bought and named *The Larooco*. This was a combination of the names Lawrence, Roosevelt and Company.

While FDR was in Florida Governor Cox paid him a visit. It was the first time Cox had seen FDR since he was stricken and he was delighted with the way he had met his misfortune. "He was the same vibrant person as of old," Cox said. "He almost seemed to enjoy the contest he was waging."

Louis Howe used similar words in telling how Mr. Roosevelt fought the battle of recovery in those days:

"In Franklin's office, when people came in and asked him how in the world he managed to attend to business, he'd ask them just how much running to and fro is a man expected to do in an office. 'Maybe my legs aren't so good,' he'd say with a grin, 'but look at these shoulders. Jack Dempsey would be green with envy if he could see me!'

"I used to go to Franklin's room in the mornings," Louis said, "and, as he lay there in bed, you could see that he was struggling mightily to move the muscles in his feet and legs. It was a sort of stubborn game with him. He'd made up his mind that he'd get those muscles to move and he never gave up for a minute, though the exercises and massages didn't seem to have much effect for a long time. One morning, though, when I went in he was lying there grinning from ear to ear, though I could see the sweat standing out on his forehead in great beads.

"As I closed the door he yanked the covers back and pointed gleefully to one foot, shoved out over the side of the bed.

" 'Look, Louis!' he shouted, 'I can wiggle my toe!'

"Well, it was one of the biggest signs of improvement I had seen, and I knew it had done a hell of a lot for his morale, and that was all important."

In the spring of 1924 Charles F. Murphy, still leader of Tammany, but an older and more chastened Tiger than the one who had battled FDR so tenaciously in Albany, came to see Franklin Roosevelt. Could he, because of his association with the "Federal end of things," undertake to round up some delegates for Al Smith for President, Murphy wanted to know.

"Louis Howe and I began at once," Roosevelt said, "though it was of course very late in the year to start. I remember telling C. F. (with his complete agreement) that with hard work and good luck we might be able to get three hundred delegates to the National Convention for Al, but that in all probability we could not nominate him. However, it would be a good thing to do and we might be able to get him the nomination in 1928."

Early in May Roosevelt became Chairman of the "Citizens for Al Smith." It was not the custom to have a campaign chairman put a man's name in nomination so Al tried out several others for this job, but finally came back to FDR and told him he was the only one to do it. Louis Howe's heart leaped. For the first time since he was stricken Franklin was to appear before the public, in the national political spotlight. Knowing the great importance of the occasion Louis carefully charted every step.

"Louis really went into so many details and arrangements for Franklin's appearance at the convention when he was to nominate Governor Smith," Mrs. Roosevelt said, "that although I was beginning to be interested in politics, I just could not understand it all. He was in a perfect fever of activity, planning, arranging, conferring with people and bringing the various leaders in to see Franklin before the convention began."

The convention met in Madison Square Garden, in the shimmering heat of late June. On the day FDR was to nominate Al, Louis, his plans completed, took an inconspicuous seat high in the gallery where he could see it all. Cordell Hull, then Chairman of the Democratic National Committee, sat on the platform with other state leaders grouped around him. As arranged beforehand, strong arms carried FDR in his chair to the speaker's platform, out of sight of the crowd, but before starting his walk to the "pulpit" as he called it, FDR turned to Joseph F. Guffey of Pennsylvania, who sat on the platform.

"Joe," he whispered, "go up to the pulpit and shake it, will you?"

"Why?" Guffey asked.

"I want to see if it will support my weight," FDR said.

Joe Guffey strode to the speaker's stand and shook it vigorously, smiled at FDR and told him it was all right. Then, carefully adjusting his crutches, and taking the arm of his son Jimmy, stalwart and strong at seventeen, FDR made his slow and painful way to the stand, while the crowd watched, breathless, and up in the galleries Louis Howe gripped his hands together so hard that his knuckles showed white against the brown leather of his skin. The stand came nearer and nearer, the tense lines began to fade from FDR's face, and suddenly there he was, gripping the "pulpit" with his strong hands and, as Louis Howe let out his breath in a long sigh, FDR threw back his head and smiled confidently at the thousands before him as though to say, "See, I made it!" Then he launched, with pride and confidence, into his great speech for the "Happy Warrior."

"He is the Happy Warrior of the political battlefield," FDR said, "this leader whose whole career gives convincing proof of his power to lead; this warrior whose record shows him to be invincible, in defense of right and in attack against wrong; this man beloved by all, trusted by all, this man of destiny whom our state proudly dedicates to the nation—Alfred E. Smith."

When FDR finished the roar of thunderous applause beat upon the blistering air of the Garden. The applause was as much a tribute to the gallantry of the speaker as it was for the leader he extolled, and there was a split second when Louis Howe wondered, half in panic, if this was it!

"His appearance there when he put Smith's name in nomination," he said later, "remains a historic incident of modern Democratic victory. The party hesitated on the verge of a stampede—to Roosevelt!"

John W. Davis broke the Smith-McAdoo deadlock and was nominated, the ticket went down to defeat that fall and Calvin Coolidge sat in the White House, but Louis Howe was not an unhappy man. Franklin was taking his place in national politics. Against the background of his Happy Warrior speech was the admiration the country felt for his game fight to live a normal life, but when insistent talk of "FDR for Governor" began to hum around Louis' ears again that fall he firmly shook his head. There was time. They could wait.

In the fall of 1924, FDR, having heard of the healing qualities of the waters at Warm Springs, Georgia, went down with the hope that they would help restore the use of the muscles in his legs. Two reporters, who went from Atlanta to ask him what he thought of the national political situation, found him in the pool, and one of them was so intrigued by the waters and what they were doing for FDR that he wrote an article called "Swimming Back to Health," illustrated by pictures of FDR and Annette Kellerman, the famous swimming star who was said to have had polio as a child.[2] But the story was not to FDR's liking and he complained to Louis about it. He was afraid the story might bring many others rushing to Warm Springs before there were facilities to care for them, and he said to Louis, "I don't want any sob stories written about my legs." Louis Howe just smiled. "Human interest stuff never hurt

[2] Ernest K. Lindley, *Franklin D. Roosevelt: A Career in Progressive Democracy.*

anybody," he said, "especially if it brings help to others in some way. It can't do you any harm."

Louis believed, of course, that any favorable publicity that would keep FDR in the public eye during this period was not only to be desired but worked for unceasingly. Later, when Al Smith was on vacation at Sea Girt, New Jersey, Louis wrote to FDR immediately, when he heard that Al was complaining that so many curious people swarmed over his vacation retreat that he couldn't even play golf or swim.

"Why not a line to Al suggesting that he come down to Warm Springs with Mrs. Smith for a week?" Louis said. "Al can get away from that bunch hanging around his neck at Sea Girt and not only have a chance to swim but clear up his neuritis as well. He might come, but if he doesn't no harm will be done and you might get a little good publicity. Think it over," he advised.

In April 1925 when FDR was at Warm Springs, Louis went down to look the place over, liked it, and was pleased when FDR included him, two years later, with George Foster Peabody, Herbert N. Straus and Basil O'Connor as one of the incorporators of the Warm Springs Foundation.

Al Smith was renominated for governor again in the fall of 1924 and Louis Howe helped Mrs. Roosevelt in her work with the Women's Division of the New York State Democratic Committeee, in which she was now taking an active part. He wrote their leaflets for them, drafted letters, secured speakers, planned strategy and even helped edit the magazine they issued during the campaign.

Smith's Republican opponent was Theodore Roosevelt, Jr., and Louis, who had stayed at the Navy Department three years before to help this same young man get started in his new job, now designed a plot to defeat him. The shattering story of Teapot Dome had just hit the front pages and the smell of the scandal was strong in the country's nostrils. Young Teddy as Assistant Secretary of the Navy had been an important part of the Harding administration but he was not mentioned in connection with the notorious oil deal. However, Louis saw a way to use the unsavory mess to the Democrats' advantage. He organized a caravan to tour several counties upstate and had the lead car in the caravan completely covered with a huge teapot, specially and skillfully made. Louis would find out where Teddy was delivering an open air address, and as the climax of the program was reached he'd have the car driven slowly around the edge of the crowd with realistic steam rolling upward from the teapot's spout. The effect was devastating and often broke up the meetings.

Teddy was soundly defeated by Al Smith, but to Louis Howe's credit he never claimed that this "devilish scheme" of his, as the Republicans called it, was actually responsible!

Early in 1925 FDR formed a law partnership with Basil O'Connor with offices in the Equitable Building at 120 Broadway, and Louis, who had been appointed Secretary of the National Crime Commission, now had an office in the same building. Louis' work with the Crime Commission was not merely a sideline while he kept a watchful eye on Franklin politically, for he was always enormously interested in crime and its causes, and studied the subject exhaustively.

It is worth noting, I think, that the five important recommendations which Louis made as a result of his work with the National Crime Commission were all carried out later on, either in fact or in substance:

1. Change the system of exclusive state jurisdiction on stolen goods.
2. Shorten and simplify justice.
3. Establish a United States Scotland Yard.
4. Have government monopoly of machine guns.
5. Universal fingerprinting.

His first recommendation became a reality in 1934 when Congress passed the Stolen Property Act which makes it an offense to transport stolen goods in interstate commerce.

His recommendation that justice be shortened and simplified was largely accomplished when the new Federal Rules of Criminal Procedure went into effect March 21, 1946.

His recommendation for the establishment of a United States Scotland Yard, to be used primarily as a school for training state forces, parallels closely the work of the Federal Bureau of Investigation which has for years conducted a school in Washington where intensive training is given to selected officers of state and municipal police forces.

Although his recommendation for Federal regulation of machine guns is not a complete reality, Federal legislation has been enacted which severely restricts the possession of machine guns and other similar firearms and makes their possession by criminals unlawful—namely, the National Firearms Act of 1934 and the Federal Firearms Act of 1938.

Finally, while there is no law requiring universal fingerprinting, the Federal Bureau of Investigation in the regular course of its duties, supplemented by its exhaustive investigative work during World War II, has accumulated a file of one hundred and twenty-eight million fingerprints.

Louis was a fanatic about the fact that anybody could walk into a store in those days and buy a machine gun. This was during the prohibition era when gangsters were knocking off their enemies with these deadly weapons and, while Louis might have thought this a good way to dispose of the gangster problem provided they only shot each other, he well knew the danger of letting these lethal weapons get into the hands of all sorts of individuals.

"Mein Gawd!" he would exclaim, if anyone disagreed with him on this subject, "Will you please give me one single reason why any individual should own a machine gun?" When one caller timidly suggested that it might be useful in killing a flock of ducks Louis almost threw him out of his office.

In the summer of 1925 Louis invited FDR to come to Horseneck Beach for a few weeks' rest, and when FDR accepted, Mrs. Howe, who had been hinting broadly that she'd like to go to England for a few weeks, was surprised when Louis suddenly told her to go ahead with plans for her trip. He had been turning over and over in his mind various things which might hasten the improvement in the still inactive muscles of Mr. Roosevelt's legs. He had seen what the waters of Warm Springs were doing, so was heat and more heat the answer? The hot sands at Horseneck Beach kept swirling into his thoughts. If he could get FDR up there in a spot with complete privacy, why couldn't they try out the curative properties of those sands? He could hardly wait and was full of excitement when, at last, he and FDR took off from New York for the beach.

"The car as usual will be crowded," FDR wrote to his mother. "Louis and I on the back seat with various packages tucked around and under us, one colored treasure on a little seat, the other in front with Snyder [Montfort Snyder, FDR's chauffeur], and several score suitcases, braces, crutches, canes, sandwiches thrown in for good measure. However it saves $11.00 for each person to travel thus to the beach!"[3]

When they reached the beach cottage and Snyder and one "colored treasure" had gone back, the other treasure being kept to do the cooking for the two "bachelors," FDR then put himself in Louis Howe's hands for a new and untried course of treatments. Far away from the cottage, over the dunes where none could see, Franklin Roosevelt, clad in an old bathing suit, crawled on his hands and knees day after day as the hot August sun beat down, crawled until the beads of perspiration stood out on his forehead and until at last, exhausted but smiling, he would rest in the shade while Louis Howe fixed for them both long and cooling drinks. In addition to this physical activity, however, FDR's active mind needed stimulation, so, when the setting sun cast its long shadows over the dunes, and the sands grew cool, they would go back to the cottage and there they sat and talked of politics and world affairs, read books, and, by lamplight, busily worked on the rough outline of FDR's contemplated history of the life of John Paul Jones.

And so the lazy summer days drifted by and the treatments

[3] Elliott Roosevelt, *F.D.R., His Personal Letters.*

and writing continued, with the solitude broken only once when
Mrs. Roosevelt drove up with two friends to see them and to bring
a little of the outside world into their secluded retreat.

FDR had become interested in the work of Dr. William Mc-
Donald, formerly of Albany but now of Marion, Massachusetts,
who had developed a new type of treatment for polio, and he was
anxious to try it. He decided to go from Louis' beach to Marion,
where he had rented a cottage for a month. Louis drove him over
during the last week in August, helped him get settled in the cottage, then rushed off to New York to meet Mrs. Howe, returning
from England, and to attend to several matters for Franklin in
the city before returning to the beach. Mrs. Roosevelt joined her
husband in Marion and FDR was so delighted with the treatments
that he prolonged his stay until well into December. Louis, however, had long since gone back to the city to resume his work with
the Crime Commission, to attend to Franklin's affairs, and to
continue his never-ending chore of writing political letters. He
was never sure how much his "sand and sea" therapy had helped
FDR but he knew that the rest, the salt air, and the fun had been
a stimulating tonic to them both, and his heart sang when he
heard about something that had happened one fine fall day in
Marion. Dwight L. Hoopingarner, an old friend of FDR's from
World War I days, had been invited up to Marion for a weekend
with the Roosevelts, and when he arrived he was met at the station by FDR and his secretary Marguerite LeHand, with FDR
himself at the wheel, ruddy and tanned and in high spirits.

"All the way back to the cottage," Hoopingarner told Louis
Howe when he returned to New York, "I could see that FDR was
full of suppressed excitement. When we got there and I was busy
unpacking I heard a shout to 'Come and look!' I stepped out on
a little porch and there, standing between two strong bars which
had been erected along the walkway, stood Franklin Roosevelt,
his hands free of the bars, only his wasted legs holding him up.
'See,' he shouted, 'see, I can stand alone!'

"I choked up," Mr. Hoopingarner said, "and stood there like

a damned baby, with the tears I could not control running down my face, but FDR never stopped grinning!"

Time was moving on, and so were the children of Louis Howe. In June of 1926 Louis took leave from everything to go to Fall River for the marriage of his daughter Mary. Regretful at losing her, but happy in her happiness, he proudly escorted his only daughter down the aisle and handed her over to Professor Robert Baker, head of the Observatory at the University of Illinois. And in the fall of 1927 Robert Baker, Jr., was born and Louis attained the awesome title of "grandfather."

Louis still found time to indulge now and then in his hobby of writing illustrated verses, and when FDR and Mrs. Roosevelt went to Florida for another cruise on *The Larooco* in the early spring of 1926, he made an elaborate dedication page for the ship's log:

"This Log is dedicated to St. Ananias and St. Sapphira," he wrote, "the Patron Saints of all True Fisherfolk.

"The Log of the Houseboat Larooco, being a more or less truthful account of what happened (Expurgated for the very young)." He illustrated the whole thing with colorful pen-and-wash drawings and FDR was so delighted that he carefully preserved it, with his log entries, among his personal treasures.[4]

Louis began to call himself the "go-betweener," during this time, as FDR had him doing all sorts of odd jobs, tying up the loose ends of things in which he became interested but didn't have time to carry through. When the citizens of Dutchess County appealed to him in the winter of 1926, when the water supply commission was in that section looking for more water for New York City, FDR reminded them that he had been issuing warnings about this situation for several years. He knew there was a possibility that New York City might take a vast supply of water and much land from Dutchess County unless something was done. He was greatly interested in the problem but was leaving for Warm Springs, so he asked Louis to make an investigation of the

4 *Ibid.*

situation. The problem was somewhat out of Louis' line and he found it pretty complicated, but he went into the situation thoroughly anyway and faithfully sent his reports to FDR.

FDR had him investigating oil on another occasion, when Mrs. Roosevelt's brother Hall wanted to get FDR interested in a new method of exploiting the earth's oil resources. Land was needed to carry out the experiment. FDR asked Louis to go to see Barron Collier, well-known New York businessman, who had large land holdings in the state of Florida, about leasing some land for this purpose. Louis didn't care whether the experiments were carried out or not but nothing along this line was ever wasted effort, in his opinion, if it kept FDR alert, active and interested; this was far more important, in Louis' mind, than whether anybody struck oil or whether New York City got all the water it needed.

Historians have asked whether FDR's ambition to become President grew from seed to bud and from bud to flower during those fateful years between 1921 and 1928. The question was once asked of Louis Howe who gave a dry and cryptic answer:

"You just don't go into big-time politics," he said, "without the Presidency *always* in the back of your mind!"

Later, when a biographer asked FDR when it was that he had first begun to cast his glance at the highest place of power, FDR—who by now had attained that "place of power"—answered firmly,

"I? Never! But Louis Howe never forgot!"

[7]

"Mess Is No Name for It"

WHEN the 1928 Presidential campaign arrived Al Smith had served four terms as Governor of New York and was the leading candidate for President on the Democratic ticket. The Democratic Convention was held in Houston, Texas, that summer, and Franklin D. Roosevelt, now walking with a cane, and leaning on his son's arm, stood before the cheering delegates and again asked them to nominate his Happy Warrior.

Louis was satisfied that the intervening years had been well spent. The national publicity Franklin had received at the Democratic Convention in 1924 had made him a popular and sympathetic figure throughout the country and now Louis had a definite time for him—1936. He was sure Hoover would defeat Smith in 1928 and that Hoover would probably serve two terms. Louis planned for FDR to run for Governor of New York in 1932.

Even with Louis' uncanny sense of timing and events, he did not foresee the crash of 1929, the discontent in the country, the breadlines, the rumbling that grew into a storm that finally swept the Democrats and Franklin Roosevelt into power four years ahead of schedule. Louis had kept up his stream of correspondence with Democrats across the country from his little office at 120 Broadway, and continued to shuttle back and forth between there, the Roosevelt town house, and Fall River. He was no longer worried about whether Franklin's interest in national politics had

101

been revived. He smiled. Franklin was now in politics up to his neck!

After Al Smith was nominated for President at Houston, John J. Raskob, Al's friend, became Chairman of the Democratic National Committee, and Roosevelt became Chairman of the Commerce and Industry Division at the Democratic Campaign Headquarters in the General Motors Building off Columbus Circle in New York. He put Louis in charge of the office and asked Dwight L. Hoopingarner to come in as his assistant. FDR had known Hoopingarner during World War I when Hoopingarner was head of the Employment Management Branch of the U. S. Shipping Board Emergency Fleet Corporation, in charge of the organization and procedures of the labor departments of the shipyards in the country, while FDR was Assistant Secretary of the Navy. In 1922 FDR and Herbert Hoover, then Secretary of Commerce, sponsored the organization of the American Construction Council, to unify all elements of the construction industry and to promote better construction and better relations with the public on the entire construction front. Mr. Roosevelt was President of the Council and Mr. Hoopingarner industrial economist and an executive of the organization.

Mr. Hoopingarner had other plans for the fall of 1928, but he didn't know Louis Howe as well then as he did later. Franklin wanted Hoopingarner; Franklin would have him. Louis pounded Mr. Hoopingarner with phone calls and telegrams until he finally fled for a weekend to the home of a brother on Long Island to escape. When he returned Sunday night the calls from Louis Howe were stacked higher than the telephone. "I knew that here was a man who would never take no for an answer," said Mr. Hoopingarner ruefully, "so I gave in and went to work."

About this time I went to work for Louis Howe. Besides Mr. Hoopingarner, Louis had engaged an estimable but rather severe lady, whom we'll call Miss N., to preside over the ten or twelve stenographers in the outer office. He had brought with him from 120 Broadway his secretary, Mrs. Edna Montgomery, and her assistant Margaret Durand, a merry freckled-faced girl, later known to thousands as the inimitable "Rabbit" of the White House. Louis gave her that name one day when he looked up and found her standing on tiptoe in the outer office wigwagging to him that some important dignitary was waiting to see him.

"You remind me of a rabbit," he said, "wiggling your ears and twitching your nose, so I think I'll call you that from now on!" And "Rabbit" she was ever after, not only to those in the office, but later in Washington to the President, Bernard Baruch, Cabinet members, and others. Not long after the 1928 campaign Mrs. Montgomery moved to other fields and Rabbit became secretary to Louis and remained with him to the day of his death. She died of tuberculosis in Asheville, North Carolina, five years after Louis Howe passed away. She devoted her life to him to almost as great a degree as he devoted his to Franklin Roosevelt and no tribute paid her would do her justice.

Louis soon had a nickname for everybody around the office. I had been there only a few days when the silence was shattered by a loud "Hoop" from the back office. I looked nervously at Miss N. "What's the matter with him?" I asked, "Does he have whooping cough, too?" Louis Howe, a sick man all the days of his life, had asthma, a bad heart, bad spells of bronchitis, and when he took these spells of coughing he held his sides in pain. No, Miss N. assured me, Louis was simply yelling for Mr. Hoopingarner. Soon we had a nickname for Louis, too, but not to his face. He spent a lot of time pacing the floor, with his hands behind his back, so we dubbed him "Felix the Cat" after the comic strip character. Later he became simply "the little boss" and it was not long before we found ourselves referring to Mr. Roosevelt as "the big boss."

On a hot August day during this campaign I first saw Franklin Roosevelt. We were thrilled when we learned he was coming in and we all found it necessary to arrange chores that put us in full view of the hall. Hearing a commotion at the elevator I peered out the door and saw him. He was advancing down the hallway with slow and halting steps. His legs were in steel braces and under his arms he held crutches, which he placed carefully before him as he made his tedious way, surrounded by several politicians who knew he was coming. He wore a light summer suit. A Panama hat was on his head and, from beneath its brim, little runlets of perspiration crawled down his face. But the eyes beneath the drooping brim of his hat were sparkling, his smile magnificent.

"Well, Louis," FDR said, lowering his massive frame into a chair in the inner office, where stacks of mail awaited his signature, "how goes it today?" It was hard for Miss N. to keep the fluttery girls at their desks while this fascinating man sat in the inside office, the door open, and snatches of his laughter and banter with Louis drifted out.

Often he came in at night to sign the mail and if we found it necessary to work overtime on these nights we didn't mind at all!

It was here that I first saw Mrs. Roosevelt, too, and was at once attracted by her warm and friendly personality. Under Louis' tutelage she was now taking an active part in national politics and had an office on the floor below, where she headed the Women's Division. Louis always had the greatest faith in women in politics and a healthy respect for their influence. However, he often said he couldn't see that any of them took much interest in politics, nationally, until the campaign of 1928. He had worked with them in 1924 in New York State and thought they did a good job, but didn't think their work amounted to much nationally.

"I really couldn't say," he said frankly, "that there was any real interest aroused in the female breast in 1924. Nor do I think that more than five per cent of the women voters deserted the faith of their fathers on any of the issues in the contest. But in 1928, mein Gawd! They came out fighting! They got aroused in the Smith-Hoover campaign when the country split wide open on two burning, although seemingly unrelated questions—whisky and religion!"

Mrs. Nellie Tayloe Ross, later Director of the Mint, was in charge of the field work for the Women's Division; Mrs. Mary Norton, Congresswoman from New Jersey, headed the Women Speakers Bureau, and with Louis' wise behind-the-scenes guidance, these women took a vigorous part in the campaign.

From Mrs. Roosevelt's headquarters, now and then, came a smartly dressed young woman with prematurely white hair and patrician features, and the girls in Louis' office were somewhat in awe of her when we learned that she worked for Mrs. Roosevelt and was quite a favorite with Louis Howe. She seemed so aloof that I avoided her for fear I might use some slang expression in her presence. One day, however, without warning, she marched into the office with two Catholic priests in tow. "Hyah kid," she said, "would you like to meet a couple of Holy Fathers?"

Horrified, I looked at the Holy Fathers, expecting them to drop dead with mortification. Instead they were laughing heartily. I learned then that the dignified exterior worn by Mary Eben hid the most Rabelaisian sense of humor I had ever encountered. Also, she is a born mimic and one of her best acts is an imitation of Mrs. Roosevelt. After we came to Washington Mary was regaling us in her office at the White House one day with an imitation of Mrs. Roosevelt making a speech. Suddenly a dead silence fell over her audience. Mary wheeled, and there in the doorway was Mrs. Roosevelt herself.

"Mary dear," Mrs. Roosevelt said, applauding softly, "you are wonderful! I want you to come to the party I am giving for the newspaperwomen next week and 'do' me for them. Will you?" Mary gulped and said she would. When the night came, however, she lost her nerve and didn't "do" Mrs. Roosevelt, but gave a hilarious imitation of a woman with five children going through the White House on a sightseeing tour, which had the girls entranced. We had long since found out that one reason Mary was such a favorite with Louis was that she tossed him a choice risqué story now and then, which delighted his soul! We had learned, too, that behind this little man's brilliant brain and keen sense of humor was a capacity to see every single thing that went on in the office. We began to think the man could see forward, sideways and backward, like an African chameleon. One day he called Margaret Durand in and asked, behind his hand, "Will you please find out what the heck that thing is that Miss Collins wears on her ankle—and how she gets it off at night? I can't figure the damn thing out." Marion Collins was a cute little redheaded typist in the front office, and her shapely ankle was adorned by a slender gold chain. When Margaret reported that Miss Collins said it was a slave bracelet welded on by her sweetheart, and that she never took it off at night, he was simply delighted and wanted to know how come all of us were not wearing them!

Louis seemed to consider me brainless, and I believe it was to test me out as much as anything else that he put me on a job that required me to get up at five o'clock in the morning. This one job taught me how thorough Louis Howe was when it came to running a campaign. He devised a scheme to trap votes by writing letters to the men who came to New York to buy goods for stores throughout the country, inviting them to headquarters.

"Those fellows are in touch with things back in their home towns," he said. "They have a lot of contacts there and can wield quite a bit of influence." What he really meant was "wield influence for Franklin," as well as Al Smith, but we didn't catch on to that right away. In fact, years later I said to him, "Knowing now that you never had a thought in your head except to elect Franklin Roosevelt President someday, why did you work yourself, and us, almost to death in 1928 trying to elect Al Smith?"

His answer was brief and all-revealing.

"Franklin wanted it," he said.

But about those buyers. The New York *Times* published a list of these visitors every morning and the names of the hotels where they were stopping. My job and that of Sterling Worden, an attractive young college student who worked part time, was to arrive at the office and by seven A.M. send letters out to those buyers by special delivery. Usually they reached the hotels by the time the buyers arose and, most of them, flattered at receiving a letter from Franklin Roosevelt, came. If Mr. Roosevelt was not there they saw Louis and went back full of enthusiasm, and Louis felt sure they would not forget Mr. Roosevelt who had appealed to them for valuable advice.

The campaign was well along before Louis gave any evidence that he considered me worth my salt around the place. I was only receiving twenty-five dollars a week and was sure he thought I was overpaid. One day, during the lunch hour, he looked around for somebody to do a certain job. There was nobody but me. He tossed a letter in my direction.

"See what you can do with this," he said tersely. "Some Methodist Bishop out west is raising holy hell about Al being a Catholic and a wet. He doesn't like his Tammany connections, either. He wants to know just what Al has ever done that would make him a good President of the United States. You go in and see Belle Moscowitz and tell her to give you some literature and to marshal some facts for me so I can draft a reply for Franklin's signature. This bishop is very important. We've got to give him the right kind of reply. He swings a lot of influence." Louis looked at me as though he thought, "You're too rattlebrained to do this, but there's nobody else around, so what can I do?"

I went into Belle Moscowitz's office with quite a bit of curiosity. I'd seen her around and had heard plenty about her from the New York newspapermen who called her "Al's right-hand man."

Belle was a former Republican of some prominence, who had declared her support for Al Smith when he ran for Governor the first time because she liked his views on social reform and labor legislation. She was introduced to Smith by Frances Perkins and soon began to suggest valuable ideas for his campaign. Al liked Belle's ideas so well that she became a member of his staff at campaign headquarters and, when he was elected, moved along to Albany where she was his closest adviser as long as he was Governor of New York. "Let's go up and see Belle," the newspapermen would say, "and see what's on Al's mind today."

"When Al plans to make a speech," they said, "we don't go to him at all. We see Belle. She puts her hand on a stack of manuscript and says, 'There it is boys. I haven't finished it yet. When it's ready I'll let you know!' Belle's plenty smart," the boys said, "and tough, too. Don't let her catch you trying to put one over. Brother, she can make it hot for you."

I found this female Louis Howe a rather heavy-set little woman with hair skewed into a knot on top of her head, sitting at a table so littered with papers that you could hardly see over it. She looked like any housewife you might meet in the Bronx on the way to market till she began to talk. Then you learned that behind this undistinguished exterior was a shrewd and wiry intellect. She instantly grasped the importance of the bishop and gave me a stream of facts about Al Smith that took me an hour to assimilate.

When the facts were all together on my desk I did a rash thing. Louis was out, so I drafted the letter to the bishop myself and laid it on his desk, then retired to the outer office and waited for the ax. When he returned I sneaked a look in the office now and then, but his face was impassive. When it was time to go home and I'd heard nothing I asked Miss Durand if she knew what he did with the letter. "Curiosity killed the cat," she twinkled, "but confidentially I'll tell you. He put it in the basket of mail he is sending to Mr. Roosevelt to sign and told him you drafted it, that he had not changed a comma and that he thought you ought to have a letter." I was greatly relieved, but Louis never mentioned the matter to me, nor I to him. However, I did receive a nice letter from Mr. Roosevelt.

There were times when we thought Louis carried this no "butter," which is what he called flattery, business too far. One day Rabbit laid on his desk a particularly fiendish task he had loaded on her, mission completed. He looked at it and grunted.

"Is it all right?" she asked him.

He looked up in surprise. "Sure," he said, "fine."

"Then why don't you say so?" she said in some irritation.

He grinned impishly. "Let me tell you something, my girl," he said, "when it's *not* all right you'll hear from me. Plenty!"

And that's the way he was.

Near the close of this campaign those of us in Louis Howe's office had our loyalty tested to the full. A most important letter was to go to leaders over the country—a letter signed by Franklin Roosevelt—and it was five o'clock when Louis announced that the letter had to go out that night, even though it might mean working very late hours, but he'd see that we were paid extra. He left full and explicit instructions with Miss N., then went to the town house for a conference with Roosevelt.

About nine o'clock, for some reason which we never understood, Miss N. suddenly announced that she "would not work all night for anybody," dismissed the force, locked the stamps and stationery in a file case and went home! Aubrey Mills, Rabbit's fiancé who often worked with us at night, Rabbit, Sterling Worden and myself held a council of war and decided not to be dismissed. Franklin wanted it, Louis Howe wanted it. We'd stay. But the stamps and stationery were tightly locked in that file case.

We decided on a desperate course. We "jimmied" open the file case, got the stamps and stationery, and went to work.

Dawn was coming up over Central Park when the last letter was ready for the stamping machine. Then we found that it was locked up, too. But the machine was located in a little cubicle, where the partitions did not quite reach to the ceiling. We piled up boxes, mail sacks, etc., until we achieved a sort of "Alp" up which Rabbit clambered and unlocked the door.

We didn't know whether Louis would praise us or fire us for this night's work—and burglary. He did neither. He simply said it was "good work," but we knew he was pleased. However, we did not know *how* pleased until several years later.

"You and Rabbit didn't know it," he said to me one day, recalling those days of the 1928 campaign, "but you both won jobs for life with me that night."

Incidentally, after we had finished this all-night grueling task, crawled wearily home for a shower and change of clothing, grabbed a cup of coffee and came back to the office, Miss N. docked us for being late!

Many stories were written about why Mr. Roosevelt changed his mind and decided to run for Governor of New York that fall after he had said flatly that he would not—that he intended to stay in Warm Springs where the healing waters were doing so much for him. Some of the stories said—and may still be believed—that the whole thing was a careful plot hatched by Mrs. Roosevelt, Al Smith and Louis Howe, and that Mr. Roosevelt was aware of what was going on all the time. In *This Is My Story* Mrs. Roosevelt proves she had no part in any such plot, though it is well known that Al Smith wanted Roosevelt to run to strengthen the ticket in New York and put strong pressure on him. Louis Howe, however, was against it. He wanted Franklin to wait until he could put aside those crutches.

While the "will he" and "won't he" stories filled the political columns, Louis Howe was firing telegrams to Warm Springs urging FDR to stand pat. On the twenty-fifth of September he wired:

> The World and other papers are running stories that you are being forced to run. The way things are running here, my conviction that you should not run is stronger than ever and Eleanor agrees with me in this. There is no answer to the health plea, but any other reason will be overruled by the Governor himself.

He signed the telegram "Luhowe," a nom de plume he often used in wires and cablegrams.

Three days later, as the pressure mounted, Louis wired:

> Tribune prints a long story that your declination was a frameup and that you will be drafted by acclamation. Have accordingly suggested to your friend on the New York Sun that he wire you for a statement from Warm Springs. If your telegram means what it says I recommend a reply for publication that will settle the matter.

On the first day of October, as the State Convention met in Rochester, Louis sent a long day letter to FDR at 11:05 in the morning:

> At 10:30 World man reported Al still hoped to draft you. Jim [Farley] tells me confidentially that real pressure comes from leaders and job holders who feel you will be elected and patronage made secure and that the Governor does not really consider your nomination vital to his personal success. There is certain grim

humor in this demand on one who could not get a park appro-
priation three months ago. Kelly's devotion is particularly annoy-
ing. If you change your mind and run please wire me.

LUHOWE

This message had hardly had time to cool before Louis fired
another:

Understand Governor trying to reach you by telephone. What I
hear strongly confirms previous advice. Syracuse Kelly leading
upstate demands. Beware of Greeks bearing gifts.

LUHOWE

The following day, October 2, a long straight telegram went
to Warm Springs at 1:29 P.M.:

Jimmie Walker nominated you and it was carried unanimously.
Dispatches from Atlanta saying you did not intend to run being
shown Smith in Rochester. He made this reply, quote "The convention has the consent of Mr. Roosevelt to do what it did, nominate him and he will run" end quote. Mess is no name for it. In
any event I would not change plans about returning, but clean
up there. Mrs. Moscowitz asks that you defer arrival in New York
until Monday as they are planning to get most of the populace out
in a demonstration. Suggest you lay over Sunday in Hyde Park,
convention being adjourned. I support you could demand time to
reconsider. Imagine usual committee to fill vacancies was appointed.

Louis Howe ended this telegram with one of his few defeatist
touches. "For once," he said, "I have no advice to give. Luhowe."

Louis changed his mind in a hurry about having no advice to
give, however, for he offered some the following day in a letter
which flashed out on the heels of the other messages: "Suggest
you insist on limiting your speeches to the four big cities with a
radio hook-up and generally making your campaign on the 'Never
mind me, vote for Al basis!' That will have the effect of avoiding
the necessity of debate on state issues, with practically no prepa-

ration. Your telegram to convention arrived after adjournment and has not been made public. I stole a copy off the wire."

I was working in the outside office the day Mr. Roosevelt was nominated when I heard the newsboys yelling down on Columbus Circle. I leaned out the window to listen: "Roosevelt Accepts Nomination," they howled.

Knowing nothing then of the telegrams to Warm Springs, but only that the boss had not wanted FDR to run, I cautiously stuck my head into his office.

"Boss," I said, "the newsboys are yelling that Mr. Roosevelt has decided to run."

He looked up and made a terrible grimace. "Yeah," he said, "so I understand." He picked up the phone. "Give me Warm Springs," he snapped. I tiptoed out.

Louis Howe lost fights the same way he won them—with calmness. And before the day was over he had started his battle to elect Franklin Governor of New York.

Mr. Roosevelt came back from Warm Springs and immediately embarked upon a program that would prove the truth of Al Smith's cryptic remark, "Hell, a man doesn't have to be an acrobat to be Governor." He'd show them he could make a campaign with the best of them.

Wearing the battered old campaign hat he had worn in his first race for the state senate, he barnstormed gaily over the state by automobile, sometimes averaging 175 miles per day and making a dozen speeches. Marguerite LeHand, his private secretary, went along as did Edward J. Flynn, Democratic political leader in the Bronx, and Jim Farley, Secretary of the State Democratic Committee, who knew practically every precinct worker in the state. FDR's friend, Samuel Rosenman, furnished the necessary legal advice, while back in New York at the Biltmore Hotel—where the headquarters of the State Democratic Committee were located—Louis Howe plotted strategy, dividing his time now between the General Motors Building and the Biltmore, a day and night assignment.

But one thing soon began to bother Louis. Now that Franklin was in the race he certainly wanted him to win. And what was Franklin doing on these barnstorming tours? Worried about the tide of anti-Catholicism and bigotry sweeping the country, he talked Al Smith at every crossroads, a sort of one-man committee against intolerance in the state.

"Mein Gawd!" said Louis, who seemed to have forgotten that he had advised FDR to do this very thing, "has Franklin forgotten that he is running? Plugging Al is all very well, but if he doesn't look out he'll pull Al through and fall by the wayside himself."

Mr. Roosevelt's opponent was Albert N. Ottinger, the Republican Attorney General of the state, elected at the same time as Al Smith, who said he was running on his own record but that Roosevelt was running on the record of Al Smith. He charged that the Democratic party had been the "sponsor of practically every economic fallacy that has burdened this country. It tried free trade and was forced to discard it. We all recall its attempts to put a cross of silver on our shoulders. It tried tariff for revenue only and threw that overboard," and so on.

As time went on and Roosevelt continued his efforts to stem the tide of sentiment running against Al Smith because of his religion, Ottinger went after him for that, and said Roosevelt was "fanning religious bigotry" with his speeches, while Ottinger's campaign manager declared that the campaign had "sunk from the sidewalks of New York to the sewers of New York!"

FDR warmed to his own candidacy, then, in a way that satisfied even Louis. He accused the Republicans of failing to take a stand on vital issues such as water power, prohibition and farm relief while the Democrats had taken a clear stand on all three. As for their claim that he was fanning religious bigotry, said Mr. Roosevelt, it was the Republican party that "step by step in the campaign has descended into the lowest depths of unspeakable slander, calumny and even obscenity. They have condoned every vile attempt to revive passions which have been dead in our nation since our ancestors burned witches in Salem!" Louis Howe chuckled gleefully, "The donkey's got his ears back now for sure," he said.

Louis was spending less and less time at national headquarters now and more and more time at the Biltmore. He'd come in, scan the morning papers, read his mail, dictate some replies, go over the day's plans with Mr. Hoopingarner and, if it was lunchtime, eat his hasty apple, gulp a glass of milk, and dash off to the Biltmore. If FDR was in town between speeches, he'd scuttle off to the Roosevelt town house to review plans and strategy, and he spent more time pacing the floor in his "Felix the cat" routine, as the rival forces began to make fantastic claims about their strength. Hoover and Ottinger confidently insisted that they would carry upstate New York by 500,000 to 700,000 votes, and all the counties outside of New York City with the exception of Albany. "Ridiculous!" said FDR, and pointed out that the Republicans had made the same claims in 1912 and 1916, and had been wrong each time. Louis, avidly scanning the papers each day to see how they rated FDR's chances, felt wonderful when the New York *Times* reported that at the big rally in Brooklyn where FDR and Smith both spoke from the same platform, FDR, who arrived first, drew a bigger reception than the one for Governor Smith.

In most speeches FDR had avoided calling Ottinger by name and always referred to "the Republicans" or "the Republican party." At the big rally on Saturday night before the election, however, he took the wraps off. Tossing his head in the familiar Roosevelt gesture, he poked fun at Mr. Ottinger's "hope chest" where "he kept his various bundles, gingerly pulling out the ones he thought best to place on view."

"The bundle marked 'water power,' " Mr. Roosevelt jeered, "was hastily thrust back when he saw it meant leasing state-owned water power sites to private companies." As to Mr. Ottinger's claim that the election of Herbert Hoover meant "insuring a continuance of prosperity," FDR called that "Ottinger's last stand."

"To all this calamity howling," he said joyfully, "the public yawns and waves Mr. Ottinger goodbye."

"That's telling 'em," Louis remarked contentedly, "if only that will sink into the dear public's consciousness, all will be well."

On election night Louis arranged for Mr. Hoopingarner and various members of the staff to stay at national headquarters, while he established himself early in the state headquarters at the Biltmore, checked with the tally sheet workers and, armed with sandwiches and milk, prepared for his grueling vigil. He was not alone, for many of FDR's well-wishers crowded into the hotel to share his vigil with him. Among these was one who a few short years ago had battled with Louis to keep her son out of just such a situation as this, but who now sat tensely by, rejoicing with Louis when the returns were good, grieving with him when the tally sheets stared coldly back with the awful news that Ottinger was winning.

Sara Delano Roosevelt, who had wanted her son to abandon politics forever after he was stricken, and Louis Howe who never wanted him to get into this race, were the two now pulling hardest for him to win. Louis' face was pale as he bent over the tally sheets on which Ottinger was leading, but he held doggedly on as the tide ebbed and flowed, and hope battled with despair. It was plain by midnight that Al Smith had lost the election, and Louis Howe's blood thinned when he heard that Ottinger had pulled ahead with such a lead his election was being announced in the early editions of the morning papers. At four o'clock in the morning Sara Delano Roosevelt quietly slipped away. Then slowly, maddeningly, the pendulum began to swing in the right direction and daylight was streaking the sky when the weary tabulators announced that Roosevelt was "in"!

FDR, who had been following the night's proceedings in his town house, was called by reporters for a statement. "Any possibility of my own election," he said regretfully, "is clouded by the defeat of Governor Smith. I am deeply disappointed."

If Louis Howe was disappointed about anything, those who saw the dawn touch his face would never have believed it. Franklin had cleared his first hurdle—he was on his way! And the little man who had brought him this far quietly straightened his shoulders, drew deep on his Sweet Caporal, and plodded home for a few blessed hours of rest.

[8]

"I Cast That One Vote"

THE defeat of Al Smith in the fall of 1928 was so decisive, so overwhelming, that Democrats throughout the country were in despair. But not Louis Howe. Franklin had carried New York State by a substantial majority, even though the national ticket had gone down to defeat. Louis, looking ahead with X-ray eyes, early saw the tiny cloud that later materialized into a storm that finally shattered the friendship between Franklin and his Happy Warrior. A few days after election Louis ran into Charlie Michelson, then with the old New York *World*, but later director of publicity for the Democratic National Committee for many years.

"Charlie," Louis said, "Al Smith isn't going to like this one a damn bit. He has lost New York and Franklin has carried it. The country isn't going to forget that, you know, when 1932 comes around and the Democrats pick a candidate for President."

"It's easy to see, Louis," Michelson said, "what's in your never idle mind."

Michelson was right, for it was then that Louis began to see that his goal for 1936 was backing up on him and that 1932 might be Franklin's year after all.

Belle Moscowitz, who had been as close to Al Smith as Louis to Roosevelt, knew all the political angles in the state and Al seemed to think that Roosevelt would need her and would retain her. FDR did not know Belle too well, although he appreciated

117

the fact that she had been a tower of strength to Al during his terms as governor. He knew, however, that she was a domineering person used to having her own way, and might try to tell him how to run things. Louis Howe recognized this trait, too, and figured one close adviser was all Franklin needed. That Louis intended to be that adviser nobody had any doubt, least of all Mrs. Moscowitz, as time went on and FDR did not take the broad hints that Al tossed in his direction, about how much help she could be to him in Albany. Belle blamed Louis Howe for much of her trouble, and no doubt built up some resentment and bitterness in Al's heart over the whole affair. What she thought worried Louis not a whit, and his offside remarks were full of acid as Mrs. Moscowitz faded from the Albany scene.

Louis himself didn't want any official position at Albany as this would have interfered with his real job of building up national contacts for the future. Besides, FDR had to have a strong and vigorous man at his side since he could not get about freely, so he appointed Guernsey Cross as his official secretary. Louis, as usual, functioned as unofficial adviser, running a "three ring circus," as he called it, with a couple of days each week in Albany, three in his Crime Commission office, and two in Massachusetts.

The tension between Smith and Roosevelt increased. Robert Moses had been secretary of state under Al Smith, was an able man, and Al thought FDR should continue him in office. But Roosevelt didn't see eye to eye with Moses, and that he received a nudge from Louis to ignore Moses there is little doubt.

Governor Smith had once appointed Roosevelt as a member of the Taconic Park Commission, and FDR, so the story goes, asked Moses, who had jurisdiction over the parks, to appoint Louis as Secretary of the Commission, a job that paid about $5,000 a year. Moses refused and told intimates he didn't believe Louis Howe was interested in parks and that he "would continue to advance Roosevelt's interests as he had always done." There was truth in this charge, though Mr. Moses may have been overzealous. We heard no complaints about Louis' work with the National Crime Commission though it was an open secret that he was working all the while for Franklin's interests, too. As a consequence of this park affair, however, there was never any love lost between Bob Moses and Louis Howe.

Louis once summed up the whole Smith-Roosevelt break in a few words. "Smith," he said, "considered Franklin a little boy who didn't know anything about politics; that left Franklin free."

The ballots had hardly been counted in the 1928 election when Louis Howe and Franklin Roosevelt began a program to buck up the party's shattered morale. Immediately after the election FDR went to Warm Springs again, leaving Louis to conclude the work at State Headquarters and to take care of the congratulatory mail. On November 12 Louis wired him:

Six hundred letters came in this morning of which 400 out of state refer to national affairs. Want to send the following letter to them and also to selected list of 2000, omitting the first paragraph. No time to get mail approval as must use force at headquarters which disbands next week. Please wire immediate approval, disapproval or alterations. This is the letter I want to send quote: I appreciate very much indeed the nice things you had to say in your recent letter as to my election as Governor of the State of New York. I shall try very hard to deserve your confidence during my two years of office.

The defeat of Governor Smith was of course a very great disappointment but I have no patience with those who deduce from it that the Democratic Party is in any danger of extinction. On the contrary, the fact that an organization largely composed of inexperienced people hastily thrown together two weeks after the nomination was able in six weeks to convince so many millions of people that Governor Smith was the proper man to be selected for our next President shows that the Democratic Party and the Democratic principles are very much alive in this country. When you consider that this was done against a powerful organization which had been working for four years to perfect its machinery of reaching the public and that the machinery was unscrupulously but effectively used to arouse bigotry and passion by the dissemination of unspeakable slander, I feel certain that had we kept our national organization going in between elections we certainly would have won. I think the time has come to imme-

diately start work in between elections. I want to enlist your aid
in a campaign to have this done. I do not believe we should even
think of who should be the candidate or what should be the issues
four years from now. Let us prepare so that we will be able to
present our candidate and our issues to every voter in the United
States next time. Please get in touch with the leaders of your local
organization and impress upon them the necessity of this. The
amount of money needed is surprisingly small. It should be obtained in small sums from a great number of people. I am going
to ask you to write me frankly if you agree with me, and if, for
your part, should a militant organization be decided upon with
the winning of the next Congress as its first objective, would you
be willing to make an exceedingly modest contribution to its
support each year for the four years between now and the next
Presidential campaign. I shall appreciate it if you will write your
views frankly. End quote. LUHOWE.[1]

By return wire came this reply from FDR:

Change letter to read as follows: Quote, I greatly appreciate
your kindness in writing me and I shall try hard to deserve your
confidence during my term as Governor. The defeat of Governor
Smith was of course a deep disappointment but I have no patience
with those who deduce from it that the Democratic party is in
any danger of extinction. Of the additional votes cast in the election the Democratic nominees apparently received many more
than half, and the casting of fifteen million votes for our ticket
shows that our party has gained tremendous strength since 1920
and 1924. Paragraph, I am of course convinced that had we kept
our national organization going in between elections we should
have done better and I hope that steps will be taken to have this
carried out during the next three years. This is no time to discuss
candidates but it is time for putting into effect a permanent working organization. I hope you will write me your views. End of
quote.

The above seems all that it is advisable to use at this time.
Stationery not yet received. Please renew order.

FRANKLIN D. ROOSEVELT[2]

---

[1] Elliott Roosevelt, *F.D.R., His Personal Letters.*
[2] *Ibid.*

Louis hated long letters, yet often he let his own enthusiasm run away with him and wrote involved missives which had to be cut down, as in the case of the letter above. The content was about the same, it will be noted, but stated in crisper language. Also, it may be noted that FDR apparently thought it was a little early to get into money raising.

The "selected list of 2000," which Louis mentioned and to whom the letter went, included delegates to the Democratic National Convention, National Committeemen and Committeewomen, State Chairmen, successful and defeated candidates for Congress, and so on.

This letter was just what the beaten Democrats needed. Most of them, through Louis, had been corresponding with Franklin Roosevelt since 1920, and his startling New York victory caused them to listen with new respect.

In their replies the Democrats not only told FDR what they thought should be done for the future of the party, but commented, many of them with bitterness, on the reasons for the defeat of Al Smith. In Mississippi, for instance, the opinion was that the religious issue defeated Al, but that the prohibition issue also played a big part. "Let them have a dry platform next time," said Mississippi, "and nominate a man who will stick to it." Strangely enough the replies from Oklahoma—now the only dry state in the Union besides Mississippi—gave religion as the cause of Al's defeat and none of them mentioned prohibition at all. In Wisconsin they said it was religion—religion in the south, that is. From Nebraska: "Never raise the wet and dry issue in this country again for fifty years!" North Carolina writers gave religion as the chief reason of defeat, with prohibition a contributory cause.

A disgruntled old Democrat in South Dakota wrote that the troubles of the Democratic party could be straightened out by using a huge western boot, with South Dakota as the toe, to kick everything south of the Mason-Dixon line into the middle of perdition!

Another hotheaded old gentleman from the same state thought matters could be helped if "old Peter Norbeck's failing health would hurry and fail, so the Governor could appoint a Democrat in his place." (Peter Norbeck was the distinguished Republican Senator from South Dakota at that time.) The old gent added hastily that he "hoped Peter would go to Heaven."

In Tennessee the wet and religious issues ran neck and neck, but one embittered Democrat stormed that he was against "Roosevelt, Smith, Raskob, Catholicks, Jews, Niggers, North, South, East, West and Pontius Pilate!"

Louis Howe pored over these replies avidly and his eyes glinted when he noted how many declared that Franklin Roosevelt was the one to lead the party out of its slough of despondency. He was not too surprised, of course, that so many of them mentioned Franklin as the man. It was proof to him that his work was bearing fruit.

In Texas, Pennsylvania, Michigan, North Carolina, Illinois, Kentucky and Maine half of the writers said definitely they'd be for Roosevelt in 1932—in New Hampshire two-thirds of them said so, while every letter from Maryland stated firmly that FDR was the one, and so it went. Louis gave all these replies to me to read and digest, then make up a report showing the sentiment in each state. These were all on easily readable charts. He then called in Mary Eben and had her make a colored map to go with these charts. A red state, for example, might mean that Al was defeated there because of his religious views, a green one would show prohibition as the cause, purple a combination of each, and so on. When the job was finished he went over these charts and maps with Mr. Roosevelt, had them bound into a big volume which he turned over to the Democratic National Committee and, according to Louis, this data played an important part in forming a year-round Democratic organization before the next Presidential campaign.

While all these letters went out over Mr. Roosevelt's signature, it was impossible for such a busy man to sign them all so Louis handed that job to me. He gave me several copies of Mr. Roosevelt's signature—a tough one it was to imitate—but I labored over it until I achieved what Louis considered a reasonable fac-simile of what later became one of the most famous signatures in the world. I always felt guilty after I went to work in the White House and folks sent these letters in to show how long they had known the President, asking earnestly that they be returned as they cherished them so because of his signature!

When Mr. Roosevelt was sworn in as Governor of New York in January 1929, Louis called me in and said cheerfully, "Well, your forging days are over. Franklin is Governor now and his signature will have to be on the level. Besides," he grinned, "if I don't call you off you'll be signing his name to get your ornery friends out of Sing Sing."

I barely knew at the time that Sing Sing was the New York State prison and, so far as I knew, I had no friends there. But since it pleased him to associate us with rakehells at all times I let it go.

All letters with a slant on the national political situation were taken care of by Louis or sent to Albany with his scribbled notes on how he thought they should be answered. Now and then, when a letter would stir his wicked sense of humor, he'd send along some rather quaint notes. An example was the zealous Democrat who, seeing FDR as a potential candidate for President, wrote him a long letter telling him how he could make his speeches more effective. He advised Roosevelt—the old master even then—on how to have his audience eating out of his hand.

"If you are talking to farmers," he advised, "you should say 'It is my delightful privilege to address that great body of people the American farmer, etc.' If you are talking to people in New York State tell them, 'I am glad to talk tonight to the people of my own state, the great state of New York, which is the financial center of the union,' and so on.

"You could carry this out in addressing any and all classes of people," he said. "This goes a long way in appealing to people's sympathies and especially in these depressed times when people need help and encouragement by a kindly word.

"I find that the man who addresses his audience in a kindly and sympathetic manner is the one who is the most popular," he said helpfully.

This was too much for Louis. He sent the letter to the Governor with the following memo:

DEAR BOSS:
This is heavenly. I wish you would follow this man's advice. I have noticed that your present method is to start out your addresses by saying, "Now you blankety-blank poor idiots, try and listen to a little sense." That perhaps is not the most tactful way. It is never too late to learn.

All this activity went on in Louis' little cubicle of an office at the National Crime Commission. Mrs. Montgomery had resigned and Miss Durand had moved up as his secretary. I had expected to devote all my time to my newspaper column after the campaign was over, but when Louis asked me to stay and do the charts, and other chores, I did my column on the side for Sunday papers. Perhaps because of Louis' own newspaper background he was greatly interested in my little column and tried in many ways to help in its promotion. "Send it to at least one editor a day," he urged, "and you may be able to pick up several new clients." I promised, but I didn't do it and I blush now to think how I muffed the opportunities he tried to open for me.

In the spring of 1929 FDR went to Warm Springs again and Al Smith's good friend, John J. Raskob, who was still Chairman of the Democratic National Committee, invited Lieutenant Governor Herbert H. Lehman of New York to take part in a National Committee finance conference. Louis was immediately suspicious. Franklin, the Governor, not invited? What went on? The thought began to ferment in his brain that this might be a move on Raskob's part to build up Lehman to offset Franklin. After brooding over it awhile he took matters into his own hands by personally going to see Mr. Lehman about it. When the Lieutenant Governor assured him that there was no thought of such a move and if there had been he would not have been a party to it, Louis was satisfied.

Henry Morgenthau, Jr., was another man now thinking about a bigger role for Franklin Roosevelt. He wrote FDR that he believed a Democratic Press Bureau should be established in Albany to "feed material to the rural newspapers which were overwhelmingly Republican." FDR thought the idea a good one and asked him to talk to Louis about it, and Louis submitted the name of William J. Crawford, an old newspaper friend, to head the Albany Democratic Press Bureau. "I think your plan for Crawford is very good and I have no suggestions to offer," FDR wrote to Louis. "Please think over the question of my going on the radio when I get back." FDR told Louis he was thinking of covering the state in a survey and then talking to the people about it by radio, with one speech about July 1 and another at the end of August. Maybe Louis didn't think it a good idea for, while FDR made several speeches in June and July, none of them were "radio reports."

On May 21 he wrote to Louis: "I am keen to hear all about your confab with H. H. I wish he would put you on the Crime Commission, but in any event I hope you will be able to keep in very close touch with their proceedings. I have been definitely asked to lead the discussion on Crime at the Governors' conference at New London (Connecticut) on July 16 so give me all the data you can."

The H. H. referred to was Herbert Hoover, now President of the United States, who on May 20 had set up a commission headed by George M. Wickersham to study law enforcement. If Louis Howe ever talked to Herbert Hoover there is no record of it anywhere—but at any rate he was not appointed to the Commission.

In August of 1929 Louis went to Kedgemakooge, Nova Scotia, taking Hartley and Elliott Roosevelt and some of their young friends on a camping and fishing trip. When the newspapers reported that FDR was not very well Louis wired at once: "What's this I hear about your 'slight indisposition?' Be back next week.

Luhowe." FDR immediately wired a reassuring message: "Indisposition not serious. How about the salmon? Keep away from the deep water. FDR."

In the fall of 1929 the New York *World* was pressing Roosevelt to make an investigation of municipal corruption in New York City, and FDR wired Louis from Warm Springs asking him to see James W. Barrett, city editor of the *World,* and explain that the Governor had only three ways to make an investigation. The first was to use the Moreland Act, which applied to state business; second, a grand jury with a special attorney or the local district attorney; and third, the unofficial investigator who would have no power to issue subpoenas or swear in witnesses. He asked Louis to explain that the first and third would have to be ruled out and that, under the second method, the investigation could not be begun "unless definite facts were alleged."

Fiorello H. LaGuardia was running for Mayor on the Republican ticket, the incumbent James J. Walker on the Democratic ticket, and Police Commissioner Enright on a ticket of his own. The investigation, or lack of it, was a hot political issue. "In regard to the Mayoralty fight," FDR wrote to Louis, "I am keeping in reserve the thought of having both LaGuardia and Enright come before me and demanding, in the presence of a stenographer, that they back up their demands for an investigation with definite facts. If they have the facts I will start the investigation; if not they will look silly. Think it over. FDR."

Matters went along this way, with Louis carrying on an ever-widening correspondence with national leaders in FDR's name, until the summer of 1930. The state convention was to meet in the fall and it was a foregone conclusion that FDR would be renominated for governor. In August Louis was at the beach and FDR on a cruise. Perhaps because it was election year Louis thought it wise to "butter" Al Smith a little. At any rate he wired FDR on August 30:

> Al was not named by Tammany as a delegate to state convention, they say by oversight. This is stupid. Suggest you quietly arrange for vacancy, not proxy from Dutchess County, prefer-

ably Hyde Park district, but do nothing till you return, to give Curry chance to correct blunder. I can be reached by telegram care Hammond's store, Westport Point, if you want me to go over and see Curry Sunday or Monday. Will be in New York Tuesday morning.

LUHOWE

Several of Al's friends had this same idea for, it is said, he was offered several proxies but accepted none of them and just went on to the convention without credentials.

After FDR was renominated Louis went confidently into the campaign, for had not Franklin made a fine record in his first term as Governor? "He was successful in establishing the executive control over the budget," Louis said, "reorganizing the power commission; establishing several liberal labor measures—including the limitation of the use of injunctions and an extension of the eight-hour day and lightening the burden of the farmer by re-apportioning road taxation. In the controversy with the legislature over an investigation of the municipal affairs of New York City he upheld the principle of home rule, but appointed an investigating committee after the local authorities had shown their inability to deal with the matter."

However, Mr. Roosevelt's opponent, Charles H. Tuttle, United States Attorney for the Southern District of New York, didn't see it that way. He bore down hard on FDR's "failure" to make an investigation, and insisted that Roosevelt's judicial appointments in the City of New York were the worst ever made. "The matter of the judiciary," he said, "is one of the outstanding issues of the campaign." He poked fun at FDR's assertion that "all he needed to make a campaign was a bow and arrow." "Was he thinking of a big wigwam down in the city?" Tuttle jeered, "and was this a delicate compliment to state that he would use a bow and arrow?"

Louis snorted over these "fool statements" but insisted that FDR let the people know what *he* thought the issues were. FDR declared there were ten major issues in the campaign, and named them all clearly from Number One: "Rural tax relief and the enlargement of the whole agricultural program in the state government"—to Number Ten: "The enactment of further laws for the protection of labor and for women and children in industry." He made a whirlwind campaign, visiting every one of the sixty-two counties, some of them several times. Tuttle, he said, was "making an obvious effort to get votes from both the wets and drys by being for repeal in some places and against it in others." "The Republican speakers," he said, "change their attitude so much that the caravan becomes like a chameleon as it goes along!" Louis was perfectly satisfied that Franklin was letting them know what the issues were.

Earlier that summer I had gone to Kentucky for a vacation with a promise to Louis that I'd come back in time to work in the campaign. When I returned in August, however, headquarters were not yet ready, so I took a job for a short time on Heywood Broun's Non-Partisan Committee in Broun's one and only race for Congress. I sought this job for the same reason I sought the one at the Democratic National Committee two years before— to get "names" for my newspaper column. Besides, I knew Broun, who lived in a penthouse atop the apartment house where I had a modest apartment and, in fact, I had been one of his volunteer workers in the spring when, troubled by conditions in New York during this depression year, he had started a one-man employment bureau in his column called "Give a Job till June." He urged employers to try to give at least one person a job until some of the worst of the winter's hardships might be over.

Heywood's opponents in the so-called "Silk Stocking District" were the incumbent Mrs. Ruth Pratt, Republican, and Judge Louis Brodsky, Democrat. Heywood hadn't a chance to win, of course, but it was fun working in his headquarters in the famous Hotel Algonquin. My job was to usher callers in to his campaign manager, Miss Ruth Hale, who, in private life, was Mrs. Broun. Many "names" became easily available, with Alexander Woollcott, Franklin P. Adams, Morris Ernst, Edna Ferber, and others constantly dropping in.

"Miss Hale," I'd say, "Mr. Blank is here. Shall I send him in?"

Miss Hale was a brilliant and resourceful newspaperwoman but her language at times was that of a longshoreman.

"Yes," she'd say, "send the sonovabitch in."

In my native South ladies at that time did not use such uninhibited language, at least, not in public. Naturally, I was fascinated.

One day the phone on my desk jangled sharply. It was Margaret Durand.

"Brace yourself," she said, "the boss wants to talk to you." Louis came on the phone.

"Listen, Democrat," he cooed, sarcastically, "don't you think it's time you came on over here with your own crowd before you get so infected with all that 'glammer' you won't be worth killing? Or don't you care whether we elect a Democratic governor this year?" Hastily I assured him that I did and that I'd be right over. But I left with some little regret as Heywood had just been arrested for joining a picket line on fashionable Fifth Avenue and our office was full of excited newspapermen, hoping ghoulishly, for the sake of a story, that Heywood would be thrown in jail. He escaped that, but he didn't escape defeat, of course, and Louis never ceased kidding me about my "Socialistic" tendencies.

In that campaign Louis gave Rabbit and myself the most terrifying jobs we ever had. He made me head of publicity for the Women's Division with four women bosses, and made her office manager. I knew nothing about publicity and satisfying one woman boss seemed a big enough job while the thought of four sent cold chills down my spine. These estimable ladies were Mrs. Caroline O'Day, vice-chairman of the New York State Democratic Committee, later Congresswoman at Large from New York; Miss Nancy Cook, office manager of the Women's Division; Mrs. Frederick Stuart Greene, head of the Women Speakers Bureau, whose husband was State Superintendent of Public Works; and last but not least the formidable Mary W. Dewson. Miss Dewson, a tall, sedate woman with piercing eyes, was a close friend of both Mrs. Roosevelt and Louis Howe, and Louis leaned on her heavily then and later for anything pertaining to women's activities in the Roosevelt campaigns.

I shied away from "Mollie," as she was called, for a good reason. A short time before she had appealed to Louis to lend her one of his "bright young girls" to help her with a special job. Foolishly he offered her my services. But Mollie had seen me around. She withered him with a blast.

"What!" she shrieked, "that flibbertigibbet? I wouldn't have her in my office on a bet."

Louis relayed this remark to me with glee, and I knew that he was chuckling into his high collar when he handed me over to her and the other ladies. Mollie finally picked Mary Eben as her assistant, though she thought as little of Mary at first as she did of me. But Mary surprised her by turning out to be a splendid assistant. Mollie dubbed her "the expediter" and had her at her side in all subsequent campaigns.

As for Rabbit, she was having a terrible time in the job Louis had given her. We did not know that since the all-night job in 1928 he thought we could move mountains, and the jobs he gave us put us way beyond our depth. Rabbit had the thankless job of hiring and firing the help, installing furniture, getting the printing done, and seeing a stream of visitors. She and I used to go out to lunch and cry into our soup over these impossible assignments. We even toyed with the idea of quitting. We could always sell apples! But we discarded this thought as worse than folly. Louis had given us our battle stations in "Operation Roosevelt" and we could not let him down.

Mrs. Greene and Miss Dewson shared an office, Miss Cook was two doors away and I shared an office with Alice Disbrow, Mrs. O'Day's beautiful blonde secretary. Louis had an office down the hall and around a corner, purposely removing himself from these feminine scenes, I felt, just to make sure that my anguished cries never reached his ears. There he mapped strategy, met with state leaders, schemed his schemes, and left us to sweat it out.

The lines from every department led into Louis' little corner office and many of the department heads became irked at his way of running things. The Finance Department, especially, had a tough time with him. Louis, who usually paid little attention to money, became very money-conscious during campaigns, and when he needed it he saw no reason why the Finance Department didn't produce the funds immediately and do the necessary replenishing and bookkeeping later.

He'd call Howard Cullman, treasurer in this campaign, as well as in FDR's first race for governor, and say, "Look, Howard, I need thirty thousand dollars for upstate and I need it right away," or "I've got to have ten thousand dollars for some important newspaper advertising," or printing, or something of the kind.

"All right, Louis," Cullman would say, "all right. We'll get it for you, but we've got to have the proper vouchers, checks, etc. I can't just run down the hall to your office with the money in my hand."

"O. K.," Louis would say, "keep your shirt on. I'll sign whatever papers you want signed. But make it snappy, will you?"

"I'd go down the hall with the necessary papers," Cullman would lament, "all set to tell him how the matter should be handled and apt as not he'd throw the papers in the wastebasket, spit in my eye and tell *me* what to do."

Cullman might admit today that this estimate was slightly exaggerated, but his description of Louis Howe is the same now as it was then. "He," said Cullman, "was the rudest and most loyal man I have ever known."

Louis got a laugh out of what he called FDR's "two cents worth" in the campaign and showed it around the office. "Here," said FDR, in a memo to Louis, "is a suggestion for a cartoon:

"Caption: Are you carrying the Hoover banner?

"Below this: Picture of a man holding his trousers pockets turned inside out.

"Underneath: The words, 'Nuff sed.' "

While Cullman and the others were having their troubles, I was going from bad to worse in the job Louis had wished on me. Women speakers would come to headquarters for a briefing before going out on their various speaking dates. Mrs. Greene would call me in and introduce me to these ladies. "Here," she would say in her calm, gentle voice, "is the little girl who writes all our nice blurbs. Give her some data and she'll write advance stories and send them to the towns where you are to speak. She will—" about this time Mollie Dewson, hearing my name, would whirl in her chair and hurl a mass of papers at me. "Here, kid," she'd shout, "run down the hall quick and give these papers to Louis." I'd run, because I was afraid of Mollie, and also because I wanted to get to Louis' ear with what I thought of this job. Rabbit would take the papers and shake her head sadly. "It's no use, kid," she'd say, "he won't see you. He won't listen. He won't listen to me, either. We'll just have to get through this mess the best way we can."

Later on, Mollie, a grand soul, became more tolerant of me and we became good friends, but that didn't help me any then. One day Miss Cook called me in and dictated a story for an upstate paper in a town where Mrs. O'Day was to speak. In it she mentioned that Mrs. O'Day, Mrs. Roosevelt and herself were all associated with the Val-Kill Furniture Factory, a small factory located on the Hyde Park estate which turned out replicas of early American furniture and gave employment to the local people. John Stuart, now with the New York *Times,* was head of General Publicity that year, and my stories had to clear through him. When I turned this one in, John's usually ruddy face turned a dark purple.

"God Almighty damn!" he roared. "This will be a fine story for the Republican papers. Their reporters pick up our releases just like the Democratic papers do, you know. First thing you know they'll be running stories to the effect that Roosevelt's head-quarters are being used to advertise a furniture factory. Haven't you got any sense?"

"No," I said, slamming the story down, "and I didn't want to do this cussed publicity job anyway. If you don't like the stuff go to Louis Howe and tell him so! He told me to 'obey the ladies' and I'll write what they say if it kills me. Did you ever try to keep four women happy at one time?"

"No, God forbid," said John, hastily calming down, "but we won't bother Louis. You just bring these stories to me. I'll take care of 'em." So whenever I appeared in General Publicity after that John, with a sigh, automatically reached for the blue pencil.

John was so shaken by all this, however, that now and then he had to rush out for something to calm his nerves. It was bathtub gin, I think, for one night he and some other newspapermen took me with them. Later in the evening they decided to go back to headquarters, where Louis was still working, to see if there was any late news. This was a bad mistake. Charlie Bayer, Bill Crawford, John and myself trooped merrily into the Biltmore. I picked up the phone in John's office, called Louis, and asked if there was anything I could do.

"Yes," he said crisply, "you can go home and go to bed."

Bill Crawford then called him, with the usual headquarters query, "Is everything under control, Louis?"

"Everything is under control," said Louis drily, "except your 'girl friend.' "

From that night on, I never tried to put anything over on the little boss.

He never referred to this aberration but he never forgot it either, just as he never forgot anything that happened around the office. This fact came out later when a group of us sent him a humorous petition asking, since he had given us such tough jobs, that he give each of us a title, which was the least he could do. This petition amused him and he dictated an elaborate reply in the form of an Executive Order, complete with gold seal and ribbon and fancy blue cover.

"Know all men by these presents," the order read, "that Colonel Simon Ananias Lothario Legree Howe does hereby issue the following executive order." Then followed an impressive list of titles for each of us, with appropriate comments on our duties. Anxiously I searched the list for my own, and lo, like Abou Ben Adhem, it led all the rest as "Official investigator of all new speakeasies." Ed Brown of the publicity staff was made "Chief of all Press Notices" and warned that "while supplying several copies of any one press notice would not be counted against his efficiency, failure to discover a single complimentary line will result in his immediate dismissal." All received fitting titles which were carefully preserved and cherished.

As election day drew near and the Tuttle and Roosevelt speeches became more caustic, each side began to make extravagant claims of victory, many from our side inspired by Louis, and all from the other side absorbing his attention as they appeared. He snorted when William J. Maier, Chairman of the Republican State Committee, claimed that "reports from upstate counties and from Republican leaders showed, without a doubt, that Mr. Tuttle would be the winner," and exclaimed, "Well, this is more like it!" when John F. Curry, leader of Tammany Hall, predicted that Roosevelt would have a margin as high as 575,000 over Mr. Tuttle in New York City, which would overcome anything the Republicans could bring down from upstate.

Somehow, in spite of our individual difficulties, we managed to survive until election night, and it all seemed well worthwhile when we heard the news that Roosevelt had won over Tuttle by a sweeping majority of 725,001 votes!

"I cast that one vote," FDR said.

When the tumult had died sufficiently Franklin Roosevelt made a gracious speech of thanks to all the faithful who gathered in the ballroom of the Biltmore Hotel to hear him. I listened as earnestly as I could, but my eyes kept sliding away from him to a figure huddled down in a chair far back in the room. His face wore its usual melancholy, faintly ironical look. But I knew, as I stole a glance at Louis Howe now and then, that I was looking at a truly happy man.

[9]

"Friends of Roosevelt"

THE day after the 1930 election Louis Howe came out in the open with his candidate's bid for the Presidency, keeping his own name well out of the announcement, however. Knowing that some kind of statement was expected after this sweeping victory, Louis loosened his collar, grabbed a pencil and a Sweet Caporal, sat down at a desk, and went to work. The statement was issued in the name of Jim Farley, chairman of the New York State Democratic Committee, who collaborated in its preparation. He fully expected, Farley said, that the call would come to the New York Governor in the first Presidential primary which was to be held late in 1931.

The Democrats of the country would certainly want as their candidate for President a man who had shown himself capable of carrying the most important state in the Union by a record-breaking majority. "I do not see," the statement read, "how Mr. Roosevelt can escape becoming the next Presidential nominee of his party even if no one raises a finger to bring it about."[1]

Louis Howe must have chuckled slyly into his high collar when he penned that phrase, "even if no one raises a finger to bring it about"!

Louis and Farley claimed that they had not even consulted FDR before issuing their statement and who was to argue with them? When Farley phoned the Governor at Albany and told

[1] James Farley, *Behind the Ballots* (New York: Harcourt, Brace and Company, 1938).

him the statement had been issued, FDR, if innocent, was at least agreeable. "O. K., Jim," he said heartily, "you know that anything you do is all right with me." Louis and Farley then prepared a tabulation revealing how well Roosevelt had fared in the rural counties upstate, normally Republican. The tabulation covered a period of from ten to twelve years and showed what a vote-getter FDR was in those areas, compared to Democratic candidates who had preceded him. This tabulation was sent to Democratic leaders all over the country, designed, of course, to make them take notice of this vote-grabbing Governor in the Empire State.

This splendid upstate vote didn't just happen, however. Louis had always been annoyed by the disposition of Democratic leaders to assume that upstate New York was so solidly Republican that there was little use to bother with it and, instead, concentrated on getting out such a big vote in New York City that it would make up for the meager vote the candidates always "came down to the Bronx with," as they expressed it. Fortunately, Harold Payson, a Democratic leader in New York State, a close friend of FDR's, had been thinking along the same lines, so Louis conferred with him and "Democratic Unions" were formed in every upstate county under active, enthusiastic chairmen. Soon reports of increasing Roosevelt strength began to pour into Louis' receptive ears. On election day the big vote in those areas proved that the new venture had been well worthwhile.

Louis was not the only one now thinking in terms of 1932. When Roosevelt returned to Albany after the election, five thousand people lined the streets in the rain shouting at the top of their lungs, "Our next President!" while a dripping band played the rollicking tune, "Strike up the band, here comes a sailor."

Early in 1931 Louis opened modest headquarters at 331 Madison Avenue, across the street from the Biltmore Hotel at Forty-third Street, in five or six rooms on the seventh floor which was all the space he could afford. He was not running a campaign—not at all. "Friends of Roosevelt" is what he called this little project. He gathered around him the workers who had been with him in the two gubernatorial campaigns and I was lucky enough to be included, but since I had not yet come back from my Christmas vacation I missed the party on January 14, a combined birthday party for Louis and the "send off" for the preconvention campaign. The girls at the party presented Louis with a book for his birthday. I do not recall its title but it must have been about a "perfect secretary" for he thanked them with the following original verse:

A Ballade scriven for ye Damoselles Alice Disbrow, Malvina Thompson, Mary Cottrell, Marguerite Pascocello and Margaret Durand, in grateful remembrance of a volume they presented the author, and which he hopes they did not read.

Ye Secretary reaches Heaven.	Because of Satan's false allures, He always had been wary, At Heaven's gate, arrived on time, The Perfect Secretary.
He findeth great ado	He found the golden streets a-buzz With violent agitation— St. Peter was accused of graft, "We want investigation!"
Caused by two who entered by error.	(It seems there recently had come Unto these realms of light— Through some Recording Angel's slip— One "Macy" and John Knight)
Ye Secretary is called in consultation	The Secretary soon was called Before the Great White Throne, The guarding Seraphim dismissed That they might be alone.
By a bewildered Deity	The Deity confessed his wrath And also consternation At this unheard-of clamor for "A real investigation."

On account	"I understand," He said, "on earth
of his	You met the same obsession
skill	And proved yourself as rather good
	At methods of suppression.
And is given	"So take my thunderbolts and go,
extraordinary	This matter cannot wait,
power.	For ending this absurd demand
	All power I delegate."
Peace falls	Calm fell on Heaven. Peter sat
on	A-nodding at the door—
Heaven.	The Saints sang hymns and everything
	Was quiet as before.
He is	Again the Secretary stood
questioned	Before the Great White Throne
	"Oh tell me," asked the wondering God,
	"How didst thou this alone?"
And explains	"It was easy, Lord, to do this thing,
how it was	And simply done as well—
achieved.	I took both Macy and John Knight
	And sent them down to Hell."

Louis Notting Howe,
January 14, 1931.[2]

John Knight was Republican leader of the State senate in New York. "Macy," whom Louis did not identify further, was probably W. Kingsland Macy, chairman of the New York State Republican Committee at the time.

The biggest drawback facing the Friends of Roosevelt was lack of money. Most of the big-money boys wait cautiously to see which way the cat will jump before setting down a big saucer of cream. That's why such early stalwarts as Frank Walker, Jesse Isidor Straus, Dave Hennen Morris, William H. Woodin, Henry Morgenthau, Jr., Herbert H. Lehman, Edward J. Flynn, Joseph E. Davies, Laurence Steinhardt, James W. Gerard, Guy Helver-

---

[2] Elliott Roosevelt, *F.D.R., His Personal Letters.*

ing, Joseph P. Kennedy, John E. Mack, and others were so appreciated and rewarded when victory came. They believed in Franklin D. Roosevelt and they showed that faith in the most practical way—they laid the money on the line. Other early stalwarts were Senator Clarence C. Dill of Washington, Senator Burton K. Wheeler of Montana, who later changed his mind, and Senator Cordell Hull of Tennessee. Louis felt great admiration for Cordell Hull and told many people in 1928 that he thought Hull would have been the ideal candidate for Vice-President that year. Nobody was happier than Louis when FDR selected Hull as his first Secretary of State.

Another early supporter was Colonel Edward M. House, adviser to Woodrow Wilson, who joined the group supporting the Roosevelt cause shortly after the gubernatorial election in 1930. Louis, always thinking in terms of delegates for 1932, lost no time in going to see the Colonel, who came from Texas with its important forty-six elective votes. Robert M. Field, aide to Colonel House, who was present, gave a vivid account of this conference between the two men. "Louis Howe arrived right on time," Field said, "which made an immediate impression on Colonel House.

"The picture as these two men faced each other was a striking one. Both were slight physically, each a mental giant in his own way, one the friend and co-worker of Woodrow Wilson, the last Democratic President, the other the devoted and resourceful friend of Franklin Roosevelt, destined to become the next Democratic President. The oddest thing about the conference was the initial, prolonged silence, unbroken by either. These two warriors, scarred from many a hard-fought political battle, instinctively understood each other and seemed to communicate their thoughts without the necessity of words. Finally they settled down and Louis outlined briefly some of his plans as Colonel House listened attentively. Suddenly Louis said abruptly, 'What about Texas?' 'You can count on Texas,' the Colonel replied. 'Why?' Louis wanted to know. 'Because,' answered the Colonel, 'I will send word to my friends there that Roosevelt is our best bet.' That seemed to satisfy Louis who abruptly concluded the conference and shuffled off.

"He reminded me of Alberich," said Field. "The only difference was that the gold which Louis guarded was the political destiny of Franklin Roosevelt."

Louis conferred frequently with Colonel House after that, and, in March 1931, the Colonel wrote to FDR, "It was pleasant to read the letters in regard to the promotion of your political fortunes throughout the United States, which Louis Howe brought me yesterday." Louis took a suggested draft of a reply to these letters and Colonel House made some suggestions, but in the final letter, "Every word was taken from Mr. Howe's draft," the Colonel said in a note to FDR, "and I do not believe it could be bettered. We never have arguments and have no difficulty in reaching conclusions satisfactory to us both. I congratulate you upon having such a loyal and efficient lieutenant."

In June Louis also took a list of proposed key men and women in thirty-seven states to Colonel House and they agreed on key figures for campaign managers for Roosevelt.

State leaders went quietly in and out of Louis' little corner office that spring of 1931, and late in June Jim Farley, whom Louis had picked for this job, started on his famous "Elks Tour," stopping all along the route to Seattle, Washington, where the Elks convention was held, to tie up the threads of Louis' correspondence contacts. To Indiana, Illinois, Missouri, Nebraska, Wisconsin, Nevada, Wyoming, Utah, Idaho, Montana, South Dakota, Washington and California went Jim, the busy "drummer," his bald head agleam with the heat and earnestness of his mission. Louis, sitting in his little office back in New York, hurled a steady stream of instructions as Jim traveled westward, and, in a steady stream the heady reports of Roosevelt strength came back. Jim reported when he reached Seattle that there was apparently an almost unanimous sentiment for Governor Roosevelt in every one of the states he had visited and that the organizations in every state were with him wholeheartedly.

That the Democratic leaders in these states were for Mr. Roosevelt was no surprise to Louis Howe, who had been in almost constant touch with them by letter since the fall of 1928. One leader, who had been a strong Al Smith man, told Farley, "I think Roosevelt is a winner and I'm going to support him. I'm getting damned sick and tired of backing losers."

The biggest stumbling blocks encountered by Farley were "favorite sons." Every state has its favorite son, not that it expects him to win, but he is always useful in tying up blocks of votes, to be used for trading purposes at the national conventions. Louis tried to shut off these candidates where it could be done without actually offending the state organizations, and he even insisted that Farley swing entirely around one state which was putting forward a favorite son, lest he get tangled up in a situation that might hurt Franklin's chances. This state was Missouri and its favorite son was the irascible but popular ex-Senator James A. Reed. The local politicos had already arranged a luncheon in Mr. Farley's honor, however, so he could not turn back, and headed right into the storm while Louis fumed. It was quite a storm, too, for Jim Reed, who didn't like Tammany Hall any better than most Midwest Democrats, announced that he would not attend the luncheon. He considered Farley a rank "Tammany-ite" and wanted no part of him. He'd go fishing, he said. However, his friends persuaded him that, whether he could stomach Tammany or not, he had better not insult the representative of the Governor of the great State of New York. Reed finally calmed down and attended the luncheon, and the two Jims tried to outdo each other in encomiums tossed across the luncheon table. Louis breathed easier, however, when Jim was safely out of the state.

The trip was an education to Farley who, as Secretary of the New York State Democratic Committee and now State Chairman, had learned his state politics as well as the next one, but who had had no experience in national politics until he was picked for this job.

"Governor," Jim Farley said to FDR, "this Presidential job

must be a great one judging from the way they are all anxious to have it."[3]

It is possible that Jim Farley did not realize when he said those words how prophetic they were. That he himself later was bitten by the Presidential bug is now history.

Farley, who had gone against Louis' advice in the case of the Missouri luncheon, mistakenly thought he could do the same on another occasion early in 1932. By this time Jim Farley had become a widely traveled man. Since Christmas he had been all through the New England states, had doubled back to the Midwest, had taken in Michigan, had hopped to Washington, D. C., and back until his strong frame sagged a bit as he loped down the hall to Louis' office to make his reports. After a particularly grueling round of hops he'd planned a weekend of rest. But Louis had different ideas.

"Jim," he said, "you've got to do a Paul Revere out to the state convention in Iowa. Things need looking into out there." Jim Farley rebelled. He had talked to the state leaders by phone and had been assured that everything was O. K. "I see no sense in going out," he said. But Louis didn't care anything about ordinary sense. He had a sixth sense. He put the pressure on, but when Farley stood firm he appeared to let the matter drop. Farley breathed freely and started making his plans for the weekend. He should have known Louis Howe better than that. Soon Jim got a cheerful call from Albany. The Governor wanted to know if he didn't really think it would be a good idea for him to "drop on out to Iowa and look things over." Farley was fit to be tied, but he started packing.

"In time," said newswriter W. E. Mullins, reviewing Farley's story about his break with Roosevelt years later, "Farley grew into the proportions of a big man, but truth to tell, in the early days he was little more than a front man for Louis Howe and he did only what the gnome-like figure in the background directed him to do."

[3] James A. Farley, *Behind the Ballots.*

It was a good thing Farley went to Iowa, for he found that some of the legmen for rival candidates had been there before him and that an "uninstructed delegation" was in the making, the very thing Louis was trying to avoid. Farley found himself in the middle of quite a fight. Fortunately, about this time Bob Jackson, one of our own legmen, phoned from Maine to say that that state had instructed for Roosevelt. Farley relayed this news to the Iowa delegation and it had the desired effect. Iowa, with its twenty-six delegates, swung into the Roosevelt column.

It was always a joy to be around the office when Farley came in from a trip with his glad tidings. Louis would hunch up in a chair with his knees drawn up, his feet resting on the lower rungs of his chair, his chin cupped in his hands, and listen with rapt attention to Farley as he unfolded the story of Roosevelt strength in the land. No teen-age girl, listening to protestations of love from her first sweetheart, was ever more enraptured than he. He had never met most of these people except through correspondence, and after fifteen or twenty minutes of briefing, he would turn and look out of the window, one foot swinging as he rocked back and forth. Then he'd turn back and give Mr. Farley an accurate opinion of each man, what he thought of their motives, and what they would do in the long run. Mr. Farley was continually amazed by the accuracy of these observations and would come out shaking his head.

"That little guy," he would say, "has a knack I've never encountered in anybody else—that of accurately sizing up a man simply by hearing him described to him by somebody else."

This pose of the little boss—sitting with one knee up with his hands locked around it, swinging his foot back and forth—was a favorite one. One day one of the staff girls said, "Didn't the boss look cute at the lunch table today, swinging back and forth like a kid in his bye-buggy!" Ed Brown, of the publicity division, clapped his hand over her mouth. "Don't let the boss ever hear you say he is 'cute,' " he warned. "He'd kill you."

We professed to be scared to death of Louis at all times—and the newcomers weren't kidding—but we knew that his bark was worse than his bite. He liked you to stand up to him—no impudence, you understand—but timidity never did appeal to him.

One new girl had a frightening experience with him. Often when he had a knotty problem to thrash out he'd close himself in his office, curl up on his dilapidated couch, or sit at his desk and stare out at the tops of the tall buildings on Madison Avenue, and dream out his solution. One night he was sitting at his desk in a deep study when the door opened and a girl stepped in. Mr. Farley, whose office was down at the other end of the hall, had just hired an attractive black-haired girl named Ellen and had sent her with some papers for Louis.

She opened the door and there, in that small, almost pitch-dark room, sat a little man with only a desk lamp that threw a green, eerie shadow on his face. He looked up, stared at her wildly for a minute, then shouted at the top of his lungs, "Get out!" She turned and fled down the hall, told Mr. Farley she'd gotten in the wrong office and that there was a madman in the corner room. Mr. Farley laughed. "Oh, that's Louis Howe, all right," he said. "Take the papers back. Pay no attention to him. He doesn't really mean anything by that. Go on back."

"Well," Ellen said, "I'm Irish and so I went back. I flung that door open as wide as I could and slammed the papers on his desk and said, 'Jim Farley sent these whether you like it or not.'" Louis looked up, startled. "Well," he roared, "you needn't get so mad about it." Then he burst into laughter, and Louis Howe and Ellen, known to thousands of post office officials as the efficient Ellen Canning, secretary to an Assistant Postmaster General, were good friends from that night on.

Jim Farley was a girl-frightener, too, though I doubt that he ever suspected it. It was a well-known fact that he was a demon to take dictation from and, when he started in, he made the rattle of a machine gun sound like a soft shoe dance in waltz time. After the girls worked for him awhile, they grew used to him. They'd pick up phrases now and then and weave them into a letter so that it all came out right in the end. But a new girl came in one day who didn't know this. Jane Duffy, Mr. Farley's secretary, who needed somebody in a hurry, sent her in for dictation. Farley started in, racing along like a trotting horse down the homestretch. She jotted down a word or two, then she lost him and never found him again. Unaware of this, he kept right on dictating, while she sat with a dazed look on her face and made meaningless marks in her notebook. Finally, he said cheerfully, "Well, all finished. Thanks a lot, young lady." She arose and, with unseeing eyes, walked from the room. But once outside she was galvanized into action. She threw down her notebook, grabbed her hat and went away from there. We never saw her again.

Louis was nervously watching the moves of all other candidates and their backers, and he saw that news of what was going on in the other camps reached FDR's ears at once, and that FDR made the proper moves. When a story was circulated that Jouett Shouse, executive secretary of the Democratic National Committee, had made a trip to Alabama for the purpose of heading off the Roosevelt movement down there, FDR dropped him a polite note saying that he had heard such rumors but felt sure Shouse and Chairman Raskob were not active for any candidate at this time as this would be "unethical" for officers of the Committee.

Louis was more concerned about a rumor that Barney Baruch had joined forces with Raskob and Al Smith to stop Roosevelt, particularly in view of the fact that a friendship had existed between Roosevelt and Baruch since World War I days. FDR sent a note to Baruch saying he felt sure the rumor was not true "because the situation from the national and party viewpoint is too serious to engage in such tactics—and also because you are personally above them." Baruch, when asked about these rumors by well-meaning "go-betweeners," simply said that he did not have any favorite candidate and that he knew that if FDR was worried about it he would talk to him personally, as their long friendship did not require an intermediary.

Another thing getting under Louis' skin was what he called "those damned Southern Clubs." Enthusiastic FDR supporters all over the South were popping up with clubs every day, many

of them headed by people who were going counter to what Louis'
hand-picked key men were trying to do. Criticism of Farley because of his "amateur standing" was also beginning to show up
among many well-meaning but rash supporters. These criticisms
of Farley were also getting to the ears of Colonel House, and he
took them seriously enough to call Louis on the telephone from
his summer place in Massachusetts. On August 17, 1931, Louis
wrote to him as follows:

> You spoke to me over the phone about the possible danger of
> using Mr. Farley as our representative in the field. I have of
> course kept that in mind, but I am anxious to have you meet Far-
> ley and have you talk with him yourself. I doubt if Mr. Farley
> would be a good man to send anywhere in the South, and I want
> to talk to you sometime soon about where we can find a man
> familiar with Southern ways to use for that purpose this fall, but
> my judgment has been that Farley is temperamentally and physi-
> cally the ideal man to use in the Western states. He has a whole-
> some breeziness of manner and a frank and open character which
> is characteristic of all Westerners. In addition I think he gives a
> distinct impression of being a very practical and businesslike
> politician, as well, and the reactions I have received from many
> letters which came to the Governor after his trip have been ex-
> ceedingly complimentary and favorable to him.
>
> I think in dealing with the regular organizations of these West-
> ern states, and so far we have not found a single state where the
> organization has not professed a friendliness to us, we need
> exactly this type of man; one who will impress the politicians
> with whom he talks with the fact that he is a politician of expe-
> rience and that the Governor's affairs are being handled by real
> political experts. Should we unfortunately come in conflict with
> the regular organization machinery in any state, it will be neces-
> sary to appeal to the electorate on high economic and moral
> grounds and we will need someone decidedly more of the intelli-
> gentsia to enlist prominent men in such states who are not ordi-
> nary political workers. For this purpose Farley is utterly unsuited.
> As a politician, however, he is winning spurs, in my judgment,
> and I cite the Missouri complication as proof. [Louis then went

on at great length about the Missouri situation, described earlier in this chapter, and praised Farley's handling of this difficult task.]

He has also one very great recommendation. He does not attempt to dictate, but follows implicitly any advice or instructions which the Governor gives him and his loyalty and unselfishness are beyond question.

In spite of these flattering words it was not long after this that Mrs. Roosevelt made a discreet visit to Farley to tell him that Louis was somewhat hurt because he felt that Farley was not taking him fully into his confidence. Farley, who was not aware of holding out, went to see Louis at once, presumably about something else, and while he did not mention Mrs. Roosevelt's visit to him, he did bring Louis up to date on everything he had been doing since he had seen him last. The little boss worked in mysterious ways and Farley always wondered if Louis really did think he was holding out on him or whether this was Louis' way of letting him know he'd better not!

On the other hand, Colonel House, with whom Louis had conferred so frequently about key men, now began to feel that Louis was holding out on him. The Colonel's advice had been helpful, and he was an early contributor, but as time went on and he was not called to headquarters, he began to feel that the part he was playing was not big enough and not worthy of his background of experience in Presidential politics.

"Louis Howe," he complained to a friend, "is trying to do it all and, at times, seems unwilling to let others know what is going on." No doubt the Colonel had reason to feel this way. Louis asked advice freely, and even took it, but he never tipped his own hand too much nor let his political cat so far out of the bag that it might come back with some mismated kittens to yowl on his doorstep.

The fact is that Louis used all these contacts without mercy and he staggered some of his visitors by his method of appraising them. Well-wishers were always sending somebody in who "could do big things for Mr. Roosevelt." Louis would talk to them, all the time looking them over much in the manner of a horse trader. Then he'd tell them frankly why he thought they "could be useful to Franklin"—or why they couldn't. This made some of them mad, but never bothered Louis who didn't care for thin-skinned people.

Louis' cavalier manner in this respect was distressing to his friends and certainly was not diplomatic, but he had such a single-track mind he simply could not waste time on anybody who could not be useful to his cause. Once Frank Walker, an old friend and early supporter of FDR who knew quite well how Louis treated callers, told him he wanted to bring wealthy Joseph P. Kennedy of Boston to see him.

"Louis," said Walker, "as a special favor to me, please be nice to Mr. Kennedy when I bring him in, will you?"

"Oh sure, sure, Walker," Louis said, "you needn't worry about me. Bring him right in."

Walker was only partially reassured by this glib promise, and took the advice of a member of the staff, who told him he'd better come in a few hours before Kennedy arrived to remind Louis.

Louis was cooperation itself. "Don't worry, don't worry," he said. "I'll put on my very best company manners for him."

When Walker marched confidently in with the beaming Mr. Kennedy, what was Louis doing? He was sitting behind his desk, with his head resting on his folded arms in an attitude of sleep. He gave no sign that he had heard the visitors until Walker gave an embarrassed cough. Even then he never raised his head. He merely opened one eye and fixed Kennedy with a baleful glare while Walker, thrown into confusion, began to talk about the weather and other subjects, all the time frantically trying to catch that eye himself so he could give Louis the signal to cut out the act. It was at least five minutes before Louis raised his head, sat up, and took a desultory part in the conversation.

Mr. Kennedy made a generous contribution in spite of this, and was afterward rewarded with some excellent appointments, one of them being Ambassador to the Court of St. James. No credit to Louis, however, as he didn't care for Mr. Kennedy for reasons known only to himself, and I am sure after that meeting that this feeling was mutual.

Another man, however, who "thought he could be useful to Mr. Roosevelt," was joyfully welcomed by Louis. One day in July we found him gloating over a statement he had prepared for the press. He tossed it over. "Read that," he said triumphantly, "it's a strong endorsement of Franklin by Joe Guffey of Pennsylvania." Many of us, at that time, had never heard of Joe Guffey, who later became a two-term United States Senator from Pennsylvania. So in all innocence we asked, "Who is that Pennsylvania Dutchman? Never heard of him."

Louis looked disgusted. "Mein Gawd!" he said. "He's not a Dutchman. He's the Democratic leader of Pennsylvania, has been for years, and his uncle Jim Guffey was leader for years before that. Joe has a knack of reading the political barometer and he's for Franklin because he knows Franklin is a winner. Catch on?" We caught on.

Another early friend was Cornelius (Neil) Vanderbilt, Jr., who felt the stirrings of the unrest of the times and had broken away from social activities and gone out on his own, later writing his valedictory in the book *Farewell to Fifth Avenue.* In the winter of 1931 Neil, then a roving correspondent for *Liberty Magazine,* was in the South on an assignment. He had covered forty-four states and had become increasingly alarmed by what he saw— hitchhikers, soup kitchens, apple sellers, breadlines, want and desperation. In Florida he went to see Bernarr Macfadden, who owned *Liberty Magazine,* and voiced his fears for the future.

"Well," Mr. Macfadden asked, "who do you think can get us out of this mess?"

"I believe," Neil said, "that Franklin D. Roosevelt, governor of New York, is the man."

Macfadden, no admirer of FDR at that time, shrugged impatiently. "Why, that fellow is nothing but a jellyfish," he said. So Neil dropped the subject.

Somewhere in a Southern paper, however, Neil had seen the

name of Louis Howe and wrote him a letter. Louis, who was in Albany, wired him to come see him at once.

Neil, who had just started a two-weeks vacation in the Florida sunshine, didn't go, but he asked Craig Kershow, an old friend going north on business, to drop in on Louis. Three days later Kershow sat down to talk to Louis Howe. That night the phone in Neil's hotel in Florida clattered impatiently. It was Louis from Albany.

"Vanderbilt, I want you to get up here at once," he said with a fine disregard for the fact that the Florida sun was good and that Neil, though interested in Mr. Roosevelt, didn't see the need for such haste. He saw why, though, before Louis let him off the telephone, and next morning Neil left for the cold northern snows. Two days later he was basking in the warm, friendly smile of Franklin Roosevelt in the Governor's Mansion at Albany. He told FDR what he had seen and heard in the country and that FDR was mentioned most frequently as the man to lick the depression.

FDR, clad in an old blue sweater, was sitting up in bed, and he and Neil were having breakfast when the door opened and Louis walked in. It was the first time Neil had ever seen him. Louis looked Neil over from top to bottom, asked him what he weighed, and walked out.

"What do you think of Louis?" asked FDR, waving his cigarette holder toward the retreating figure.

Neil shook his head in bewilderment. Louis, he said, looked somewhat like a combination of Colonel House and Calvin Coolidge. FDR laughed. "Pretty good," he said, "and do you think that he, too, was raised on a quince?"—a reference to Alice Roosevelt's famed quip about Coolidge.

"I didn't know what he'd been raised *on,*" Neil said later, "but it wasn't long before I realized what he had been raised *to,* for there was no doubt in my mind, after I'd gotten to know him better, that this little man, this Louis Howe, was the undisputed Talleyrand of the Roosevelt movement."

Louis held a long conference with Neil and decided to send him to North Dakota to do some fence building before the state convention, and to take the pulse of the country on the way out. Neil agreed, and promptly sent in his resignation to *Liberty Magazine*. Fulton Oursler, the managing editor, wouldn't accept it, but asked him to go ahead with the survey and also to tie FDR up for a series of exclusive articles for *Liberty* on how he expected to lick the depression. The tie-up was made and there was only the matter of Neil's salary. Louis sent him to Jim Farley about that. It was the first time the two men had met and Farley, figuratively rubbing his hands when this Vanderbilt appeared before him, put the bite on him for a contribution. This wasn't what Neil had in mind and, somewhat annoyed, he phoned Louis that he'd work for nothing, but he'd like his expenses. Louis quickly O. K.'d this, and within twenty-four hours Neil was on his way to North Dakota. He took his realtor friend Kershow with him, and John Brodix, a wealthy gentleman farmer from New Jersey, both of whom felt as Vanderbilt did that FDR was "the man." They invaded North Dakota with a sort of three-ring circus act—Neil hitting the big cities, where he talked to editors and leading citizens, Brodix touring the state, chatting with cattlemen and farmers, while Kershow talked to real estate men in the various towns. The burden of their song was "It's Roosevelt—you'd better get on the bandwagon."

It was not a coincidence that they all turned up in Fargo the night before the state convention; Louis had planned it that way, happily pulling the wires on these three busy legmen like the master in a puppet show. Late that night the three, by hook or crook (crook, probably, as they waited until the canny editor H. A. "Happy" Paulson, who would have sensed a "plant," had gone to bed), all managed to get stories in the morning paper, Vanderbilt on the front page, Kershow on the financial page and Brodix—of all places—on the animal husbandry page. All the stories, Neil's with an eight-column head, predicted "ROOSE-VELT!" As a result of these maneuverings engineered by Louis, and with the help of faithful workers already on the spot, North Dakota was the first state to swing into the Roosevelt column.

Soon Louis had Neil literally covering the United States on

this pulse-taking job, and when he had finished he had nearly 90,000 miles behind him, and Louis had his files full of valuable data.

Louis dubbed Neil "Presidential Agent," which he later shortened to "PA." The name stuck and often, after General Edwin M. Watson, affectionately known around the White House as "Pa" Watson, became military aide and secretary to the President, if someone mentioned "Pa" FDR would look up quickly and say, "Now which 'Pa' do you mean—Neilly or Watson?"

Louis treated Neil, Vanderbilt or not, just as he treated the rest of us. If he had something important he wanted Neil to do he expected him to come running. They got along all right, in spite of this, for Neil understood Louis and developed a deep affection for him. "Louis Howe's word was as good as gold," Neil said, "which was more than you could say for many in political life."

Once, though, Neil was really annoyed with Louis. FDR was scheduled to speak at the Waldorf-Astoria at a big banquet. Neil had a date with a beautiful blonde that night, daughter of an admiral stationed at Newport, and she was coming to New York for a dinner-dance date of long standing. Neil rushed home to the Vanderbilt mansion to have tea with his mother and change into dinner clothes before meeting the young lady's train at seven o'clock. On the hall table he found a note to call Louis Howe immediately. Knowing Louis, his heart sank. Cautiously he called the office and breathed easier when he found that Louis was out. But Jim Farley came on the wire.

"Louis is looking for you everywhere," he said. "He says you have been around long enough to know all the political bigwigs and he wants you to get into your soup and fish and hustle down to the Waldorf right away to act as chief usher at the banquet." (Louis thought no more of asking a Vanderbilt to be an usher, if it would help Franklin, than he did of asking him to be a doorkeeper, which he did once, but that's another story.)

In an anguished voice, Neil tried to explain about the blonde.

"It's no use," Jim said. "You know Louis. Better get on down here as soon as possible."

Neil couldn't even meet the young lady's train, but managed to send a note and some flowers to her hotel saying he'd pick her up at ten-thirty. When that time came FDR had just finished speaking, but there were others on the program. Neil, anxious to escape, figured he could slide down from his seat into the orchestra pit and leave the hotel that way. FDR saw him. Leaning across the table he said in a loud whisper, "And where are *you* going, Neilly?"

"I've got a date with a blonde," said Neil desperately.

"Good luck, my boy. Good luck to you," said FDR with a straight face, but with twinkling eyes. "I wish I had one, too."

The next time Neil saw Louis he was still nettled and proceeded to tell him how he'd messed up his evening. Louis sat there and listened with an amused smile on his face.

"Don't you ever crave feminine relaxation?" Neil asked him.

Louis grimaced. "My boy," he said, "you'll be surprised how much difference it makes to you when you lose the urge. Then only is a man worth the salt in his body."

"I have often thought," said Neil, "how right he was."

Once you were in Louis Howe's confidence he trusted you implicitly. None of this "don't mention this" or "don't mention that" with him. If he thought you'd mention it you wouldn't be there. That's why I was surprised one day when he asked me—and this was the only time—not to mention something that happened in the office.

At that time in my native state, Kentucky, there were two Democratic factions (at what time isn't there?). But this was a very special cleavage, and backing one faction was Judge Robert Worth Bingham, publisher of the powerful Louisville *Courier-Journal,* and his faithful aide and alter ego, General Percy Haly of Frankfort.

Feudin' days, those shot out with firearms, were over in Kentucky, but the political feuds were hot and no quarter asked or

given. Many candidates for office tried to walk a tightrope between the factions. Louis was a past master at side-stepping these
ticklish situations and I was sure that he was making no move in
Kentucky at this time.

I was surprised, then, to see General Haly leaving Louis' office
one day as I came in from lunch. When I mentioned it to Louis he
said, "Look, the *Courier-Journal* is going to support Franklin.
General Haly came up to talk to me about it, but it would be just
as well if you didn't mention this back in Kentucky right now."
I promised to hold my tongue.

The *Courier-Journal* supported FDR, and Judge Bingham was
the first Ambassador to the Court of St. James when FDR went
to the White House.

High above Madison Avenue, set to do the most important job
of his life, Louis Howe holed up in what was undoubtedly the
most disorderly office in the city of New York. In the center of the
room he had a big desk, in one corner a dilapidated couch, and
a chair or two. But what made the room look like a rat's nest was
his method of disposing of his mail. He would sit down, light a
Sweet Caporal, roll up his sleeves, and rip open the letters in the
pile Rabbit laid on his desk every morning. He always liked to
open them himself. Once when he was opening Mr. Roosevelt's
mail we asked him what he did with those marked "personal and
confidential." "Oh, those," he said with a sly twinkle, "I always
open them *first*."

One look at a letter was all he needed. If he didn't like the contents he just threw the letter back over his head like a peevish
child disposing of an unwanted toy. There the letters accumulated
until they made a pile that reached almost to the lower rung of his
chair. These letters were salvaged by Rabbit, or some of the rest
of us, and answered—usually by briefing them, if they were too
long, and putting them back on his desk again. He had no use for
long-winded letters. "Filibuster letters" he called them, and
claimed if a man couldn't put all he had to say on one page it
wasn't worth reading. Many of these long-winded letters had
merit, though, and when cut down and brought to his attention,

were answered. I soon found myself in charge of the "cut it short department," which grew to include newspaper editorials, newspaper stories, reports, and all sorts of things that landed on Louis' desk. This "cut it short department," which he inaugurated, became so popular with him that he carried it right into the White House. Many important officials, no doubt, would have been horrified had they known that long, impressive reports they sent to the White House, complete with seals, ribbons and all, found themselves in the C.I.S. Department and laid on Louis Howe's desk as one-page memos.

As the campaign gathered speed, the mail was so heavy that it began to stack up on Louis' desk, the chairs, and even the couch. Louis, who hated to dictate, let it stack. About this time, Henry Morgenthau, Jr., sent Mrs. Gabrielle Forbush, a friend of the Morgenthau family, to Louis and asked him to give her a job. Mrs. Forbush and her husband had both been with prosperous advertising agencies, but like many other businesses in this depression period these agencies were no more. Louis took her on, but the fact that Mr. Morgenthau sent her didn't mean that he gave her anything important to do till he found out "what made her tick"! She filed cards and did odd jobs around the place for awhile, but every time she looked at the stacks of mail, she winced. One day she timidly asked Louis if he'd like her to take some of the letters and try her hand at answering them. "If it'll keep you out of my hair, go ahead," he said. To his surprise she turned in some splendid drafted replies and he sent them up to Albany for the Governor's signature. Back came a memo from FDR saying, "I don't know who G. E. F. is, but tell her to draft some more letters." After that Louis had her getting out letters by the score.

Mr. Forbush came in to help and eventually they had a staff of some fifty or sixty people, many of whom had held important jobs but who had been thrown out of work because of bad times. One woman had been the editor of an important woman's magazine, but she sat in the staff room dictating letters, happy to have work to do.

Louis didn't bother this department until one day somebody sent in one of FDR's letters to a child, which had been published in the paper in a little Western town. Louis fired the letter to Mrs. Forbush with this notation, "This letter is too damned gooey." Mrs. Forbush went into her files and got a copy of the letter she had drafted and took it to him. When he compared it with the published letter he found that the editor—or the family—had added a "gooey" paragraph or two to make it sound better in the paper!

George Gordon Battle, famous New York lawyer, wrote Governor Roosevelt that he had seen some of the letters from headquarters, that he didn't know who was drafting them, but they were darned good. The Governor sent this letter to Louis, who graciously sent it to the Forbushes with this memo, "Why don't you just swipe this letter for your private files? I won't say a word."

It was Mrs. Forbush who, with Isabel Leighton, authored the book *My Boy Franklin,* from material supplied by the President's mother, and which appeared in the bookstores just before FDR's first inauguration.

If Louis Howe had "swiped" something for his own files this book you are now reading would have been far easier to write. But he kept almost nothing. He simply did not care whether history noticed him or not. All he cared about was seeing that it remembered Franklin. When I appealed to Mrs. Howe for something the little boss left that might be helpful to me, she just shook her head. "You know how Louis was," she said. "He didn't seem to throw things away. He just had the happy faculty of letting them get lost by themselves." If Mrs. Howe herself had not kept pictures, clippings, programs, letters, and a few documents, and if FDR had not been the magpie that he was, hoarding all the bright things that fell under his eyes—which, fortunately, included many of Louis' papers—this task would have been almost impossible. Many papers which Mrs. Howe thought might have been helpful were, alas, swept away in the hurricane and flood which destroyed the Horseneck Beach cottage in 1938.

In his search for efficient help for Friends of Roosevelt, Louis appealed to Eddie Anker, old Albany friend, who was now with the New York Telephone Company, to send him one of their best operators for a tryout as head of our switchboard. This switchboard was a simple "one position" affair then, and such was the state of our finances that the switchboard, my desk, Rabbit's mimeograph machines, file cases, and the "kitchen" were all in one big corner room. The kitchen was just a two-burner hot plate, a few dishes and some pots and pans behind a big screen, presided over by an amiable colored girl named Ruby. About a dozen of us supported this kitchen setup which we grandly called "The Roosevelt Luncheon Club."

Into this hodgepodge came Miss Louise Hachmeister—later the well-known "Hackie" of the White House—who had been sent up by Mr. Anker. She never forgot her interview with Louis Howe about that job. Miss Durand met her first and took her in to see Louis. After briefing her a bit he looked her up and down. "Did Rabbit tell you what you are expected to do around here?" he asked gruffly.

"Yes sir, I think so," gulped Hackie.

"Well, I don't see that there's anything more for me to say then," he barked. "Rabbit, you show her the ropes. We'll give her a two weeks' trial and if she's no good out she goes. Out!"

Hackie, a handsome dark-haired girl with a gorgeous smile, had a sense of humor that saved her.

"I staggered from the room," she said, "and took my place at that dinky little switchboard where the girl who was already there tried me out in the mornings, and in the afternoons I pasted clippings in a scrapbook. All for twenty-five dollars a week, too."

Hackie had held down some important jobs in Wall Street, but she would tell you herself that she didn't know a politician from a wood tick. She speaks of those first days as a nightmare of names, addresses, callers, the Roosevelt clan running in and out, Louis Howe's shouts and murmurs, the whir of the mimeograph machine in one corner of the room, the rattle of my typewriter in the other, the clang of Ruby's pots and pans. Louis briefed her on his most important contacts and expected her to remember them all. His method of making a long distance call was unique, but baffling. He'd simply pick up the phone and say, "Get me Smith [or Brown or Jones]" and expect them to be in his ear in nothing flat. Hackie kept a card index of all his contacts, but often, when she looked in the file the little man wasn't there, Louis' contacts multiplied so fast.

One day I came in from lunch and found her all a-jitter. "Now he *has* gone crazy," she said. "He just picked up his phone and said, 'Give me fits.' What's the matter with him?"

"Oh, nothing serious," I told her. "He just wants you to get Judge William Fitts down in Birmingham, Alabama." Miss Hachmeister, vastly relieved, got the judge on the wire and Rabbit reported that Louis, after talking to him, turned to her all a-beam. "That Hackie," he said, "is a very, very smart girl. She is going to be very valuable to me." That she was valuable indeed is attested by the fact that she went through that campaign to Louis' satisfaction, then on into the White House with FDR, as chief operator, with a staff of five working for her. President Roosevelt always called her his "telephone detective," for once he or Louis set her on somebody's trail she always got her man. Only once did Hackie admit failure. It was in the early days of the Roosevelt administration when Louis told her to get a certain judge in the Midwest on the phone. Louis had had some dealings with the judge in the campaign, and Hackie knew who he was, but when she tried to find him he had disappeared. She chased him all over that section of the West only to learn, finally, from a mail carrier in a little crossroads town, that the judge had passed away.

"I quit then," said Hackie. "I know that there are two places, each in the 'H' listing, that are beyond the reach of the chief operator of the White House. I gave up and reported to the boss."

Later, at Friends of Roosevelt headquarters, when the switchboard had been expanded a bit and Hackie had taken on an assistant, the new girl was startled out of her wits when Louis picked up the phone and said, "Get me the Rabbit." The poor girl, who had not learned that this was what Louis called his secretary, looked cautiously around the room expecting to see a flock of rabbits jump out of the file case. She went to the door and whispered to Malvina Thompson, Mrs. Roosevelt's secretary who was working in the next room, "That little man says he wants a rabbit. I thought I had come to work in a political headquarters. What is this anyway, the zoo?" When Malvina told her he only wanted his secretary the operator was relieved, but not much. She kept wondering what she'd do if he picked up the phone and demanded an elephant, a monkey, or a lizard.

Hackie and I always had an advantage over the others, for here in the corner room we always knew what was on the menu for lunch. The "Roosevelt Luncheon Clubbers" pitched in forty or fifty cents per day to Ruby, then waited for results. Now and then we persuaded Louis to eat with us, if we could make him abandon his regular diet of an apple and glass of milk.

"Ruby," we'd say, "shake a leg! Mr. Howe is eating with us today. What's for lunch?"

Ruby would roll her eyes heavenward. "I'se got Spanich ryess," she'd intone, "and I'se got liver-rich sangwiches—both!"

This was Ruby's way of saying she had Spanish rice and liverwurst sandwiches, but she made it sound like a feast. Louis always enjoyed these brief respites from his hectic day and threatened to bring Franklin in to eat with us sometime. But to both our disappointment and relief, he never did.

The four Roosevelt boys and Anna were in and out often, and Louis was like a doting uncle to them, helping them with their various problems and giving them advice. In his heart, I believe, he was always partial to Franklin, Jr., or perhaps he leaned to him because he saw in him the same qualities he had seen in the other youthful FDR twenty years before. One day he suddenly interrupted a conversation with Joe Guffey to say, "Joe, do you know that one of Franklin's boys is destined to have a great political future?" "Which one?" asked Guffey, thinking he'd say, "Jimmy," who was already being spoken of in some quarters as "the Crown Prince." "It will be young Franklin," said Louis quietly. "Watch him, he's got everything." Franklin, Jr., was only seventeen years old then, but Louis saw those qualities in him that eighteen years later made him smash to victory in his first political race as candidate for Congress in a special election in the 20th Congressional District of New York. Joe Guffey, who has a long memory, sent him a telegram on that occasion: "Congratulations!" he said. "You are bearing out what Louis Howe said about you many years ago."

Louis, though doting, could also be a stern uncle if he caught any of the tribe up to something he thought might "hurt Franklin's chances." One day Jimmy, then living in Massachusetts, made a speech at a Democratic rally in Worcester, in which he said that if his father became President the first thing he would do would be to call a special session of Congress to repeal the Prohibition amendment. This prohibition question was a touchy one and Louis saw no need to twist its tail, at least until after Franklin was nominated. The day the story hit the papers Jimmy was yanked to New York. He dashed into Louis' office and we figured there was some hot telephoning to Albany. After awhile he dashed out again and headed into our office looking for the water cooler—oh, yes, it was in there, too—and took a long drink. "What's the matter?" we asked him. "Did your father give you the works?"

"Father!" he exploded, as he took off his hat and mopped his brow. "No, he wasn't so bad, but you should have heard *Louie!*"

The repercussions of this incident soon died down, but we noticed that James did not issue any more statements from Massachusetts.

We found out during this period that Louis could be just as tough with FDR as he was with Jimmy, if he thought he was making a wrong move. We froze in our tracks one day when we heard these words coming from Louis' office, while he was on the phone to Albany.

"Franklin, you damned fool! You can't do that. You simply can't do it, I tell you!" We had no idea what Franklin was doing that Louis objected to, but it was only a minute before we learned just how strong his objections were. The next thing was a shout, filled with fury.

"But Franklin," he yelled, "if you do it you're a fool—just a damned, idiotic fool. And if you do it you will live to regret it. Mark my words, you'll live to regret it!"

The Governor put in some licks then, and he must have been giving Louis a hot argument, for Louis was shut off for a few minutes while he listened, but his angry breathing could be heard all the way to the outer office.

"All right, all right, pighead," he shouted. "Go ahead and be a damned fool, if you insist. But don't say I didn't warn you. What's that, what's that? You're going for a swim? Well, go ahead, dammit, and I hope to God you drown!"

The telephone slammed back on its cradle and there was such a complete silence for a minute that we feared the little boss had suffered a stroke. He survived though and the next time he talked to Albany he was calm.

This telephone battle with FDR came during the time the New York *World-Telegram* was putting pressure on FDR as Governor to have a legislative investigation of Tammany Hall and the battle might have been about that, but we didn't know for sure, and naturally we didn't dare ask Louis.

One thing we did know though—to talk to a man as Louis talked to FDR, you have to hate him or love him very much. And we knew that in Louis Howe's case it definitely was not hate.

Louis was now busily engaged issuing pamphlets adorned with Governor Roosevelt's photograph, and bearing such titles as:

Franklin D. Roosevelt—Who he is and what he has done.

Roosevelt and Human Welfare.

A leader in Progressive Democracy—Roosevelt.

Labor, Unemployment and Care for the Aged—What Roosevelt is doing about it.

These pamphlets went far and wide over the country from our little headquarters, with no identifying marks except the words, "Issued by the Friends of Roosevelt, 331 Madison Avenue, New York City." But they definitely made the political leaders in the country take notice.

One Sunday morning Louis called us out of bed and told us to get down to the office quickly for a special job. Rubbing sleep from our eyes we went—Ed Brown and Tom Peters of the publicity staff, Margaret Durand and myself, and one or two others.

"I'm sending you down to see Harry Hopkins about something Franklin wants done," he said. "Hopkins will explain it to you."

Some of us had heard of Harry Hopkins, but the name didn't mean much at the time. He had a small office downtown, as head of the New York Emergency Relief Administration, but he was not conspicuous in any of the councils.

"Here's what you are to do," Louis said. "Franklin has been asked to write a magazine article about an experiment he and Hopkins are trying out. I need some material before I can get the story ready. Hopkins has the data in his office. Let him do the talking and show you some exhibits he has. You write up the story in your own way and let me have your drafts. I may then send some of you upstate to write some stories from there."

With mild curiosity we trooped down to Hopkins' office. He was there before us, with his secretary, and had the material spread out on a long table in the middle of the room.

The first thing that struck me about Harry Hopkins was his extraordinarily beautiful eyes. Deep and dark, set back in his long, pale face, they dominated his features and made his plain countenance almost handsome.

This was the plan as he explained it to us:

Several plots of land had been secured in upstate New York and impoverished families were being sent there from New York City, given a cow and some chickens and a small garden, with the idea that they might become self-supporting. This was in the very depth of the depression and every effort was being made to help stricken families who, cold and hungry, faced a hopeless winter. Hopkins spread out on the table pictures of these families "before and after." Here would be a family in a Bowery environment, pitiful bare rooms, pinched children's faces, discouraged, beaten parents. Then there would be a picture of the same family in the new environment, the children well fed, the parents' faces full of hope and courage, the little garden plot blooming, the cow sleek and fat. It was a heartwarming sight but there was another side to the picture. Some of these New York families simply didn't take to rehabilitation. Bewildered by country life, longing for the sight and smell of New York, even in poverty, they had in many cases fled from this paradise back to their old haunts and holed in. The experiment, in these cases, was of course a failure.

The thing that we marveled at, though, was that Harry Hopkins laid these failures and their case histories out for us to see, right along with the successful ones. He didn't have to do it. He might have soft-pedaled these failures for, after all, he was in charge of the experiment and they could have reflected discredit on his handling of the problem. But he made no effort to do so.

"That's an amazing fellow," somebody remarked as we left. "He knew we were sent there to get material for the Governor's story. How would we have known the difference if he hadn't shown us a single one of those bad pictures? There is an honest man."

We all agreed on this point and I, for one, never had any reason to change that opinion in the years that followed.

It was during this period that, as a rare treat, Louis arranged for five of us girls to go to Albany and spend a weekend at the governor's mansion—Margaret Durand and myself, Mary Cahill and Margaret Pascocello who worked for Mr. Farley, and Alice Disbrow who now worked for Mrs. Roosevelt. The Roosevelts were away and we were chaperoned by Malvina Thompson, Mrs. Roosevelt's secretary, and Marguerite LeHand, secretary to the Governor. We had the run of the place. We visited the Capitol building, we swam in the Governor's pool, we went to the races at Saratoga, but the big thrill for Rabbit and myself was that we were allowed—since Louis had removed himself to Fall River for the weekend—to occupy his room. When we went to Saratoga we wanted, most of all, to see Louis' old home and visit some of his haunts, but there was no time. It was a thrill to zoom through the countryside in the Governor's car but a big disappointment that we were not allowed to bet on the races when we got there.

"You see," Malvina explained, "racing is all right here, but betting is illegal. So steer clear of those 'betting boys' who go through the crowd. You are in the Governor's box and everybody will be watching you. We can't do anything that might embarrass him." However, we "made book," when Malvina went off to visit friends, and laid bets among ourselves, keeping a wary eye on Mrs. Graham Fair Vanderbilt in the next box, and others who might have their eyes on us. We got by with this, but when we announced that we were going back to New York on the Albany night boat Malvina set her foot down. Too many jokes had been made about this famous boat; she said it was no place for five unescorted girls, but we pleaded so hard she finally gave in. However, she insisted on getting on the boat with us and seeing us safely to our staterooms. It was a lovely moonlit night and as soon as she had gone, Rabbit and I scurried up to the upper deck and had a few dances with some summer vacationers. Fearing that the little boss might hear about it some way, we told him after we got home, and also about those race bets at Saratoga. Simultaneously, he bestowed upon us a sort of fatherly forgiveness along with a bit of unshirted hell. "I believe I noticed though," said Rabbit, as we slunk from the room, "a slight twinkle in one eye, didn't you?" I can't say that I did.

In the fall of 1931, however, when Louis had us all in our proper niches ready to go on with him right into the convention the next summer, his astonishment and rage were something to behold when I marched in one day and told him I was going to Kentucky to build a house.

"Build a house!" he exploded. "I never heard of such a damn fool idea. What about electing a President? Build your house some other time. Campaigns won't wait. Houses will."

I told him that this one wouldn't, the plans were all made, my folks wanted me to be there and I had to go. He fussed and fumed and swore he couldn't find anybody to do my work and delayed me three weeks before he finally sent me off, warning me that I'd better bring back a picture of a completed house to show for all this "wasted" time. He simply did not consider anything important except the campaign to elect Franklin Roosevelt. He expected everybody around him to feel the same way and infected most of them with this idea to such an extent that when Mrs. Mabel Fickel, one of Mollie Dewson's lieutenants, asked for maternity leave in the middle of the campaign, Mollie shrieked, Howe-like:

"Well! All I can say is, this is one helluva time to have a baby!"

I sent Louis post cards from time to time that fall, to let him know how the house was progressing. Once I got a short note from him, enclosing a stamp and asking if I was too "d——— stingy to spend money on a stamp to write him a letter."

It was after Christmas when I returned and Louis' first words were, "Well, where are the pictures of that dream house?" I handed them over. He settled back and studied them, turned them over and around admiringly, then looked up with a grin.

"Congratulations," he said, "I never thought you'd do it. Isn't there an old saying that you have amounted to something in life if you've written a book, had a baby or built a house? Well, you've built a house."

The implication that this was the best I'd ever do brought a burst of laughter from Rabbit and myself in which the little boss finally joined with great relish.

"Now," he said, "let's all get back to work and build a President."

Room 1702

EARLY in 1932 Louis' organization, Friends of Roosevelt, fooled no one as to its objective. If there had been any doubt, it was quickly dispelled when Governor Roosevelt wrote a letter to the secretary of the Democratic State Committee in North Dakota, one of the states that could not instruct for a candidate unless he admitted in writing that he was in the race. Roosevelt's letter went to North Dakota on January 23, 1932, and Louis Howe drew a long breath, took a deep drag on his Sweet Caporal, and moved one step closer to his dream of twenty years.

Louis' plans had been so thorough and he believed that things were so good for Franklin that he sat down with the Governor in February, mapped out a campaign trip, with pins stuck in the map where campaign speeches were to be made, and planned the type of speech for each section! At a town in the farm belt they'd plan a farm speech, somewhere else a power speech, another place an economy speech, and so on. So carefully were these plans worked out that after FDR was actually nominated in July, and the trip begun, only one major change was made. No speeches were canceled—they merely shifted one speech from the town they'd first "pinned" to another town, after the trip got under way.

A fainter heart than Louis Howe's, however, might have been dismayed by the impressive array of candidates taking their places at the post or being tentatively trotted along the judges' rail.

166

Favorite sons were all over the place, with the convention only a few short weeks away.

In spite of his vigorous statement in 1928 that he would never run again, there was Al Smith, his brown derby poised to hurl into the ring for the third try. Illinois was busily grooming the pink whiskers of its perennial favorite, J. Hamilton Lewis; Missouri had its favorite son, James A. Reed, pawing and snorting at the paddock; down Virginia way, Governor Harry Flood Byrd stood apple-cheeked and ready; Maryland flew the banner of its good-looking, white-maned governor, Albert C. Ritchie; while deep in the heart of Texas, there was a roar from the grandstand for its own John Nance Garner. Louis watched them as if they were figures in a chess game.

"Howe thought of nothing else during his waking hours," Jim Farley said later. "Rebuffs never discouraged him and he was as grim as a bulldog in hanging onto what he wanted."[1]

Louis worked so hard that summer that his always thin frame grew thinner, his neck scrawnier, his coughing spells more frequent, but he never stopped. He put in fearful hours at his desk with only his apple and glass of milk for lunch. One thing carried him through the day: after this meager lunch he curled up on his dilapidated little couch for an hour and told Miss Durand to tell callers "that he was dead," and no matter how big the wig who waited in the anteroom, he simply waited till Louis came alive again.

Then, suddenly, it was June and the Chicago convention was just ahead. Louis planned down to the last detail what he wanted each of us to do, briefed us on it, and expected us to deliver. Miss Hachmeister was to man the special switchboard, set up in our headquarters in the Congress Hotel, Rabbit was to be at Louis' side for dictation, errands, telephoning. Malvina Thompson, loaned to him by Mrs. Roosevelt, was to help him with mail and telegrams. Aubrey Mills, Rabbit's fiancé, took along an elaborate card system of delegates' names, where they were staying in Chicago, when they would arrive, and how they could be reached on

[1] James A. Farley, *Behind the Ballots*.

the telephone, and Mary Eben, on Mollie Dewson's staff, was subject to calls from Louis if he needed her. He sent Fred Roper, son of Daniel Roper who later was FDR's first Secretary of Commerce, to Chicago two weeks in advance with Rabbit and two or three others to open the headquarters. Fred was then just out of college and his father and Colonel House, who was an old friend of the Ropers, decided that a little political experience might be good for him, so they sent him to Louis in February to see if he could use him. Fred was only twenty-three at the time and had grown a mustache to make him look older and more sophisticated, but this didn't fool Louis. He gave him the same treatment he had given "Hackie" and the others.

"Can you do anything that an intelligent female couldn't do better?" he asked. Fred swallowed and said he wasn't sure.

"Well, then," said Louis abruptly, "can you frost a mint julep glass from top to bottom?" When Fred laughed and said he didn't know, but if Mr. Howe wanted one he could damn well try, Louis was satisfied. This trick of Louis' of asking irrelevant questions to throw an applicant off guard was used frequently. If the applicant grew huffy, that was the end. He decided young Roper would do, hired him, gave him the nickname of "the keeper of the sacred mustache" and set him to all kinds of odd jobs, and he finally, with Beale Jensen and Fred Palmer, ran the "Roosevelt Clubs" from headquarters after the convention. These clubs were similar to Louis' "Democratic Unions" in New York State and, as they sprouted like mushrooms over the country, he knew what was going on in the grass roots sections of the country.

One of the odd jobs Louis gave Fred was to call on the producer of the then popular musical comedy, *Of Thee I Sing*. One of the hit songs in the show was "Wintergreen for President," and those of us who had seen the show promptly substituted the name "Roosevelt" for "Wintergreen" and went around chanting it from office to office. Louis heard us and immediately sent Fred to see the producer to ask him if he wouldn't change the song in the show and make it "Roosevelt for President." The producer, who certainly had no wish to alienate all the Republican voters who came to see the show, to say nothing of the supporters of Al Smith and other Democratic candidates, emphatically turned down the request. When Fred reported this to Louis he only grinned. "I thought he would," he said, "but it was worth a try, anyway."

Louis warned Fred that when he arrived in Chicago the first thing he must do was secure two or three rooms at Convention Hall, where Jim Farley could hide away and get the various leaders off the floor for conferences when the convention started. Louis knew that Jouett Shouse, executive director of the Democratic National Committee, had taken over practically every available room at the hall in the name of the Committee, and that they definitely would not be available for the Roosevelt people. Fred bashed his head against a wall everywhere he turned. He called Louis on the phone.

"There is simply no chance to get a room at that hall," he said, "unless, well, unless—"

"Go on, go on, Roper," said Louis impatiently, "unless what?"

"Well, unless I can bribe the caretaker to take over a few rooms and put locks on the doors for us," Fred answered.

"Roper," said Louis sweetly, "I told you to get those rooms. I didn't tell you *how*, did I? That's up to you, my boy." So the "keeper of the sacred mustache" laid the proper amount of silver across the palm of the keeper of the sacred rooms and secured an office that Farley could use, and locked off two more—one on each side—to make it soundproof. Louis had warned Fred to make it foolproof, too, so he had a telephone booth installed in the inside office just to make doubly sure that no prying ears listened to any of the Farley conversations!

When Fred reported the success of these maneuvers Louis promptly told him to put a cot in the rooms and sleep out there, lest the opposition slip out in the middle of the night, take off those locks and get the rooms back. Fred stuck to this grisly routine for three or four nights. Then the spookiness of the place unnerved him and he appealed to Louis by long distance to let him go to the hotel for a night's sleep.

"You wait a day or two," Louis said, "then if you can't take it any longer I'll send my boy Hartley out to sleep in the rooms until the convention starts." Fred managed to stick it out, however, but it was an experience he never recalled with any great enthusiasm.

My job at Chicago, since I had read and briefed mail from the delegates for so long and was expected to know them all, was to serve on the reception committee, greet each delegate, and see that he was promptly ushered into our headquarters where Jim Farley awaited him.

Louis, who wanted no part of this handshaking routine, holed up in a big suite high on the seventeenth floor, 1702, prophetically known as the "Presidential suite," which faced the magnificent vista of Lake Michigan and the boulevard. Mrs. Howe and Hartley, now twenty and a student at Harvard, came on from Massachusetts. Mrs. Howe stayed in a quiet room in another part of the hotel and Hartley acted as doorkeeper for his father.

Before Louis left New York he worked out a little project which he thought extremely clever, and why it was never carried to a conclusion I do not know. He planned to have Mr. Roosevelt record a special greeting to the delegates on a phonograph disc and mail it to them before they left their homes for the convention. Louis felt that Franklin would be handicapped by not being there in person, as so many other candidates would be, and this was his plan to offset that disadvantage. When we asked him what would happen if the delegate *had* no phonograph to play the record he turned on us. "Mein Gawd!" he said. "What if he doesn't have one? Don't you think that if a man gets a personal greeting from the Governor of New York—the next President of the United States—he'll have sense enough to take it in his hand and hotfoot it over to some neighbor who has a machine?" We agreed there was merit in this thought, and never knew that the record was not made and sent until several members of that 1932 delegation were polled about it, and the Franklin Roosevelt Library at Hyde Park made a complete search of the Roosevelt campaign material to see if they could locate one.

Louis, juggling funds to meet the terrific expenses of the convention, sent the staff out in relays to keep from putting too great a strain on the exchequer all at one time. When he had settled affairs to his satisfaction in New York, he took off for the big scene himself with Dwight Hoopingarner who was now secretary of the Business and Professional Men's League for Roosevelt.

The president of the League was Jesse Isidor Straus, an early FDR supporter who had done some fine spadework for the Roosevelt cause. But something bothered Louis. Somewhere he had picked up a rumor that Straus had taken quite an entourage with him to Chicago, including a high-powered publicity man on his personal payroll. Was the man running for President? Most people thought Mr. Straus merely had hopes of being a cabinet member, but Louis kept an eye on him.

"Look, Hoop," he said to Hoopingarner as they parted at the Congress Hotel, "this League crowd is your baby out here. Keep an eye on them and see that they deliver for Franklin. And," as a parting shot, "see that *you* don't forget who's running for President!"

Louis had barely taken his hat off when he found that all hell was a-poppin' among the Roosevelt delegates. The day before, in the midst of an enthusiastic rally, Senator Huey Long of Louisiana threw a bombshell into the meeting by proposing that the Roosevelt people pledge themselves to the abolition of the two-thirds nominating rule in favor of a majority rule. Jim Farley hedged and stalled, and pointed out that the meeting had no power to take such action. Besides, he said, it would not be fair to take it without consulting the candidate. But Huey delivered one of his stomping, shouting speeches which swept the delegates into such a state of excitement that they adopted the resolution, pledging the Roosevelt forces to fight for the abolition of the two-thirds rule before the meeting broke up! Louis almost had a stroke. He told them how silly they'd been to go out on such a political limb, and that they'd better climb off it before it broke with their weight.

"Farley and I took a lesson in national politics then and there," said Ed Flynn. "I cite this as an example of the inexperience of the men who were handling Roosevelt's campaign in Chicago. Louis Howe was probably the most experienced of us all."[2]

In the meantime Farley had reached Roosevelt on the phone and FDR had told him not to worry, that he felt sure the difficulty could be solved, and they ended doing what Louis said they would. They had to back down and Roosevelt issued a statement disclaiming any intention of trying to change the rules. But Louis kept his eyes open from then on, to make sure something like this didn't happen again.

Copying his own strategy after the election in 1928, when he had Mary Eben make up the colored maps to go with the book which went to the Democratic National Committee, Louis had Mary make up a huge map, showing the states that had instructed for Roosevelt in red, while states instructed for others were in less gaudy colors. Since we had most of the Solid South—except Maryland and Virginia, I believe—a huge block of western states, Maine, New Hampshire, Vermont, West Virginia (and several other eastern states), even Alaska, which was one of the first to board the Roosevelt bandwagon, the whole map was dominated by these spectacular splashes of crimson. This map nettled the other candidates and their managers, and they ridiculed it. "Field Marshal Farley's map," they said scornfully, "doesn't mean a thing. Showy, but what else?" Up on the seventeenth floor Louis, who didn't care who had credit for the map so long as it struck the sensitive spots, grinned happily when these peevish slurs reached him.

Another scheme Louis worked out to keep the delegates intrigued was to have them come to his suite in relays and talk directly to Governor Roosevelt on the phone. Louis had a voice amplifier rigged up from Miss Hachmeister's switchboard, down on the first floor, and when he gathered a group of delegates in his suite the Governor talked to them, his words piped into Louis' room, almost as though he was speaking on the radio. We never knew when we went into Louis' room whether we'd trip over a Senator, a Governor, a farm delegation, a labor group, or a bunch

[2] Edward J. Flynn, *You're the Boss* (New York: The Viking Press, 1947).

of coils and wires Louis had on hand to rig up some Rube Gold-berg trap for the delegates.

Some of the remembered ones who came and went in 1702 were Senator Jimmy Byrnes of South Carolina, Senator William King of Utah, Justin Miller of California, Benjamin Marx of Ohio, Bruce Kremer of Montana, and Arthur Mullen of Nebraska.

The fact that we were so short of money brought us all a brief-ing from Louis on economy before we left New York.

"Just because you are on an expense account," he warned, "you don't have to eat your fool heads off out there. Go slow and remember the battered old budget now and then, will you?"

Dutifully we gals doubled up three and four in a room which we called "the bull pen," and when we ate we kept a watchful eye on the right side of the menu.

However, after a few days, Rabbit and I worked out a system we figured would win us some kind of decoration from the little boss. We hastened to lay it before him.

"Boss," we said, "we haven't cost you much money since we've been out here. We've been going to lunch or dinner, nearly every day, with some men from New York who are out here, men who used to come in and out of the office. When we eat alone we are careful, but when we eat with them we shoot the works!"

He looked at us sharply. "Who are these summer Santa Clauses you've trapped?" he wanted to know.

When we started to enumerate them he doubled up with pain or laughter, we couldn't tell which at first. We knew it was both when he cried out:

"Stop, stop, you're killing me! Every one of those guys you've mentioned is on my payroll, too!"

Cliff Scott, canny political friend of Louis from Arkansas, Cornelius Vanderbilt, Jr., and I were the members of the "three man" reception committee at the headquarters on the first floor of the Congress Hotel. Neil, in his leg work for Louis, had been so helpful that when he came to Chicago and wanted to be useful, Louis assigned him to this job. Neil, however, hadn't been in touch with many of the delegates and was not familiar with their names and faces. One day, in the confusion, he failed to recognize Lieutenant Governor Lehman of New York and tried to stop him from going in to see Farley. John Stuart, also on hand in Chicago, leaped up to Room 1702. "Louie, Louie," he yelped, "you've got to get that damn fool off the door down there."

Louis looked up and scowled. "What damn fool?" he asked. "I brought several damn fools out here with me."

"Why, that damn fool Vanderbilt," John panted. "He doesn't know the delegates and he's keeping out some important people."

"Tell her to kick him in the shins," Louis said laconically.

"Tell who to kick who and why?" asked John, in grammatical confusion.

"Tell Lela," said Louis irritably. "She knows who these people are, or if she doesn't she ought to. Tell her to watch Neil and if he tries to keep any of the delegates out, kick him in the shins."

John didn't think this made sense, but he relayed the message to me anyway, and I relayed it to Neil, who took it with great good humor and for several years afterward swore he still carried scars from those shin kicks. We bore scars, too, from being pushed around by photographers, who jammed the reception room as soon as they heard of Neil's job in order to get a picture to run with the arresting caption, "A Vanderbilt as Doorkeeper."

Louis was now busy on another project which occupied all his time when he wasn't with the delegates. FDR, Judge Rosenman, and Professor Raymond Moley—FDR and Rosenman in Albany, and Moley in Chicago—were putting their best efforts into FDR's acceptance speech, but Louis kept Rabbit busy jotting down things *he* thought should go in it. To say that this upset Moley would be an understatement, as he could get absolutely nothing out of Louis about what he was writing, and Louis drove him frantic with hints and innuendoes. Louis himself had brought Moley into the Roosevelt circle in the campaign of 1928. Moley was then Associate Professor of History at Columbia University and Louis thought his ideas would be useful to Franklin. But that didn't mean that he wanted Moley's ideas to supplant his own. Moley had left his speech draft, on which he had been working with FDR in Albany, and was getting other ideas and suggestions at the convention which he was passing back by phone. Finally FDR and Rosenman phoned the gist of their draft to Moley in Chicago. He had the speech typed and tried to persuade Louis to read and approve it. Louis refused to look at the draft for an agonizingly long time, and when he did finally condescend to read it, he let out a howl that it was not what *he* wanted at all. He yelped at Moley, blamed Rosenman, fumed that FDR ought to know better, and so on. Then he dictated an entirely new draft of his own which he would not even let Moley see, nor give him a hint as to what was in it. Finally he refused to discuss it at all, saying he was too busy, and Moley was in a state of black despair.

The convention was in full swing now, with Senator Thomas J. Walsh, the avenging nemesis of the Teapot Dome scandals, as permanent chairman, and Senator Alben W. Barkley, Kentucky's great orator, as temporary chairman. A faction in the Democratic Committee wanted Jouett Shouse for permanent chairman, but they were definitely not Roosevelt people, for it was plain by this time that Shouse, head of the Executive Committee, and John J. Raskob, chairman of the Democratic National Committee, were doing all they could to block Mr. Roosevelt's nomination. Our side won with the election of Walsh and Barkley, but Shouse had his revenge. He tied up the tickets to Convention Hall so tightly that it was almost impossible for the Roosevelt supporters to get in. Jim Farley, bombarded on all sides for these bits of pasteboard, had Vincent Dailey of the New York State Democratic Committee sitting in the back office, away from the crowds, juggling the thin stream of tickets that found their way in and passing them out where they would do the most good. World wars have their undergrounds and so do political conventions. There is no doubt that many tickets handed out by Shouse to supporters of other candidates, especially to supporters of Alfred E. Smith, later found their way surreptitiously into the back office and into Vincent Dailey's hands. We found out early that there was no use to take up the ticket situation with Louis. "Tickets are not my business," he said curtly. "I'm working on the delegates. The tickets are Jim's baby."

With Walsh's and Barkley's elections an accomplished fact, however, this thin trickle of tickets turned into a golden stream, thanks to Ambrose O'Connell, now Judge Ambrose O'Connell of the United States Court of Customs and Patent Appeals in Washington, who was assistant to Frank Walker in Chicago. Ambrose put on his hat and went looking for Shouse. In spite of efforts to stop him he pushed on until he reached the inner office. Shouse was not there, but his assistant was.

"I've come for the tickets," Ambrose said.

"What tickets?" the young man asked, as if he didn't know.

"The same tickets you would be planning to use if you had won and we had lost," said Ambrose.

The young man handed them over.

Jim Farley was proclaiming "Roosevelt on the First Ballot," a statement which the Roosevelt decriers heard with mingled fury and alarm. This big talk started before Louis even arrived in Chicago, for Farley had run into the "Stop Roosevelt" movement as soon as his feet hit the station platform. He phoned to Louis to pour out his woes about this alarming movement. Louis listened carefully, no doubt counting in his mind what all this long conversation was costing his skinny budget. Suddenly he cut in, "Sit tight and claim everything, Jim," he said. He turned around to those in the room and grinned. "Jim sounds a little excited," he remarked, "but it's all right. Texas and California will flop when the time comes." And it was "Roosevelt on the First Ballot" from then on in Chicago.

Al Smith, still in New York, hearing all this "claim everything" talk, gave some pungent interviews before he left for the convention, snorting at what he called the "Farley Fairy Stories." His supporters were already busy in Chicago. Heywood Broun who, like a lot of other newspapermen and women from New York, was strong for Smith, wrote a column for the Scripps-Howard papers called, "Feather Duster Roosevelt," a blistering attack on what he termed Roosevelt's "weak-willed" policies. The Smith forces immediately had thousands of copies of this column reprinted, and hired stooges to stand around in the lobby at the Congress Hotel handing them out. We went into a quiet huddle in our own headquarters, and soon we had a "clean-up squad" passing along the corridors, taking great handfuls of these offending leaflets from these hired "hander-outers," quietly tearing them up and tossing them into a wastebasket.

But now, in the heat and confusion, a worry as big as the fate of our candidate began to plague the staff of Louis Howe. We thought the little boss was going to die. His weight had fallen off so alarmingly that his clothes hung on him like rags on a scarecrow, and his always frequent coughing spells had now become constant, rasping things.

The intense heat, which he always hated, the excitement and suspense, the long hours with no sleep, were beginning to take their toll. His skinny frame had shrunk to less than a hundred pounds. He looked ghastly. The only thing we found to encourage us was a remark by a newspaperman who had known Louis for many years.

"Hell," he said, "Louis Howe has come this far, half alive, and you know damned well he isn't going to die until he sees Franklin Roosevelt nominated for President."

Just the same, on the third day of the convention I was sure Louis' time had come. It was one of the most blistering days of the session. I had been sent up to ask him if he would receive a group of farm leaders from the Midwest, who were anxious to have Governor Roosevelt's views on the farm problem in those troubled days when embattled farmers, in some sections faced with foreclosures, were standing off the sheriff with shotguns.

When I entered the room Louis was alone, seated in a chair near the open window, struggling for a breath of air. He was leaning forward in his chair, his shirt collar open at the neck, his head in his hands, and his labored breathing could be heard all the way across the vast living room. He looked up at me with eyes dulled with pain. "What is it?" he whispered. "What do you want?"

Panic caught me by the throat, and for a moment I could not speak. Finally I gulped out the message about the farm leaders. "Yes," he whispered. "Yes, I'll see them. Tell them to come up. Give me half an hour." I turned and literally fled from the room, with tears streaming down my face. As I entered the hall, a hand suddenly reached out from the next room where Malvina Thompson was working.

"What's wrong, child?" she said, "Did the boss scold you about something?"

"No, no," I choked, "but he is dying, the little boss is dying. Please do something, tell somebody—"

She took my arm, pulled me into the room, then led me into the bathroom and shut the door.

"I know he's pretty bad today," she said, "but you know he has these spells and gets over them. He'll be all right. I'll have somebody go in. Stop crying now, wash your face and go back downstairs." I washed my face, then began to dab powder around my eyes. Suddenly I heard a choking sound and looked at Malvina. She was leaning against the wall rocking with laughter. She grabbed my hand. "Stop," she said, "stop, or you'll never quit crying. That's powdered soap you're slapping in your eyes." This broke the tension, we both laughed, and I was able to go down and tell the delegation that Louis would be able to see them in half an hour. And, amazingly enough, he did.

One newspaperman wrote a story from the convention that accurately summed up Louis Howe's whole relationship to Franklin Roosevelt.

"Room 1702 in the Congress Hotel. Keep that number in mind. In all human probability a candidate for President is being nominated in that room this day. And it is by no means improbable that Room 1702 may be the anteroom to the White House—one has that strange feeling in passing its threshold—the feeling that destiny is at work within these walls.

"Hunched down within the depths of an overstuffed chair is the most singular personality in American politics. I defy anyone to find his counterpart outside the pages of Charles Dickens or

Victor Hugo. A diminutive, incredibly thin, gnome-like individual
who seems scarcely to belong to this day and age. There is something utterly medieval about him. His head, full-domed and thinly-
thatched, is overlarge for his body. His forehead is high and furrowed.

"His eyes are set back deeply under heavy brows. His face is
narrow and points from high cheekbones to subtle chin. The
whole face is amazingly creased and wrinkled.

"This amazing man is Louis McHenry Howe, the closest man
alive to Franklin Roosevelt; his alter ego; the real head and directing mind of the Roosevelt drive for the Presidency.

"Every moment of his waking and sleeping hours has been
spent in Room 1702 or in an adjoining room. Day or night he
has not taken a step out of that place. I doubt if he has even
glanced out the window upon the stirring panorama of Michigan
Avenue and Grant Park—the surging crowds, the marching
bands, the squadron of Army airplanes. . . . These spectacles leave
him cold.

"His one and only interest is to finish the job and get back to
Governor Roosevelt's home in New York's East Sixty-fifth Street,
his home also, and to his books and private papers. To get the job
done he applies the inexhaustible energy and concentration that
is the astonishment of all who watch him work. He sleeps maybe
four hours in the twenty-four, and eats when his nervous energy
permits, a sandwich and a glass of milk. Anything serves. Food
means nothing. The only thing that means anything is votes for
Roosevelt—that and the insistent calls of the Albany wire. Personal appearance means even less. His clothes hang on him,
baggy, unpressed; his trousers confined perilously by a carelessly
buckled belt. But there is nothing baggy about his intelligence.

"He is a rare bird in political life, this curious little man who
serves his master with the unhesitating fidelity of a loyal dog; this
remarkable Louis McHenry Howe, who presides in this new
throne room where history is in the making."

This newspaperman was not the first to refer to Louis as
"gnome-like" and the word had begun to irritate him, possibly be-

cause he knew it fitted him so well. Charlie Bayer of the New York
American, a great favorite with Louis, was in Chicago and wrote
an "inside story" about the convention which he showed to some
of his colleagues. In it he revealed some of Louis' behind-the-scenes
machinations which, just now, Louis wanted to soft-pedal as
much as possible. Charlie's colleagues warned him about this, but
he hastily assured them he would submit the story to Louis before
he sent it to his paper. "That's the worst mistake you could make,"
they said. "You've called him a gnome, a wart-like individual, etc.
That will make him so mad he'll throw out the whole story."
Charlie winked. "That's where you're wrong," he said. "That's
exactly why I put those phrases in. To make Louis mad. He'll
insist on cutting them out. Then I'll make a deal with him to cut
all references to his physique if he will pass the rest of the story."
And that's the way it turned out. Just an example of one smart
newspaperman outsmarting another smart newspaperman.

Events were now rapidly moving toward the nomination of the
candidates. The air was electric. People milled around the halls
of the Congress Hotel, betting, sweating, swearing, scheming.
Theme songs filled the air. Down the hall in the Ritchie headquarters a phonograph ground out, all day long, the strains of *Maryland, My Maryland;* the Smith forces were whooping it up with
The Sidewalks of New York; the Byrd supporters were humming
Carry Me Back to Old Virginny, while the Garner forces were
tearing off *The Eyes of Texas Are Upon You.* All the candidates
had their marching tunes ready for the big parade around Convention Hall. All but us! Incredibly, until a short time before
Roosevelt was nominated, we had not decided on a song, and the
arguments about it almost split our forces into fighting camps.

A lady from New York State named Rhoda Hinkley, a great
admirer of Franklin Roosevelt, came into headquarters with what
seemed to some of us a marvelous suggestion. She was sure that
the election of Roosevelt would bring happier days to the country.
Why not nominate him to the strains of the then popular song,
Happy Days Are Here Again? She talked to Harold Payson about
it and to Ed Brown of the publicity staff, and others. Harold knew

her, thought her suggestion good, and tried to present it to Jim
Farley, but Farley was so busy with the California and Texas
delegates, talking "shop and swap," that Payson couldn't reach
him.

Some members of the staff insisted that the logical song for
FDR, a Navy man, was *Anchors Aweigh*. But nobody knew the
words! We needed a snappy song everybody could sing when
Roosevelt's name was put in nomination. A few of us were strong
for *Happy Days* but others tried to hoot the suggestion down.

"Hell," said Fred Roper, "that's the theme song for a brand of
cigarettes."

"Hell," we responded, "that's just the idea. They play it on the
air three times a week. What publicity for Roosevelt! People,
hearing it on the air, will automatically associate him with the
song. It's publicity you'd have to pay a million dollars for if you
bought it." Finally, we decided to let Louis settle the issue, but
who would bell the cat? Desperately, I said I'd do it, and I left
with their raucous laughter in my ears. "Bet he'll tell you he never
heard of it," they chortled. "Also bet he'll throw you out on your
ear." But time was running out, so I chanced it.

Louis was alone, stretched out on the big couch, when I dashed
in. He raised his head.

"Mein Gawd!" he cried. "What's the matter with you? Is the
hotel on fire?"

I launched into my plea for *Happy Days*. He clapped his hand
to his head. "You too!" he yelped. "They're driving me nuts out
at that hall. What'll we play? What'll we play? That organ player
calls me every five minutes. I don't give a damn what they play."
When I rushed on about *Happy Days* he stopped me cold. "I never
heard of the damned song," he said, just as they had predicted.
"Then I'll sing it for you," I said. He looked on in horror as I ran
up and down the room, snapping my fingers, trying to sing the
song. With a groan he motioned me to stop, reached up over his
head and picked up the phone.

"Give me that organ player," he said. "When Roosevelt is
nominated play that song, 'Happy Days Are Here Again,' " he

told him. He threw me a withering look. "Are you satisfied?" he asked. "If so, get out of here." I got.

Edward J. Flynn in his book, *You're the Boss,* has said that he and Louis always argued about who told the man at Convention Hall to play *Happy Days,* thus establishing it as the Roosevelt theme song. Flynn said he was the one but that Louis always insisted he was. Louis was. Mr. Flynn admitted that the memories of politicians are faulty after a lapse of fifteen years, but that's the way he remembered it. The memories of reporters are faulty, too, after so many years, but this reporter kept notes at the time, to be used in her newspaper column, and is more than happy to place the original idea where it belongs—with Rhoda Hinkley who, I am sure, was the very first to mention *Happy Days* as a Roosevelt theme song.[3]

We all dashed madly out to Convention Hall to see Roosevelt nominated, but Louis stayed right there in 1702 and listened to it on the radio. We wanted to see how our little surprise worked, too. Under Louis' direction the publicity department had prepared an enormous picture of Roosevelt on canvas, which was tied up along the railings of the third tier. It was not noticeable until Roosevelt's name was put in nomination; then Ed Brown and a couple of lieutenants cut the ropes and the huge picture unrolled, and swung for the thousands to see, as Judge John E. Mack of Poughkeepsie, long-time friend of Franklin Roosevelt, put his name in nomination.

"His reputation is unsullied, his character spotless . . ." said John E. Mack. "Notwithstanding all the honors that have been heaped upon him, in rounded and complete measure, he still remains natural and unspoiled, frank and open but with all that persistent determination which is his heritage to carry on, and carry through for the good of his state and his country."

Then the wild shouting, the rush to the state banners, the cheers, the stamping feet, the bedlam. We leaped from our seats and joined the marching throngs, shouting to each other as we marched, "If the little boss could only see this!" But back in 1702,

[3] Edward J. Flynn, *You're the Boss.*

the heat waves rolling in upon him, the little boss, exhausted at last, completely and utterly, lay on the couch, his knees drawn up to his chest, and between spasms of coughing said over and over, "Tell them to repeat 'Happy Days Are Here Again.' "

As other nominations went on, we rushed back to the hotel to watch the maneuverings around headquarters. To our untrained and optimistic eyes things looked good for us on the first ballot; but, alas, after we had gone back to the hall for the voting, Roosevelt only received 666½, 100 short of the number necessary for nomination. Then came that long, grueling all-night session which none who attended that convention will ever forget.

Again Louis Howe stayed in 1702 and this time he lay on the floor, his head on a pillow near the open window to catch a breeze, a radio on the floor beside him. And he lay there all night long.

We all knew that if Texas would switch to Roosevelt, releasing the forty-six delegates it was holding for Garner, we were "in." We sat in the galleries and chanted, "Texas, Texas, come on Texas! The eyes of the nation are upon you, Texas!" until their ears were deafened with our cries as the maddening count of the ballots went on. Almost every state had to be polled individually and this slowed things down until the suspense was almost unbearable. Yet Texas never moved.

One of the most dramatic moments of the convention came when the roll was called for the State of New York. There sat James J. Walker, at that very moment under fire from the Seabury Investigation, and in danger of being removed from his post as Mayor of New York by Franklin Roosevelt, now a leading candidate for the Presidency. When Walker's name was called a great hush fell over the hall. Jimmy rose to his feet, stepped forward, and as the spotlight played full upon his slight, dapper figure, he leaned to the microphone and said in a firm, defiant voice:

"I vote for Alfred E. Smith."

A rustle went through the vast hall and a newspaperman, sitting with us, said in an awed whisper:

"My God, that man's got nerve! Voting against a man who has

the toe of his boot right against the seat of the well-pressed Walker trousers."

This Jimmy Walker matter had caused great anxiety back at 331 Madison Avenue. The whole country, it seemed to us, was sitting out there watching to see what FDR would do. If he didn't remove Walker from office the country would say, "Tammany-controlled." If he did remove him, Tammany Hall would go against him. And we had to have New York to win.

It was during this worrisome period that I went into Louis' office one day and found him gazing out the window in deep contemplation. Sure that he was thinking about the Walker matter, I said:

"Boss, what do you think the Governor ought to do?"

He looked up. "I'm not thinking at the moment," he replied.

"But boss," I persisted, mindful of the talk at headquarters that the Governor didn't make a move without talking it over with Louis, "what have you told him he ought to do about it?"

He swung around in his chair.

"I have never mentioned the Walker matter to him but once," he said, "and then I told him, 'Franklin, never mind what "they" say about all this. You just search your heart and do what you think is right. You can't go very wrong if you do that—and never mind the consequences.' "

He looked at me for a moment to see if I believed this. I did.

Then he continued, "As a matter of fact that's all I ever tell Franklin."

He looked at me to see if I believed that. I didn't.

Fortunately, the problem of Jimmy Walker was solved, suddenly and advantageously, when he resigned right in the middle of the investigation and the Governor didn't have to remove him after all. Louis gave Margaret Durand and myself a ride uptown in a taxi that night and sat in a corner of the cab, hunched up in a knot, with a smile on his face which can only be described as that which adorns the face of the cat when the canary has mysteriously vanished.

Howe, Mrs. Howe and Hartley on election night, 1932.

Election night, 1932. James Farley, FDR, Edward J. Flynn, and campaign workers. The author is fifth from the left.

James Farley, Louis Howe, and FDR, November 3, 1932.

"Boss," said Rabbit, just to get a rise out of him, "do you know what I think? I think this guy Roosevelt is just a fool for luck."

"You said it," was his surprising answer. No argument.

"Of course," she said hastily, "his luck and having a smart man like you back of him make a pretty good combination."

"You kids are too fresh," he said. "I think I'll put you out and let you walk." As a parting shot he stuck out his tongue at us as he rolled happily on his way.

After the hectic all-night session in Chicago the convention adjourned at nine in the morning and we rode back to the hotel with heavy hearts. The "Stop Roosevelt" forces were boasting that they had us licked and things looked black indeed.

Ours were not the only heavy hearts on the way back to the Congress Hotel. Rolling along in another cab, urging the driver to greater speed, was big Jim Farley, the generalissimo of the Roosevelt forces. When he reached the hotel he immediately went into a huddle with Ed Flynn, Joe Guffey, Frank Walker, and one or two others.

"What is the next move?" they asked.

"Frankly," Farley said, "I don't know. I have no authority to do anything until I see Louis Howe and hear what he has to say. He will have talked to the Governor by now. I'll give him my suggestions and he can tell us what he thinks should be done next."

They went hurriedly to Room 1702. There on the floor, just as he had lain all night, was Louis Howe. His shirt was open, his tie was off, his head rested on a pillow, and his harsh breathing filled the room. They looked at each other in silence. Then, as the others quietly withdrew, Jim Farley laid his great bulk down beside Louis' wasted form and there the strategy was outlined, Louis' voice barely audible as he whispered in Farley's ear. When Farley lifted himself from the floor and joined the others, Joe Guffey said gravely, "This is the end for Louis, isn't it, Jim? He can't possibly last through the day, can he?"

Jim Farley brushed his hand across his eyes almost angrily.

"Of course he'll last," he said. "Anything else is nonsense. You know he's not going to die until he sees Roosevelt nominated. He's one of the gamest little guys that ever lived."

Now, more than ever, Texas was the answer to our prayers. But John Garner, popular Speaker of the House of Representatives, had those forty-six votes tied up as tightly as a sailor's knot, and solidly behind him was California, with its forty-four important votes. Another thing in Garner's favor was that he had popular, smooth, tough Congressman Sam Rayburn, who later became Speaker of the House, managing his campaign.

Sometime during that morning Jim Farley conferred with the canny Rayburn. What a splendid ticket Roosevelt of New York and Garner of Texas would be, was the burden of Farley's song. But the wily Rayburn did not hastily commit himself. After all, he was there to nominate John Nance Garner. But he realized that Roosevelt was the man he had to beat and he blanched when he recalled the fearful deadlock in 1924, when Al Smith and William Gibbs McAdoo locked in a death struggle that finally defeated both.

Louis had his moments that day when he wondered if time was not being wasted on these negotiations with Rayburn. Bulldogging ahead for Roosevelt, he looked with amazement on any manager who would think for a moment of giving up "top billing" for his candidates, no matter how tempting the bait. If somebody had come to Louis Howe with a reverse proposition, say a "Garner-Roosevelt" ticket, he would have strangled him with the ropes and coils lying around in the back room.

During this time Harry Byrd was brought over to the Roosevelt forces. Louis sent for Byrd and asked him bluntly what would induce him to swing into the Roosevelt column. Byrd told him he wanted to be United States Senator from Virginia. Louis bent his head in thought for a moment. Carter Glass and Claude Swanson were then firmly entrenched in these two jobs. Finally Louis looked up. "Is that your price?" he asked. Byrd replied that it was. "Very well," Louis said. "We'll put either Glass or Swanson in Franklin's Cabinet." Glass was later offered the job as Secretary of the Treasury. He turned it down, but Senator Claude Swanson became Roosevelt's first Secretary of the Navy.

After a frenzied day of shuttling back and forth between 1702, the Garner headquarters and other points, Jim Farley finally brought Louis Howe the news he had been waiting to hear.

"It's in the bag," said Jim. "Texas is with us."

Louis, always calm to the point of ennui in a crisis, looked at Jim Farley for a moment with nothing whatever showing in his tired, closed-off face. "Jim," he said, "that is fine." A strange reaction to the most thrilling words he had heard in twenty years. But that was the way of this strange and unpredictable little man.

The anti-Roosevelt people rushed around all day fondly believing they had Roosevelt licked. They wouldn't have been so cocky if they could have peered behind Louis Howe's iron curtain! They even had telegrams pouring in to the delegates from their folk "back home" (so-called) demanding that they "quit Roosevelt." Louis quietly offset this maneuver by having FDR send them a long, cheerful telegram urging them to stand firm. And they did.

Mr. Garner, by long distance, had released the Texas delegation, Mr. McAdoo had released the California forces pledged to Garner, and the stage was set for the big finale that night.

Still Louis Howe never left 1702, but sat at the radio while we all rushed off to Convention Hall and seated ourselves right across from the stage so we would miss nothing. The hall was packed to the rafters when William Gibbs McAdoo stepped to the center of the stage and, as the blinding lights played on him, said:

"California came here to nominate a President of the United States. It did not come here to deadlock this convention—"

Knowing this was *it*, our taut nerves gave way. We leaped to our feet and began to shout like wild Comanches, our yells mixing in with loud boos that were shattering the rafters from the galleries above.

For up there was a crowd of rough-looking characters who had been planted there, according to a story that went around the first day of the convention, for the sole purpose of "booing" Franklin Roosevelt's name every time they heard it. Mayor Anton Cermak, who was strong for Ritchie for President, had had his city minions go into the streets and gather up the unemployed and·the bums, so the story said, get them seats in the galleries, furnish free sandwiches and coffee for them, and let 'em shout. This incessant booing sawed on the nerves of the Roosevelt forces like a steel file, but there was no way to stop it. However, Cermak, who was no fool, had also switched to the Roosevelt forces that day, and was riding high on the bandwagon when the convention met that night.

Incidentally, both Louis and Farley gave me a chance to play cops and robbers in connection with this switch of the Mayor's. Sometime during that day the venerable Adolph Sabath, Congressman from the 5th District of Illinois, came into the reception room and drew me discreetly aside. "I have an envelope here," he said, "which Louis Howe and Jim Farley want you to carry to Mayor Cermak's headquarters upstairs. They want you to give it to the Mayor personally and wait for his answer, but under no circumstances let the newspapermen know where you are going and what you are up to." I promised and slipped out and made for the elevators. But my newspaper friends, who had taken note of this little conference, were at my heels. I took the elevator up two floors and stepped off. So did they. This was not Cermak's floor, and I was baffled for a moment till I saw a Powder Room down the hall. I strolled in and slammed the door. Sometime later when I ventured out, the hall was empty. I took another elevator. The boys were on it. I got off two floors up, rounded a corner, and took to the stairs. By riding the elevators and running the stairs, I finally shook them off and made for the Mayor's suite. I was admitted by a suspicious-looking man who stepped aside to let two other men carrying a tub full of ice go in. I told the man I had to see the Mayor, that I had a message from Roosevelt headquarters and was to wait for an answer. He snatched the letter from my hand and ducked through the door where the ice had gone and I heard loud, excited voices. I never saw His Honor, but in about ten minutes the same man came out and laid an envelope in my hand. I dashed back by the same route I had come—stairs, elevators, elevators, stairs, until I reached 1702, where Louis and Farley waited. I passed the message to them not knowing what those mysterious envelopes contained, but it all became clear that night.

Nobody thought, however, to pass the word to the "faithful" in the galleries that things were different. So when McAdoo began to speak for Roosevelt they yelled and booed. Angrily, McAdoo appealed to the Mayor to restore order. The good Mayor hastily scrambled to the platform, waved his arms, and frantically tried to stop them, and they booed *him!* Finally he quieted them down, Illinois released its delegates from their pledge to Senator J. Ham Lewis, Ritchie's Maryland followed with its sixteen votes, and the rest tumbled to Roosevelt like a row of ninepins. When the final tally came it read: "Roosevelt 945." This was the fourth and last ballot.

The minute FDR was nominated Ed Brown, as instructed by Louis, rushed to the "inner sanctum" as we called our little hideaway at Convention Hall, darted into the telephone booth and phoned Louis. "Hold the phone," Louis said, "while I get Franklin on the wire." Ed, phone gripped in his hand, waited while Roosevelt dictated a message for Chairman Walsh to read to the convention. He thanked them for nominating him, asked them to stay in session so that he might appear before them in person and be notified, and told them he could arrive between two and three o'clock the next afternoon.

Louis read the message to Ed, who took it down, typed it on a machine in the hideaway, and rushed to the platform with it, where Chairman Walsh read it to the convention amid thunderous applause.

One of the first to go to see Louis was Bernard Baruch, who had been in Chicago all week, and had been almost pulled apart by the managers of the various candidates who wanted his support. Many assumed that he was there in the interest of Al Smith, but he was there, he said, as an observer only and took no active part until the final ballots were counted. When he reached Room 1702 he said to Louis, "Reporting for duty—my President has been nominated. What can I do to help?" Louis, who had been hurt by stories that Baruch was in on a "Stop Roosevelt" movement the fall before, and had remained somewhat miffed in spite of Baruch's disclaimers, was now in a mellow mood and extended the welcoming hand to this old friend of Franklin's.

We all dashed back from the Hall, our one thought to get to the little boss as fast as we could. Hartley met us at the door. "Father has been waiting for you," he beamed. "He's having a little victory party and he wants his gang."

We rushed in, and there, all his weariness magically melted away, was the little boss dispensing champagne. By his side was Tom Lynch.

"Come and get it," Louis said. "This champagne is some that Tom Lynch has been saving for years just for this occasion." Louis then grandly served the champagne in lily cups and we each had about a thimbleful apiece, but to us it was nectar from the gods!

Finally Louis said, "Well kids, the war's over. Go out and raise hell if you feel like it. Stay up all night if you want to, but," he grinned, "I'm a working man. I'm going to get some sleep."

[II]

"And Howe!"

EXCITEMENT rippled through the crowds in Chicago when they heard that Governor Roosevelt would fly out and address the convention in person, another of Louis' and FDR's revolutionary ideas. In 1932, flying halfway across the country was not the casual action it is now, and the idea was to prove once and for all that Franklin Roosevelt was a normal man in spite of the inactivity of his legs.

Many delegates were jittery. They could wait, they insisted. Suppose something happened in this hour of victory. Some even called the Governor personally but he turned a deaf ear, and so did Louis. FDR was not only going to fly but, the rumor said, was bringing twelve people with him. Good God, thirteen in the plane! Some delegates almost had heart failure. However, FDR, who was as superstitious as the next one, brought only nine besides himself, and had the extra seats removed for desk space and baggage.

We rode out to the airport with a group of newspapermen to meet the Presidential plane, and strained our eyes in vain for a glimpse of the little boss who had gone out early, but his slight form was lost in the sea of humanity that surged around the strip where the plane was to land. Word went around that the plane had been delayed by head winds and, as the minutes ticked by and still no plane, our nervousness mounted, especially when the

191

newspapermen began to speculate on who would take Roosevelt's place if his plane took a nose dive between Albany and Chicago!

Finally the little plane appeared, a mere speck in the sky that grew larger and larger until it swooped to a triumphant landing, and then we saw the little boss's straw hat bobbing around in the group at the landing. He was one of the first to grasp FDR's hand as he came down the ramp; then Anna, Roosevelt's daughter, and Betsy, his daughter-in-law, grabbed him and gave him a mighty hug as the cameras whirred and the crowd roared. In the excitement FDR's hat was knocked off, and as his glasses slid sideways on his steaming nose, Ray Daniells of the New York *Times* suddenly had the lead for his morning story: "When they knocked off his glasses and stole his hat he knew the campaign was on."

A funny thing happened at the airport. The good Mayor of Chicago, having seen the light, now let it shine benevolently in all directions, and could not do enough for nominee Roosevelt. He sent George Gaw, the city's official greeter, speeding to the airport in the big, white greeting car, filled with beaming officials, and, in a grand gesture, ordered some planes to fly out and escort the Roosevelt plane into the airport. Somehow the little fleet became confused up there in the blue, picked up a mail plane by mistake, and escorted it grandly into the landing. The face of the aerial postman, when he alighted amid all this pomp and splendor, was something to behold!

Once the Roosevelt plane was safely on the ground, Louis Howe's thoughts were not on it, nor on the waiting people, but on a little package tucked safely away in his inside pocket—the draft of the acceptance speech he had written for Franklin. Roosevelt had his speech with him, even making last-minute changes on the way to Chicago, but as the car roared away toward Convention Hall he took the speech from Louis, scanned it, and saw that it did not deviate too much from his own. So he simply dropped the first page of his own draft, substituted Louis' first page and the rest of the speech was delivered as written. This satisfied Louis, satisfied Judge Rosenman, and brought Ray Moley's temperature down to normal.

As Louis stood between FDR and Mrs. Roosevelt on the platform in Chicago, many of the spectators wondered who the little man was, but didn't pay too much attention to Louis; their eyes were fixed on the commanding figure of their new nominee. And this was the first and last time that Louis Howe ever appeared on a political platform.

A few years later in Washington, when Louis had been dead something more than a year, President Roosevelt invited some of us over to the White House one night to see a movie, and among the newsreels was one made at the Chicago convention. When the picture flashed on the screen, showing Louis on the platform with Mrs. Roosevelt and the President, Rabbit touched the President's arm and whispered, "Look, the little boss." "Yes," FDR said huskily, "God bless him. Louis was a grand soul." Since one of the President's favorite compliments was to say that somebody was "grand," we felt that this truly represented his deep feeling for this little man who bore such an abiding affection for him.

Several traditions were shattered in Chicago at that 1932 convention. First, the plane ride and now, for the first time in history, a candidate for President came, in person, to address the delegates after his nomination. Heretofore it had been the custom for a nominee to pretend coyly that he had no telephone, no radio and no newspapers, hence could not possibly know what was going on until weeks later, when a hand-picked delegation would solemnly wait on him to inform him that he had been nominated for the Presidency. Franklin Roosevelt swept this little custom into the discard once and for all when he said, "You have nominated me for President and I know it. I have come here to thank you for the honor." Then at the close of his speech when he said the words, "I pledge you—I pledge myself to a new deal for the American people," perhaps few realized that at that moment a phrase was born which would become one of the most cussed and discussed terms ever known in American politics—the New Deal.

After FDR's speech he, Mrs. Roosevelt, Louis, and his staff hastened to the Congress Hotel—to Suite 1702 where Louis had lain on the floor and struggled for breath as he fought to bring about this moment. Impressions of that day come sweeping back. Of John Roosevelt, youngest Roosevelt son, who staggered from the plane, his face a bilious green. It was his first plane ride and he was sick as a pup. Of Gus Gennerich, the Governor's faithful bodyguard, dumping a load of baggage on the floor and yelling, "Hi Babe!" at Mrs. Roosevelt's dignified secretary. Of the two girls who pushed their way to Mr. Roosevelt's side and, as he put an arm around each and gave them a hearty kiss, reporters leaped forward asking their names. Neither would give her name, though each revealed the identity of the other. And that's how Mary Eben and Lela Stiles had their names in the Chicago newspapers as the first girls to be kissed by Roosevelt after his speech to the convention!

Louis hurried back to New York now that Franklin had been nominated, to get the campaign under way. Additional offices were opened across the street in the Biltmore Hotel and most of the executives moved in there with offices on the fourth floor. Jim Farley, who had been elected chairman of the Democratic National Committee at Chicago; Frank Walker, treasurer of the Committee, and his assistants, Forbes Morgan and Ambrose O'Connell, and Robert Jackson, secretary, with the members of their staff, were all on this floor. On the first floor quarters were established for the National Committeemen, and secretaries were provided for them as they came and went during the campaign. These men served as advisers and the first floor offices were called "Advisory Committee Headquarters." These advisers were not all National Committeemen, but were all the faithful FRBC men (For Roosevelt before Chicago). Joseph C. O'Mahoney of Wyoming, Arthur J. Mullen of Nebraska, Joseph F. Guffey of Pennsylvania, W. W. Howes of South Dakota, Colonel "Jack" Cohen of Georgia, and Richard Crane of Virginia were among them. Louis would have no part of this swank Biltmore setup. His little corner office had brought him luck and there he would stay, but it soon became evident that this cubicle was the real nerve center of the campaign. "The statements are issued from the Biltmore," wrote a reporter for a Memphis paper, "but the orders come from Louis Howe's small office in a building on Madison Avenue."

Louis reorganized his force for the big job, giving Rabbit the heavy job of managing the office, hiring help and so on, with an office of her own and a sizable staff. He placed me in charge of his and Jim Farley's mail, with an office on the fourth floor in the Biltmore, with five people to help me. These loyal and wonderful people were Mary O'Connor, Rose Tennenbaum, Eddie Miller, Bill Flynn and Leo Hochstetter. We opened, read, briefed, sorted and distributed the vast pile of mail that landed on our desks and, after weeding out those that had to have the personal attention of Howe and Farley, we took stacks of it around to the various department heads to answer.

One of Louis' innovations in this campaign was a department known as the Research and Library Division. When Louis wanted something he wanted it right now and not after a staff of researchers had spent hours digging. He sent for Miss Katherine C. Blackburn, with whom he and FDR had worked in the Woodrow Wilson Foundation, to set up and run this department.

"Rabbit," Louis said, "give Miss Blackburn fifty dollars and send her down to Washington to dig up what we need for this department to get it going at once." Two days later Miss Blackburn was back with all the necessary material and twenty-six dollars, which she turned over to Miss Durand. Rabbit immediately took her in to Louis who gazed at her in astonishment. This was positively the first time anybody had ever turned any money back to him.

"What the heck goes on here?" he said. "May I ask, Miss Blackburn, if you were 'on the town' in Washington?" Miss Blackburn, much amused, explained that she had stayed with friends and had only needed her train fare, but he was still shaking his head in a bewildered fashion when she left the room.

A delicate question about money had to be settled at the beginning of the campaign. The Democratic National Committee, the organization which had the job of electing Roosevelt, owed

$300,000 to the former chairman of the Committee, John J. Raskob, who had been dead set against FDR in Chicago. The debt was left over from the Al Smith campaign of 1928 to which Raskob had contributed so heavily. Frank Walker, as Treasurer of the Committee, went to see Raskob to find out what could be done and a diplomatic solution was reached—from the first monies collected by the Committee in the campaign, 25 per cent was to go to Raskob until the debt was wiped out. Louis Howe, who had no use for Raskob, reacted to this news as a cat would react to a jab with a hot poker. It wasn't that he didn't think Raskob should be paid. He just didn't see the need for the big hurry. After all, the most important thing was Franklin's election. Why not get the important business out of the way, then pay Raskob? He sent for Farley and Walker to come to his office at once to talk it over.

The two men were having lunch in the Hotel Biltmore dining room when Louis' urgent message reached them. They knew what was up, and decided to eat a good lunch before they went, to be better able to face Louis. Before they finished the main course another urgent message was handed them. They looked at each other and decided to order dessert. Before they finished the boy rushed in with a third message. They topped off the lunch with coffee, squared their shoulders and went. Louis was furious.

"Wait till Franklin hears about all this money business," he warned, as he grabbed the phone and called Albany. When the Governor came on the phone Louis began to sputter. Walker, cocking a keen ear, decided that Louis was garbling the facts.

"Dammit, Louis," he said, as he grabbed for the telephone, "what you are saying is putting me in a bad light with the Governor. I'll talk to him myself." And talk to the Governor he did, as Louis sat fuming. FDR, after listening to Walker's story, O. K.'d everything, Raskob got his money, Louis and Walker cooled off and continued to be good friends. In fact this was the only time in their long and close association that they ever had any words, for Louis Howe knew that Walker's loyalty to Franklin Roosevelt, like his own, was never open to question.

Little things like this, however, kept those of us in the office in a cold sweat half the time, as we often took these tilts seriously, even though they were soon forgotten by the participants. Naturally we heard about them all through the well-known "headquarters grapevine."

The atmosphere of the campaign was informal, even around the plush Biltmore, and soon everybody had a nickname. Farley was "Big Jim," O'Mahoney was "My Honey," W. W. Howes was called "Sioux" because of his habit of always spelling out the name of "Sioux Falls" when he dictated letters. Emil Hurja, the statistician, was dubbed "Weegee," by Louis, who never could pronounce his name. Katherine C. Blackburn was "Casey," Mary Dewson was "Mollie" and so on. Everybody had a name for "Wild" Bill Lyons, too, but since this is not written on asbestos we'll skip it! Bill was the doorkeeper at the Biltmore headquarters on the fourth floor, and was known as "Senator" though there is no record that he was ever elected to that office. The story was that he ran for the State Senate so often out in his native Colorado, that they finally gave him the title anyway. Farley had met him when he was chairman of the New York State Athletic Commission and Bill, who had moved to New York, was in the clothing business. Bill immediately attached himself to Farley with all the affection of a barnacle for the underside of a battleship. He was about seventy years old at the time of the campaign, had the voice of a steel file, and dressed with wild abandon, usually topping off his costume with a wide-brimmed hat adorned with a rattlesnake skin. Most of all, though, he wore a vast and visible contempt for the human race. He insulted everybody. This trait certainly didn't make him a popular doorkeeper, but Jim Farley put him there and efforts to dislodge him proved futile until the campaign was almost over; by then he had enraged most of the Democrats who dared to try to pass his gate. Most of the callers came full of good will, and some with money in their pockets, but this made no difference to Bill. He'd look at the letters they bore, letters written by Farley, signed in green ink, urging them to "drop in," then he'd spit contemptuously. "Them letters don't mean a damn thing," he'd say. "Jim wrote a thousand of 'em, but they don't mean nothin'."

One day William H. Woodin, later Roosevelt's first Secretary of the Treasury, approached the gate with a check for $10,000 in his pocket, one of the biggest contributions to date. Bill not only turned him away, he all but threw him down the elevator shaft! The timid, unassuming Woodin, no match for this violent character, hurried from the Biltmore and phoned Farley who arranged for him to return with dignity, with the much needed contribution.

On another occasion Joseph Wolf, the Democratic National Committeeman from Minnesota, tangled with Bill and lost. He retreated, full of sound and fury, to the first floor. Miss Buckner Blackerby, a soft-spoken young woman from Alabama, a receptionist for the Advisory Committee, heard his story, then phoned Jane Duffy, secretary to Chairman Farley.

"We have a Wolf down here," Buckner told Farley's secretary, "who can't get by that 'Lyon' you have up there. Do something, quick." Jane Duffy "did something quick" and Mr. Wolf was admitted, but he was a shaken man.

To say that Bill Lyons was as a burr under the tail of a fractious horse, to Louis Howe's sensibilities, is such an understatement that it's foolish to make it. He never could "see" the Senator, and as these tales came to his ears he turned purple.

"He's insulting all of Franklin's friends," he cried. "Mein Gawd! He's got to get off that door."

His orders to have him removed, however, seemed not to reach Farley's ears, so one day when Farley was away and O'Mahoney, who had moved up from the first floor to assist Farley, was in charge, Louis called him and told him to throw Bill Lyons out. O'Mahoney stalled awhile. Then Louis suddenly put the finger on me.

"Look," he said, "I'm tired of all this. *You* go and get Bill Lyons off that door. I don't care how, but do it."

I couldn't have been more alarmed if he'd told me to go to the zoo and handle a live rattlesnake. If the man had thrown out a guy with ten thousand dollars, I asked Louis, how did he expect me, a penniless minion around the place, to fare? "Go and get him away from there," was his answer.

Matters were not helped any by the fact that Farley had decided to make a joke of the feud between Bill and Louis and one day, when Louis was due at the Biltmore for an important meeting, Farley took Bill off the door and put on a new man, with instructions not to let anybody pass the gate for the next ten minutes. In a few minutes Louis came hurrying in, started through the gate, and was stopped by the new man. Louis tried to brush him off and go in anyway. Again he was stopped. Breathing heavily, Louis told him in no uncertain terms who he was, and that he was in a helluva hurry, but again the man barred his way. Louis snatched off his hat and threw it on the floor and let out such a yell of rage that we heard it all the way down the hall. We rushed out just in time to see Farley stroll casually from his office to ask Louis what was the matter. Louis was white as chalk and mad as a hornet, and so was I. I went back in my office and phoned Rabbit. "Dammit," I said, "I don't think that's funny. Mr. Farley knows the little boss has a bad heart—he might have had a stroke and died." She agreed, and while Farley thought Louis took the whole thing as a joke after he cooled off, he never polled us to see how we felt about it! We liked Mr. Farley, but we didn't like "Wild Bill," who was in on it, and we were furious because he had a chance to laugh at the little boss.

I decided to go to Jane Duffy for help in getting Bill off that door. She was as strong for Farley as I was for Howe, but we were good friends, and I thought we might work out something. After a long conference we sent for Bill and told him that Farley was being cussed out, over the country, because Democratic workers were not getting their supplies. This would not do. He'd just have to give up the door and supervise the job of shipping these supplies. There was only one flaw as far as I was concerned. He'd have to spend a lot of time in my office sorting the mail which related to supplies. Mrs. Duffy was a great favorite with the Senator, and she pulled out all the stops: she told Bill he would really be saving Farley's good name if he would only do this job.

We thought we had him sold, when suddenly he took his big, black cigar out of his mouth and said brusquely, "No, no, you girls are wasting your time. I could never leave that door. Jim depends on me to keep out the riffraff. He wouldn't stand for it."

Suddenly we both started laughing. We laughed till the tears streamed down our cheeks, while Bill looked at us in amazement. This had seemed so serious to the girls. Why the hilarity? We explained that it was our nerves, that we were merely hysterical. Our act had backfired on us.

When I reported failure to Louis I thought surely I'd be fired on the spot. He listened intently and when I reached the part where Bill would have been located in my office he suddenly slapped his knee and began to howl with laughter.

"Wonderful, wonderful," he said. "The scheme was perfect. The only trouble was that it didn't work. But I wish it had. Think how you could have put Bill through the hoops right in your office. My, my, I would have bought you a whip and a pair of pink tights and you could have tamed him right there. Too bad, too bad! Well, better luck next time."

This sudden change of pace really threw me. I thought he'd be so mad he'd spit vinegar, yet here he was laughing his head off. Sometimes the little man had me talking to myself.

But don't think for a minute he gave up. When Farley returned he was met with another barrage. He sent for Ambrose O'Connell.

"No two ways about it," he said. "We've got to get Bill off that door or Louis Howe is going to kill somebody. You figure out another job for him. Something that sounds big, with some kind of a title. But do it quick!" Ambrose put his wits to work and came up with a brilliant scheme. He put Bill to work pasting Jim Farley's press notices in a huge scrapbook "to make sure that he would go down in posterity." When Farley came to Washington as Postmaster General in Roosevelt's Cabinet, Bill came along and did the same work, though he had the high-sounding title of Administrative Assistant to the Postmaster General, which Farley bestowed on him. Behind the scenes, though, Bill was known simply as "the pastemaster general."

The mail that rolled across our desks during the campaign was fascinating and we had many quaint suggestions on how to win the election. One woman wrote in suggesting that we get a lot of adhesive tape, pass it around the country, and let the people tape up the corners of their mouths into a perpetual smile. "With everybody smiling all the time," she explained, "people would begin to feel better and the country would soon get back on its feet."

Another woman, however, wanted to call attention to how bad things were under the Republicans. "Get bunches of little children," she advised, "to stand on the street corners and sing 'Mama, are the hot dogs all dead?' This will show the people that under the Republicans all the little children are hungry, then they will elect Mr. Roosevelt."

All these suggestions amused Louis, but his favorite was a letter from a man who wrote in recommending his wife for a job. He praised her for many pages, winding up with the enthusiastic suggestion that "a careful inspection of my wife Kate will convince you of her sterling qualities." Louis promptly created the job of "Kate inspector" and it was conferred on Sam Schiff, genial friend and business associate of Farley. Sam said he was grateful for the honor but after all, he was a married man and why not give this interesting job to a bachelor? The only bachelor handy, however, was Joe Guffey and he turned it down.

Another intriguing suggestion for trapping votes was made in person by an impressive-looking Indian chief, who wanted to take a stand in front of our headquarters, somewhat in the manner of a cigar-store Indian, as a symbol that the Indian vote was "in the bag" for Roosevelt. But there was a string tied to this alluring proposition. He wanted wampum, plenty of wampum for this guarantee of the reservations' vote. He hinted darkly that if his offer was rejected, he would take his proposition over to the Republicans, whose headquarters were right up the street. When he was turned down he made good his threat. One day Louis, looking out the window, exclaimed, "Mein Gawd! Look what's going by out there. Old Rain-in-the-Face riding on a big float in a Republican parade." Sure enough, old Rain, his feathers fluttering in the breeze, was riding grandly by, glancing up now and then at our windows to see if we, crestfallen, were witnessing his triumph. We wondered mildly how much wampum he received from the Republicans, but figured they needed him worse than we did, so let him go without loss of sleep.

But while Louis ignored old Rain he was quick to see the merit in the real ideas brought to his attention. The celebrated little booklet, "Everybody's Political Primer," is a case in point.

Down in Tennessee that summer, W. C. Teague, a reporter on a Memphis paper, in collaboration with a cartoonist developed this "primer," designed to show the general futility of the Hoover administration, and to prove that it was "time for a change."

Teague, full of enthusiasm, rushed off to New York with the primer and presented himself at the Biltmore. He was received with great politeness and the primer was examined with interest, but he received no definite answer until finally somebody said, "Let Louis Howe have a look at it." Teague crossed the street without much hope, sat down with Louis at three o'clock in the afternoon, and by five o'clock Louis had given him an initial order for three million copies. The primer was one of the most widely praised campaign documents of the year and Louis had seen its possibilities at a glance. He loved cartoons, and the stories in the primer were all told by cartoons, with amusing captions. One that Louis liked best showed Hoover, dressed in rompers, with a round hat set far back on his head, busily driving nails into the head of a little wooden man named "Depression," splinters flying in all directions. Standing by were his helpers labeled "Board," "Committees," and "Commission." The lesson read:

What is Her-bert doing?

He is working.

At what is Her-bert working?

Her-bert is work-ing to abol-ish pov-er-ty.

Did he abol-ish it?

*Not pre-cisely. Her-bert just broke it up and scat-ter-ed it all
Over the coun-try.*

Louis himself worked out a pamphlet, lavishly embellished
with cartoons from the pen of F. Opper, the well-known cartoonist. Louis gave this pamphlet a British slant—his subject was
'Erbie the Anglophile.

One cartoon showed 'Erbie making a speech while two little
boys were having a fist fight alongside the platform. " 'Erbie's
little Dry playmate and little Wet playmate are still squabbling.
Which one will 'Erbie support?" the caption read. There were
other references to 'Erbie's close pal 'Ropy (Europe), and so on.
When the proofs came from the printers Louis showed them to us
proudly.

"What do you think of them?" he asked. "Clever, eh?"

We kept looking at them. "What are you going to do with these
things?" we asked.

"Why," he said, "I'm going to have them distributed by the
thousands at factory gates for the workers, just as I did so successfully in Franklin's race for the United States Senate."

"Well," we said timidly, "they are clever, but aren't they a little
too subtle for the average factory worker? How do you expect it
to affect them?"

He grabbed the proofs and gave us a withering glance. "Oh,"
he snorted, "I guess you wouldn't understand. Why, I don't expect
to do a thing, my dears, except to appeal to their blind prejudice."
He may not really have meant that, but anyway it took us down
a notch or two because we had not admired his brain child. If we
had mentioned at this moment that FDR was roundly defeated
in the Senate race where he had used this idea "so successfully"
he might really have blown his top. Maybe the others were as ig-
norant as I was; at that time I did not know that FDR had ever
run for the Senate from the State of New York.

Louis had been toying with this cartoon-primer idea as far back
as the days of "Teddy" Roosevelt. While he admired Teddy, his
admiration did not extend to T. R.'s "Progressive" Party. Among

the Howe papers in Hyde Park is a beautiful water color by Louis, showing a bull moose standing in tall, green grass, under stately trees, with a blue lake shimmering in the background. Beneath the drawing Louis had carefully printed this "lesson":

Dear Chil-dren
This is a Bull-Moose. Some times people who be-long to the Pro-gress-ive Party are call-ed Bull-Moose. This is quite Wrong, for there is a great dif-fer-ence. If you want to kill A Moose you must shoot him through the head be-cause there is where his brains are. If you hit him at the other end it does no harm. With a Pro-gress-ive it is just the other way 'round.

"Everybody's Political Primer" went over big, but the money to pay for it was a little slow in getting into the author's hands, so again Teague came to New York, this time looking for wampum. People looking for wampum naturally went to the Treasurer's office, so that's where he went. Again he was passed from hand to hand with kind words, but no wampum, and again, somewhat discouraged, he took his problem across the street. When he'd told his story Louis picked up a plain sheet of paper and scrawled on it, "Pay this man. L. H." Teague sprinted back to the Treasurer's office and was paid in full.

Louis also had some rather revolutionary ideas on the distribution of campaign literature. This literature, if it reaches and is read by the voters, is one of the most effective ways of campaigning, yet one of the most costly, if properly exploited. If the literature is sent to the state leaders for distribution, much of it never goes any further, the party leaders having a lot of other things on their minds, usually state and local elections. Yet if the literature is mailed out to individual voters, the postage and help to mail it runs into a fortune, thus is prohibitive.

Louis made a survey of national campaigns and how literature was handled, and found that in the case of literature sent to state committees only about 3 to 5 per cent ever sifted down to the actual voter. So he adopted a method of his own in this campaign. He sent a few pieces of each kind of his leaflets to about one hundred and forty thousand local committeemen and committeewomen, and found that in the long run this was most effective. Some 90 per cent actually reached the voters' hands.

Newspapermen who covered headquarters were amazed at the frank way Louis let them in on campaign secrets. Not all the newspapermen received this preferred treatment, however. Louis had his trusted lieutenants, among them Jim Hagerty of the New York *Times*, Charlie Bayer of the New York *American*, and Mike Hennessy of the Boston *Globe*. If one of them said to him, for instance, "Louis, I hear that things are not going so good for the Governor out in southern Illinois. What's the trouble?" Louis would reach for the phone.

"Hackie," he'd say, "get me Dallman." Hackie by this time knew that Vincent Dallman, editor of the *Register* in Springfield, was one of the Howe key men in that region and she'd get him on the phone.

"Vince," Louis would say, "I hear Franklin is having a little trouble out there. What's up? Is it labor, farm problems, wet, dry, Tammany Hall or what the hell?" He'd listen intently, dragging away at his Sweet Caporal, until Mr. Dallman had told him what the hitch was in that territory. Then he'd turn to the newspapermen and give them an absolutely frank account of what was wrong and what he expected to do about it. If it meant sending a man out there he'd tell them who was going and how the thing would be handled, a big help to them in writing their background stories.

In addition to his own "shop," as Louis called his offices at 331 Madison, he kept a sharp eye at all times on what was going on across the street at the Biltmore. Particularly, he kept an eye on the treasurer's office, for even then we never seemed to make ends meet, and rumor of a contribution of any size sent a wave of excitement running through headquarters like a strong west wind.

Once, while Farley and Walker were away, Joseph C. O'Mahoney and Ambrose O'Connell, who were left in charge of the Farley and Walker offices, heard that Mrs. William Randolph Hearst wanted to make a contribution and that it would be a generous one. Ambrose dispatched himself at once to Mrs. Hearst's office, and when she wrote out the check for $7,500, he hardly waited for the ink to dry before he was on his way back to his office, coattails flying. He and O'Mahoney sat down, took the bills and were happily going over them, stretching the check to cover a hundred here, two hundred there, on the accounts, when suddenly the phone rang. It was Louis.

"Ambrose," he said, "come over here right away."

Ambrose was there in five minutes. Louis, hunched over his desk, fixed him with a baleful eye.

"Ambrose," he barked, "who in the hell is running this campaign, anyway?"

"Why you are, Louis," Ambrose said soothingly. "Everybody knows that."

"Is that so?" Louis yelped. "Then where in hell is that $7,500?"

He had gotten wind of the bonanza by some underground of his own, and he had his own ideas about how it should be spent. When Ambrose told him they already had parceled most of it out he nearly had a stroke.

"I really believe," Judge O'Connell said, "that while Louis and I were good friends to the day he died, in the back of his mind he never really forgave me for spending that money before he got his hands on it.

"I'll never forget how we used to have to borrow from the bank on Friday to meet the Saturday payroll and often had to ask some of the workers if they could hold their checks till Monday just to make sure we had enough money. We drew on any legitimate source we could to meet those payrolls when we got in a tight spot. Joe Guffey came to our rescue several times.

" 'Joe,' I'd say, 'we've got to have $1,500. Do you have any idea how we can raise it?'

" 'Ambrose,' Guffey would reply, 'I think I can get it for you. But I'll have to have it back by Tuesday.'

"For some reason it was always Tuesday," Ambrose recalled. "I'd promise, of course, and then on Tuesday I wouldn't have it. I'd dodge Joe all day long and since the Treasurer's offices opened one into the other I was often able to get off the elevator and go from office to office until I reached the end of the hall where my own office was. As soon as I popped my head out, there would be Joe. He really wasn't looking for me, he never pressed us for money, and was always generous. He was there looking for Farley or someone else, but my conscience worried me anyway, and I'd try to rustle it up for him if I could. Then the routine would start all over again, we'd turn to some other member of the Advisory Committee, or tap some of Walker's friends for a loan, and so it went from payday to payday all through that campaign."

The slogan at headquarters those days was "Keep Cool, Calm and Collected" and somebody had placards made with this slogan in big black letters, and distributed around to each office. It wasn't long before all these slogans in the Finance Department found themselves with the last two letters neatly blocked out, so that they all read, "Keep Cool, Calm, and Collect."

Meanwhile, FDR traveled around the country, speaking from the back platform of his special train, which Louis Howe called the "Columbus Caravel." That campaign trip was the cause of the most shattering storm of advice ever to hit a Presidential headquarters. Louis always enjoyed telling how the old-time politicians camped on his doorstep and in the Governor's office at Albany, with pleas for the Governor to make a front-porch campaign on the order of the Harding campaign in 1920 that proved so successful.

"Their objections to Franklin making a campaign," Louis said, "were founded to a great extent on the belief that the carefully disseminated propaganda about Franklin's health must have some foundation, and that he would be unable to stand the rigors of a grueling campaign.

"This fear, however," said Louis, "never entered the minds of Franklin's intimate friends. I had seen him through two campaigns for Governor, traveling up and down the state in all kinds of weather, speaking two, three and four times a day and found him at the end of the campaigns in better health than when he started, while all the newspapermen who accompanied him were weary and bedraggled to the point of exhaustion.

"Franklin realized that the best answer to the question concerning his health was himself. So, after listening patiently and carefully to those who attempted to dissuade him from making such a strenuous trip, he turned to his advisers and with the most disarming of smiles, said:

" 'Gentlemen, I have listened carefully to your arguments against my going to the Coast and back, or even as far as Chicago. I appreciate the weight of what you have to say and think I understand all the reasons you advance against it. But there is one reason in favor of my going which has not been brought to your attention and that reason is—I want to!'

"And that was that!" Louis grinned. "From then on all discussions about whether he would go or not was abandoned, and, as results showed, Franklin was right and his advisers wrong!"

There was one important difference between that train and Columbus's caravel, however. When the land disappeared over the horizon Christopher Columbus was cut off from all knowledge of what was going on in the world. But Louis made the most elaborate arrangements to see that FDR's train was kept in constant touch with the latest political developments all over the country.

At every stop of over ten minutes, from nine o'clock in the morning until sometimes two or three o'clock the next morning, it was the job of Marvin McIntyre, who was in charge of the train, to call Louis Howe or Jim Farley; they would have their notes ready so they could tell him what had transpired since his last call.

A staff of workers read and condensed this material for the train and, in addition, Louis forwarded to the Caravel by air mail ten or fifteen pages a day of abstracts of editorials on political matters, from scores of newspapers to which he had access. Thus, Franklin D. Roosevelt was probably the best informed candidate who ever toured the country, thanks to Louis, who kept the "cut it short" and "boil it down" department working far into the night.

In the middle of the summer, however, a dark shadow fell athwart this cheerful picture. A thing that Louis Howe had dreaded was here. The rumor began to crawl slyly around the country that infantile paralysis was a disease that eventually affected the brain of those afflicted. Louis heard that the Republicans were planning to issue a statement along these lines, even though they would not dare come right out and say that it was affecting Roosevelt himself.

Louis took immediate steps. He called Dr. George Draper, one of the leading authorities on polio in the country, who had worked on FDR's case, and asked him for a statement which he could use if it became necessary. Dr. Draper gave him a full statement at once, saying there was no truth in this theory whatever. He pointed out that Sir Walter Scott had been a victim of infantile paralysis when he was a small boy, and one could hardly say that there was anything wrong with the brain of Sir Walter Scott. Louis held the statement in readiness to use the moment the Republicans issued their statement, but they never did, deciding, perhaps, that it might prove a terrific boomerang. The vicious gossip, in the main, subsided, though you still ran across it here and there, trailing its way across the country like a furtive and slimy snake, raising its head to strike where it thought harm might still be done.

People were always asking during the campaign, "Who ghost-writes FDR's speeches for him?" Many, of course, thought Louis Howe was the "ghost" but he waved this honor aside.

"There is no actual ghost-writer," he said. "What Franklin does is to take all the data presented to him on a given subject and write it in his own way, incorporating a paragraph here and a paragraph there which has been given to him.

"I, myself," he laughed, "often present him with what I think is a creditable paragraph or two when he is preparing a speech, and find it missing entirely in the finished draft. Then, to my utter surprise, I often recognize my old friend, embodied in some other speech where it is considerably more effective."

If Louis missed his paragraphs now and then when he gave them to the Governor, he began to miss whole pages when he wrote some material for the Women's Division for distribution to the women workers throughout the country. He sent the material around to Mollie Dewson, head of the Women's Division, and asked her how many copies she wanted. The next day Mollie marched into his office with her nose in the air.

"Surely," she said, "you don't expect us to send this to the women, do you?"

"Why not?" asked Louis, a little miffed. He was pretty proud of his "masterpiece" and had burned some midnight oil in its preparation.

"Well," said the outspoken Mollie, "I don't know about you men, but the women won't waste time reading through all this stuff. It's too long. You give us your own printing budget and let us write our own."

So Louis Howe, who always insisted that everything laid before him be "cut short" before he'd bother with it, had his own material sent back to him because it needed to be cut down.

"I gave them their budget though," he said, "just to show them they couldn't do it, really, and didn't pay too much attention to what they were doing until suddenly we began to get letters from the county chairmen asking for some of 'those little red, yellow and green leaflets' that the Women's Division was getting out. Everybody wanted some."

These were the famous "rainbow flyers" that Mollie Dewson and Mrs. Roosevelt prepared and sent out by the thousands, with such telling effect. Before the campaign was over, they had a little plane hopping gaily over the country, piloted by the famed woman flier, Phoebe Omlie, with Stella Akin, redheaded woman lawyer from Georgia as a speaker, literally scattering these "flyers" from coast to coast.

"Funny thing, too," Louis grinned, "those women made the same amount of money go twice as far as the men did. Miss Dewson, Miss Lavinia Engle, head of the Women Speakers Bureau, Mrs. Henry Morgenthau, Jr., in charge of radio, Mrs. Nellie Tayloe Ross, vice-chairman of the Democratic National Committee, Mrs. Ruth Bryan Owen, Mrs. Emily Newell Blair—all those women could make a campaign dollar go farther than any group I ever saw.

"In another field," Louis went on, "I found the women superior to the men in actual work among the voters. The Women's Division organized a corps of women who, without any compensation, went from house to house interviewing women in their territory, armed with leaflets and ready to debate any question with intelligence. At headquarters we called them the 'grass trampers' and they were wonderful."

The good work done by the Women's Division pleased Louis for another reason. Several "elder statesmen" in the party saw no reason why the headquarters should have a "Women's Division."

"Votes are votes," they said, "and should be treated in the same way, whether male or female." Louis emphatically dissented, and was happy when events proved him right.

In fact, Louis was always so enthusiastic about women in politics that after he went to the White House, he wrote an article for the *Woman's Home Companion* in which he said he saw no reason why a woman should not be elected President of the United States!

"If women progress in their ability to handle practical political and governmental offices with the same increasing speed as they have during the last ten years, within the next decade the advisability of electing a woman President will become a seriously argued question," he said, "and if the issues continue to be as they are now—humanitarian and educational—it is not impossible that a woman might be elected on the ground that women understand such questions better than men."

This story caused a mild sensation when it hit the newsstands, and in editorials about it Louis Howe was called everything from a "prophet" to a "crackpot," but to all this hullabaloo, he just grinned.

"I didn't say anything I haven't said a good many times before," he said, "only when I said it before I didn't say it from the White House!"

While FDR was swinging joyously around the country, down

in Uvalde, Texas, John Nance Garner, the candidate for Vice-President, was strangely silent. That is, it was strange unless it was understood that Garner didn't want to make any speeches.

"Hell," he said, "I always speak my mind, and when you are running for Vice-President you can't say what you really want to say. Somebody will try to write my speeches for me and tell me how to say them, so I just won't make any."

However, Louis, never one to take a chance, dispatched Charlie Hand, an old newspaper friend and an ardent Roosevelt man, to Uvalde to ride herd on Garner, just in case he decided to jump the corral fence and dispense some sentiments that didn't jibe with what Roosevelt was saying in other parts of the country.

Getting Charlie to Uvalde wasn't easy, however. Charlie, who loved the bright lights of New York with a consuming love, shuddered all the way to his immaculately polished shoes when Louis called him in and told him he was sending him to Uvalde.

"Uvalde!" said Charlie. "Good God, what's that? Sounds like the place where the women have those awful protruding lips."

"Shut up," said Louis. "You know very well where it is and that I don't mean Ubangi. This Garner says he isn't going to make any speeches, but he might change his mind. You go down and visit with him. If he decides to make a speech tell him we'll be glad to help him with it. Get packed and take the first train."

But Charlie didn't give up so easily. He slipped out and called FDR.

"It's no use, Charlie," FDR laughed. "Louis has picked you for that job and he isn't going to take 'No' so there's no use to struggle. As a matter of fact you'll find Jack an interesting fellow. I think you'll really enjoy yourself."

Charlie struggled, though, for three days, then gave up and took the train for San Antonio. There he put in a phone call for Garner. Garner, he was told politely, was out fishing. Charlie, who was in no hurry anyway, said he'd call again tomorrow. The next day he received the news that Garner had gone hunting. No, he wouldn't be back all day. When Charlie still couldn't reach the elusive Garner on the phone he hired a car and took off for Uvalde.

Garner's little granddaughter met him at the door. Right behind her, his frosty eyebrows beetling like mad, stood "Cactus Jack."

"I'll bet you ten dollars," he said, "that this is another one of that little devil Louis Howe's ideas."

Somebody, it seemed, had tipped Garner off and that's why he had taken to the bushes. Charlie was in no position to deny Garner's charge so he felt that he was getting off to an awful start. However, Garner cooled down and before long they became pretty good friends.

They even "struck several blows for liberty" together, as time went on, but the bucolic life was not for Charlie. Now and then he sent feeble cries of rage to headquarters directed right at Louis Howe's gnome-like head, but they bounced off unheeded. Louis, in fact, took pains to send glowing messages to Charlie ever so often, about how he and Franklin appreciated what he was doing, that he was a patriot, a great newspaperman, that he had been a big help by taking on this assignment, etc.

"All this hogwash," said Charlie gloomily, "didn't alter the fact that I fought the battle of Uvalde right up to election day."

Garner did come out of retirement once before election day, and made a rousing speech for the ticket. General Hugh Johnson, Barney Baruch's right-hand man, was beginning to play a rather important part in the campaign and decided he was the one to write this speech, which concerned finances.

"It was an awful speech," Charlie said. "You couldn't tell what in hell he was driving at. Garner, who had been on important committees having to do with money in the House of Representatives for many years, had forgotten more about finances than old 'Iron Pants' ever knew, so with a little help from Charlie Michelson and myself he wrote his own speech—and it was a rattling good one."

A little incident occurred on FDR's trip that Louis liked to emphasize, since, he said, it showed what a hold Franklin already had upon the feelings of his countrymen. At one place where the train was supposed to stop, a misunderstanding developed and the train carried FDR past the big crowd gathered to greet him at the station. They were so disappointed that some pretty bitter grumbling developed. A member of the welcoming committee went over to the bulletin board on the platform, pulled from his pocket a letter he had received from Governor Roosevelt, and tacked it up.

He called to the crowd:

"Gentlemen, step up here and read this letter," he said, "and see if you don't agree that a man who would write a letter like that would never willingly disappoint his friends."

One by one the members of the committee stepped up and read the friendly letter from FDR, then they went into the depot and drafted a resolution on the spot, regretting that they had failed to see him, but expressing the belief that it could not have been his fault. They rushed the resolution into headquarters and it beat the Columbus Caravel by three or four days.

It was not only in the hinterlands, however, that tempers grew short as time grew short. The spirit around headquarters had been wonderful all during the campaign, but with so much still to be done and so little time to do it, nerves were taut and some explosions occurred. One occurred in my own bailiwick, where the mail had grown to such enormous proportions that the little staff of five had now grown to eighteen and was scattered in several offices along the hall on the fourth floor.

One day, rushing down the hall with a basket of mail for Farley, I heard Mrs. Duffy ask Betty Trumbo if she would go in and take dictation from Farley. Betty was my best friend in Kentucky, and I had persuaded her to take leave of absence from her job as secretary to the Chief Justice of the Kentucky Court of Appeals to come up and work in the campaign through the summer while the Court was not in session. Betty had heard of Farley's reputation as a demon dictator, her nerve suddenly deserted her when Mrs. Duffy asked her to go in, and she said she believed she wouldn't. I grabbed her by the arm and ran with her down the steps to the next floor and backed her against the wall and yelled at her that she d——— well better go in and take that dictation, that I'd had a pretty hard time convincing Louis Howe that we had to import people from Kentucky to work in the campaign, with so many people out of work close at hand and if he found out she'd laid down on the job I'd never hear the last of it. Betty hopped back to the Farley office and did such a good job that she later became one of his most trusted lieutenants in Washington.

"I wouldn't have minded her tirade," Betty told a friend ruefully, "but she backed me right against a door where the Republicans were having a meeting and they heard it all."

All this tension, the hard work, the feverish activity finally came to a head on November 8—election day. Excitement was at a high pitch. Only Louis, on the surface at least, was calm. He holed up with a few close friends in his little office, where he had arranged to get the reports from the wire services. He kept Margaret Durand with him and sent me across to the "big show," as he called it, at the Biltmore Hotel.

Here, in a big room on the first floor, a long table had been placed, and hand-picked girls from headquarters manned telephones placed all along the table. At the head sat Governor Roosevelt, Jim Farley and Edward J. Flynn, Secretary of State of New York. It was my thrilling job to man one of the phones at the head of the table where the "Big Three" sat. As calls came in on the table phones they were passed up to the head so that FDR or Mr. Farley could speak to the callers direct.

"Hello Joe, how are things in Wyoming?" FDR would shout to Joe O'Mahoney, who had gone home to vote and was speeding the election news back to headquarters. Or "What's the good word in Ohio?" to William A. Julian, lieutenant on the job out there. "Is everything under control, Bill?" he'd call gaily, across the miles, to W. W. Howes far out in South Dakota. Throwing his head back in a typical Roosevelt gesture he'd chortle gleefully, "You mean I'm getting votes in rock-ribbed Pennsylvania?" after Joe Guffey told him that this Republican stronghold was rolling up a sizable Democratic vote for the first time in sixty years.

But over in his little corner, Louis Howe, now that the great moment had come, was stricken with a vast pessimism. When the good returns began to roll in he'd say gloomily, "Losers always have a big spurt at the start before they finally begin to dwindle off to defeat," and smoking nervously, he sat there hunched over the ticker until finally the glad news swelled to such a roar that there was no mistaking the outcome.

"Roosevelt wins!" shouted a newspaperman in the Biltmore. "And Howe!"

Yes, it was almost as much a personal victory for Louis Howe as it was for Franklin Roosevelt, and nobody knew it better than the newspapermen who had covered the campaign.

Now that it was settled I wanted only to get to Louis and see how he was taking his hour of triumph. Two others had exactly the same idea. Mrs. Howe, who stayed in Fall River to vote, took a train to New York to be with him. Confident that FDR would win, she wanted to be there because "I just wanted to see Louis' face when it was a certainty," she said. Hartley, who was at Harvard, drove down in a car which he described as a "real rattletrap," so that it took him all day to make the trip, but he arrived in time. It took me almost an hour, though, to fight, scratch and claw my way through the milling, shouting throngs in the hotel, and on to Madison Avenue, to Forty-third Street, and up the flights of stairs—no use trying to get an elevator—to the seventh floor.

There sat the little boss, looking at the pile of telegrams and ticker tape as a miser might regard his gold. He looked tired, but his face glowed with an inner light.

"You're late," he said, as I boldly leaned down and planted a kiss on his cheek. "You've missed a party!"

Because of my slow progress across the street I had, unfortunately, missed the high spot of the evening. As soon as Louis knew Franklin was "in" he leaned down solemnly, opened a drawer of his desk, and lifted out a bottle of sherry.

"I put this sherry away in Albany twenty years ago," he said, "right after Franklin had won his fight against Tammany Hall. I said then he'd be President someday and I made up my mind never to open this bottle until that time came."

Howe and Roosevelt, 1934.

FDR at the funeral of Louis McHenry Howe at Fall River, Mass. Mrs. Roosevelt and John Roosevelt on FDR's right, Franklin Roosevelt, Jr., on his left.

Then he filled the glasses for his guests, raised his own and said simply:

"To the next President of the United States!"

And while all the world, it seemed, was trying to get into the Biltmore Hotel to shake Franklin Roosevelt's hand, Louis Howe merely picked up the telephone.

"Hello, Franklin," he said in his tired but triumphant voice. "Congratulations! I guess I've worked myself out of a job. I'm going home and go to bed!"

12

The Little Boss

PERHAPS if Louis Howe had known when he went to bed election night that he'd wake up famous, he would have taken off to darkest Africa, FDR or no FDR. As it was, he always said Franklin played a mean trick on him, when he stood before a microphone in the Biltmore Hotel ballroom that night and said:

"I want to say just a word. There are two people in the United States more than anybody else who are responsible for this great victory. One is my old friend and associate, Colonel Louis McHenry Howe, and the other is that splendid American, Jim Farley."

When that sentence crackled over the air waves, Louis Howe's cherished anonymity was gone forever. As campaign manager for Roosevelt, Jim Farley's name had become a byword in the land, but millions of people immediately pricked up their ears and demanded to know:

"Who the devil is Howe?"

Reporters, magazine writers, cranks, cameramen and job seekers descended on him in droves. For a time he had to leave his beloved little corner office and get another one, high up in the building, where he could hole in and, dammit, get some work done. But the country was avid for news of this mysterious little man, this "king maker," and they scratched every surface for data about him. Harold Payson, who was editor of *The Jeffersonian*, a magazine published by the New York State Democratic Com-

218

mittee, was even desperate enough to ask me to do a story about him. I asked Louis what I should do.

"Oh, go ahead if you want to," he said, "but don't you dare butter me!" When the story was finished I took it to him and he went through it carefully, blue pencil in hand. Any hint of "butter" was promptly deleted. The paragraph he liked best, in fact, was this:

"Those who don't know Louis Howe very well sometimes see him as a gruff, abrupt, rude individual. Those who do know him very well sometimes see him in the same light."

After telling what he ate, what he wore, what he smoked, and what his reading habits were, the subject of his hobbies was taken up, and disposed of, in one paragraph:

"So far as anybody knows he has only one hobby—Franklin D. Roosevelt."

It was only natural that when so little was known about a man, all sorts of legends began to spring up about him. Louis was compared to Napoleon, Lincoln, Talleyrand, Colonel House, Mussolini, and even to Alexander the Great! This amused him no end. Some of the smart writers, however, alarmed at the increasing number of these legends, undertook to "debunk" this mysterious little man. One was Stanley Walker of the New York *Herald Tribune*, who wrote a magazine piece about him called, "The Gnome Nobody Knows." He pictured Louis as an ordinary enough fellow who just happened to have enough horse sense to get what he wanted. Referring to the legends which pictured Louis as a wit, an epicure, a crime expert, a journalist, a great man of surpassing modesty, a king maker, Mr. Walker said, in some irritation:

"Thus we have the fantastic creation who is to be the brains of the next administration, a perfectly amazing mixture with overtones of Colonel House, George Harvey, Harry Daugherty, Machiavelli, Frank Stearns, Mrs. Moscowitz and Talleyrand. He also reminds certain people in odd facets of his character of John the Baptist, St. Augustine, most of the Borgias and Marshal Ney. He is like Napoleon because he signs his letters 'Howe.'

"Not to make many bones about it," Mr. Walker went on, "Louis Howe is really a simple and ordinary sort of fellow. He eats, sleeps, and occasionally visits his family at Fall River, Massachusetts. He is no fop, but that doesn't make him resemble Abraham Lincoln. He is not a dolt, but there is nothing very remarkable about that. . . . All attempts to portray him as a man who conceivably could exert the same sort of influence which Colonel House exerted during the Wilson Administration must fail because Howe is not that kind of person. The Colonel looks like a statesman. Howe couldn't pass for a statesman any more than he could pass for a Tammany district leader. . . .

"The Greeks may have had a bird like him," Mr. Walker conceded, "and the Ptolemys needed one, but in modern times no one, certainly no President, has had a man of Howe's background and personality, or a man who will occupy anything like the place that this smart little introvert will fill after next March 4. Presidents have had advisers, but none like Howe; they have had cronies, as Harding did, but Howe is no man's crony. His loyalty is not to himself, or to an abstract ideal of government, but solely to Franklin D. Roosevelt."

Needless to say, Louis' friends didn't care much for this description, but he merely grinned cheerfully and said he thought it was pretty good. No butter, see.

He only laughed when they called him "that crabby little guy from Fall River," or "The Secret High Inquisitor," but when a writer dubbed him "The Roving Political Brain Cell," he clapped his hand to his head in mock anguish:

"Mein Gawd!" he cried. "This is too much. What'll I be next?"

Personally I always liked best the New York *Times'* designation, "The President's Other I."

One young reporter who came in for an interview asked in considerable awe, "Is it true, Mr. Howe, that you and Mr. Roosevelt really call each other by your first names?"

"Yes," Louis grinned, "and sometimes worse than that."

When one reporter wrote that Louis Howe often pounded the desk and shouted at FDR, "Can't you ever get anything through that thick Dutch head of yours?" it was hard for some people to swallow, but when we remembered the day he told FDR on the telephone that he "hoped to God he drowned," it sounded perfectly reasonable to us.

While Louis was not one to brag to strangers that he and FDR could beat each other over the head, his sense of the dramatic made him really enjoy the shock on the faces of visitors when they saw him for the first time and realized that this was the little man who wielded so much power.

"Louis really loved power," Mrs. Roosevelt once said. "Not for any advantage for himself or for publicity, but simply to show those of us around him what he could accomplish when he set his mind to it. Often he'd tell us of some project he'd planned that seemed to us impossible to achieve.

" 'But Louis,' we'd say, 'you can't do that.'

" 'Can't I,' he'd say, 'watch!'

"Then when he had accomplished this seemingly impossible task he bragged about it like a small boy.

" 'I said I'd do it,' he'd say, 'and I did it. You don't see me fail very often, do you?'

"And," Mrs. Roosevelt continued thoughtfully, "it's true. He rarely ever failed. He was amazing."

Even the astrologers noted this desire for power of which Mrs. Roosevelt spoke. In *Astrology for the Millions* Grant Lewi devotes a whole chapter to Louis Howe and his relationship to Franklin Roosevelt. Of Louis he said, "His pictures, his description of himself and the character he is known to have had suggest that he had Capricorn rising, with the Sun and Saturn therein, giving terrific force of personality, a burning desire for power and success, but a desire that would be satisfied by ruling the ruler, which is precisely what he did."

Carty Ranck of the New York *Times,* interviewing Louis for a post-election story, asked him where he was going to ride in this new caravan headed for Washington.

"Oh, I don't know," said Louis mildly, "I guess I'll fit in somewhere. I suppose I have an inferiority complex, really. I must have or I'd give more thought and attention to things that many persons consider so important. Politics has always interested me as a game, but I would rather stay on the sidelines than play myself. I get a big kick out of looking on."

"Don't you want a political job?" Mr. Ranck asked.

"No!" he said emphatically. "Do you?"

"No," said Mr. Ranck just as emphatically.

"There you are," said Louis philosophically, "newspapermen don't like political jobs, but just try and make some of the politicians believe *that*."

The picture that illustrated this New York *Times* story was one of the very few that Louis liked. It was a photograph of a portrait by the artist Leonobel Jacobs who had wisely made his extraordinary eyes the focal point in the painting. Most pictures only seemed to point up the lines of his face, his thin hair and skinny neck.

"I think I'll send all my friends around to Mrs. Jacobs," he said, "and have her certify that I'm every bit as good-looking as she has painted me."

"Mrs. Roosevelt and I are running a race," he laughed, "to see which one can find the ugliest pictures of ourselves. The world's worst pictures are made of both of us," he vowed, "but I am always two laps ahead."

One of the "inside stories" about Louis said pontifically that "when Roosevelt is installed in the White House, Louis Howe will be found in a cubbyhole exerting a wholesome influence over the Presidency."

"I called Franklin's attention to this alarming suggestion," he laughed, "and warned him that he might expect me to be his 'chloride of lime' man after March the fourth. We both had a good laugh over that one."

One reporter got an unusual slant on how Louis felt about "yes men," when, tapering the interview off, he asked Louis if he liked dogs.

"No," said Louis, much to the reporter's surprise, "and do you know why? Dogs are 'yes men.' I like cats much better."

"Well," said the interviewer, "that's a new one. I thought most men disliked cats."

"I suppose they do," said Louis, "but I like cats because they are always themselves. Their utter indifference makes them fascinating. Then, too, they are always laughing at us. Cats are 'no' animals. That's why I like them."

He shrugged in resignation when he was told it was going to be next to impossible for him to maintain his cherished anonymity when he reached Washington and began to feel the heat of the great white light that "always beats upon a throne."

"I suppose that's true," he said wearily. "There will be closeups and 'intimate portraits.' " He grimaced. "But," he added, brightening, "I think it will die down soon and that they'll forget about me and let me alone."

He didn't get steamed up when people began to talk about how wonderful it would be for him to go to Washington as chief adviser—and none doubted that he would be that—to the President of the United States and actually, it was rumored, live right in the White House! He didn't see that living in Washington would be so much. After all, he lived there eight years when he was with Franklin in the Navy Department. And as for living in the White House, well, he had always lived with the Roosevelts whether in New York, Hyde Park, or Albany, and he didn't take up much room, anyway. "They'll stick me away somewhere," he said.

As soon as a President is elected the Secret Service takes over and, for his protection, puts a couple of men on his trail who stick with him until he is safely installed at 1600 Pennsylvania Avenue. Then an army of them takes over. A small army, it is true, but a mighty potent and efficient one. Chief William H. Moran, then head of the Secret Service, came to New York the day after election and was closeted with Louis for a long time. Pretty soon Louis called Rabbit and myself in, introduced us to Mr. Moran and gravely told us we'd have to stay away from speakeasies and other disreputable joints as the Chief was going to have us "tailed" from now on. We didn't know whether to believe it or not!

The Chief enjoyed this banter, but he kept looking at his watch.

"I can't understand," he said worriedly, "where my two agents are. I told them to meet me here in your office and they should have been here half an hour ago. I can't imagine what's keeping them."

This was too much for Louis who bent double with laughter for a moment, then snorted derisively:

"You are certainly one helluva Secret Service head," he said. "Can't even keep up with your own men!"

The Chief, who didn't know Louis as well then as he did later, reddened a bit, then joined in the laughter.

By this time Louis really didn't mind being called "The Medieval Gnome," and often when his phone rang he'd pick it up and say in a sepulchral voice, "This is the Medieval Gnome speaking." And, tying up many of the names which had been conferred on him, he even had cards printed with the awesome title, "Colonel Louis Rasputin Voltaire Talleyrand Simon Legree Howe."

Louis' title of "Colonel" was bestowed upon him by the governor of Kentucky, and he received his commission at a little office party we arranged for him during the campaign. He was as tickled with it as a kid with a new red wagon. Jim Farley made the presentation speech and Louis beamed as he picked up the phone and called Mrs. Howe in Fall River. Mrs. Howe must have just burned the biscuits when she got the message for she said acidly:

"If you have time for all that foolishness you've got time to come home." He had planned to go that weekend, but something had come up. He looked at us when he hung up the phone, his face puckered in a wry grin.

"Never pays to get too big for your breeches," he said. "The family can always cut you down to size."

The title of Colonel pleased Louis, however, until the newspaper boys began to write stories drawing the inevitable comparison between Woodrow Wilson's Colonel House and Franklin Roosevelt's Colonel Howe. This annoyed him mightily. The final straw was when job hunters descended on him, and thinking it a way to get in his good graces, unctuously addressed him by his title. "Mein Gawd!" he exploded one day. "I wouldn't mind these sycophants just calling me 'Colonel,' but why in hell do they have to sing it. 'How dew you dew, Kurronel Howe?' " he would mimic them in a singsong voice. "I wish I had never heard of that damned title—to hell with it."

Louis' smoking habits brought him ribbing from Franklin in those days. "Ludevic," he'd say—"Ludevic" being a nickname FDR called him now and then, when in a teasing mood—"I hear the Sweet Caporal factory is closing down since there is only one man in America who smokes their brand."

"I'll wait till they close down before I change," Ludevic would answer.

Louis' clothes also came in for a lot of kidding from FDR. "When Louis gets a new suit it's news," he said one day to a caller, with Louis sitting by. "I'm pretty sure he hasn't had a new suit in ages and certainly not new socks. Louis doesn't do any darning, you know, so he just wears his socks till they don't cover his legs any more."

Louis nodded, but he wore a secret, sly grin.

"Let's have a look, Louis," FDR bantered.

Solemnly Louis lifted up his trouser leg and displayed some rather loud new socks, then flipped from beneath his high collar a tie which matched a couple of the colors in the socks. FDR stared, then roared with laughter.

"This is the revolution," he said, "absolutely the revolution!"

"No, not at all," commented Louis drily. "It's just the first dawn of that prosperity I've been hearing so much about."

Mrs. Roosevelt usually tried to keep an eye on Louis' clothes, knowing how little he cared about his appearance. However, he always wore both a belt and suspenders, whether his dress was formal or informal. "What makes the guy wear both at once? Is he such a pessimist as all that?" somebody once asked, not unreasonably.

As for Louis' hats, they were at least conversation pieces. Mrs. Roosevelt was after him all the time to buy a new one, but he loved his old hats, no matter how battered, and it was only after much resistance that finally he'd give up and go downtown with her while she selected a new one for him herself.

Once in New York, when he was taking Mrs. Roosevelt to some sort of official function, she persuaded him to dress in a tuxedo, which he always hated, and he sat at the table glumly, not enjoying anything because he was so "dressed up." But Mrs. Roosevelt was rather proud of him until she happened to glance down at his feet. To her horror she saw that Louis, in all innocence apparently, was sitting there with a sedate black sock on one foot and a gleaming white one on the other!

FDR teased Louis about his reading habits, too, especially his love for detective stories. "Louis loves those gory ones with lots of murders," he'd say. "He gets bored with them unless there's a murder on the very first page." Louis leaned especially to English detective stories. He could usually figure out what an American detective would do, he said, but the English type kept him guessing. He also liked the dry, pungent humor of *Punch,* the English weekly, and often had us scurrying around the city to find a copy, if his was mislaid. He was especially fond of Kipling, Anthony Hope, Carlyle and Robert Louis Stevenson. Once FDR asked him why, if he liked English authors so well, he didn't go for Charles Reade.

"Oh," Louis said, "he's a pretty dull fellow."

This brought a roar of laughter from FDR. Reade dull! He was anything but that. Besides, Louis and Reade really had a good many things in common. They both had the same love for the theater and a flair for stage settings and unusual effects and Louis, like Reade, collected and kept on file a vast amount of material for his study of human nature, from observation, books, travel, etc. But, unlike Reade, Louis didn't put much of it in file cases. He kept it where it was always handy—right in his gnome-like head.

"Louie" and "Franklin"—when they really got going it was tit for tat, especially about those toy yacht races they had in the summertime for the "Krum Elbow Cup," a silver cup which FDR, his sons and Anna, Louis, Ralph Cropley and Mr. Smith who worked for FDR's aunt Mrs. John A. Roosevelt, would compete for on the Hudson River at the Roosevelt estate. Each one had to design and make his own boat and they had three classes: a 42-inch over-all schooner, a 42-inch over-all sloop and a 12-inch sloop. The idea was not just to compete for speed, as the prize was not given for the fastest model but for the fastest type of any given length. Louis, assisted by Hartley, spent a lot of time on his boat in the woodworking shop at the beach, and they evolved one with a deeper keel which Louis figured would outstrip the boats FDR and his boys had made. He figured right, for his boat won the race that summer and the cup had a place of honor ever after in the cottage at the beach and is now in Mrs. Howe's home in Fall River. Louis got a bigger kick out of beating the "famous Naval Roosevelts" than winning the cup, and needled FDR about it on every occasion. "Oh yes, Louis *did* win once," FDR would concede. "Know how he did it? A gale came up one day as we sailed the boats across the river and Louis' boat was the only one in the whole fleet that wasn't dismasted." Louis would only grin triumphantly. "Well, that's the *Roosevelt* story," he'd say, "and, anyway, who has the cup?"

The little boss really had a lot of wonderful hobbies but, since he didn't talk much about them in the office, we only learned about them gradually as time went by. In addition to his woodworking hobby he loved flowers, especially wild flowers, and his children remember that he spent long hours working in his "wild garden" which he built on the north side of their home in Saratoga, with rocks and a piped rill of water rippling through. He planted only wild things in it and he and Mrs. Howe would take many long walks in the late afternoons along the little used tracks of the Boston and Maine Railroad in search of lady-slippers, his favorite flower, to put in the little garden.

He confided to one interviewer that in his youth he yearned to be an artist, and this ambition he never quite forgot. He did some really beautiful water colors and would spend hours in a little chair on the beach sketching the ocean, with its many changing scenes. "The ocean rolls directly from Spain to my place on the shore," he once said poetically. One summer Mrs. Howe's cousin Bessie Borden, who was going abroad, left her little fox terrier Petey with the Howes at the cottage, so, as a steamer letter, Louis made a diary of Petey's daily escapades, richly and amusingly illustrated with some of his best water-color drawings.

Louis even tried his hand at dry-point etching. When Mary was in her senior year at Vassar, Clarence Chatterton, her art instructor, introduced him to this form of art and he was so fascinated that he took it up enthusiastically. Some of his best etchings, along with two of his beautiful water colors, hang in Mrs. Roosevelt's cottage at Hyde Park, in addition to the lovely ones Mrs. Howe has in her Fall River home. The roller Louis used in his work on his etchings, with his name in block letters, is now in a place of honor in the Franklin D. Roosevelt Library at Hyde Park.

Louis was extremely clever with his hands, and once at a dinner at the governor's mansion in Albany he constructed cardboard replicas of the State House in Albany, and the White House in Washington, which he set up at the ends of the long dining-room table. Along the table he placed various objects, symbolic of events or incidents in FDR's career, and during the dinner he delighted the guests with a humorous monologue on the meaning and significance of all these table decorations.

Both of Louis' children inherited his pleasure in the arts and crafts, but, said Mary Howe Baker ruefully, "none of his skill." However, Robert Baker, Jr., Louis' grandson, seems to have inherited some of his skill, especially in woodworking, and now teaches woodworking at St. George's School in Middletown, Rhode Island.

"I always felt that Mrs. Howe and their children deserved special recognition for enabling Louis to carry out his plans," Mrs. Roosevelt once said, "for it often meant that he had a scant amount of time to spend with them. However, the fact that they all had similar intellectual interests and many outside interests probably made it possible for them to share and enjoy Louis' varied activities."

While it could not be classed as a real hobby, Louis admired "old things," and when some of his associates at the Democratic National Committee presented him with a gold cup after the 1932 campaign, its value increased a hundredfold after he learned that it had been made in Birmingham, England, in 1827 by Matthew Boultron, famous goldsmith of that era.

He wrote creditable poetry, too, and his first effort, entitled "Prayer," written at the age of six, was proudly published in an Indianapolis paper:

> *As the rain beats on the roof,*
>
> *It is like a shower of Grace*
>
> *As the lightning shrieks and flashes*
>
> *It is the shining of Thy face.*
>
> *As the thunder bursts and crashes*
>
> *It is Thy voice from Thy Holy Place.*

There are several of Louis' published and unpublished poems in the Hyde Park Library, ranging from the devout "Prayer" to the hilarious one about what happened to FDR's appendix during their stretch in the Navy—also the verses he wrote for the famous "Cuff Links" dinners, and birthday and holiday poems written for the amusement of the President, Mrs. Roosevelt, and the members of "his gang." At Christmas time 1931, with his goal of putting Franklin in the White House almost in sight, he laid this little poem beside the Roosevelt breakfast plate. Its title was "Success":

> *Pity him most who gaineth most*
>
> *Who won all things for which his heart aspires,*
>
> *And now must feed his hungry soul*
>
> *On bitter ashes of fulfilled desires.*
>
> *Envy him most who loveth most*
>
> *No failure chills, no labor tires*
>
> *A soul forever kept aglow*
>
> *By love's unconquerable fires.*

In this poem Louis summed up the melancholy cynicism which was so much a part of his nature, at the same time revealing that soft spot in his heart that "kept his soul aglow" and the dogged determination that kept him from tiring at his eternal labors.

Due to asthma and difficulty in breathing Louis Howe never liked places where he felt "closed in." Now and then he'd stay overnight with a newspaper friend in New York who had a penthouse apartment, and if it was summer they always had to fix him a bed on the terrace outside the apartment, with a table handy on which were mystery stories, crossword puzzles, maybe a book on archeology. His mind was so active that when he went to bed he was like a parked car with the engine running, so he armed himself with all sorts of things to keep his mind off his problems.

"If you go to bed with a problem and don't get it off your mind, your ultimate decision will be a failure," he always said. "But if you can get your thoughts steeped in a detective story or crossword puzzle you may find that by the next morning your subconscious mind has been active and your problem is solved."

Louis never liked anybody to notice his afflictions, but it was impossible to ignore them for even walking up steps at times almost stopped his breathing. Walking up the ramp at Grand Central Station in New York or even to the platform elevator in Pennsylvania Station was so hard on him that finally William Egan at Pennsylvania Station and the stationmaster at Grand Central formed a plan. They knew what car he'd be on and, as he disembarked, one of the electric truck baggage carriers would just happen to be there. "Let's get on and ride," one of the waiting men would say. Louis, who knew what the score was though he wouldn't admit it, would grin sardonically and climb aboard. The same play was worked at Union Station after he came to Washington, and passengers used to stop and peer in amazement at the hunched-up little figure on the baggage truck, riding along with his eyes closed and swaying to the movement of the truck as though this were the most natural way in the world to travel.

As soon as the election was over Louis turned immediately to the task of seeing that the original F. R. B. C. (For Roosevelt before Chicago) men received fitting recognition, and he, Jim Farley, Frank Walker and Ed Flynn formed a committee to take care of this group. Shortly after election they went down to Warm Springs where FDR was vacationing to talk things over with him. As they sat around the fire in the living room at the "Little White House" Louis suddenly brought up the name of an F. R. B. C. man who had excellent qualifications for a high job.

"I think he'd make you a good Cabinet member, Franklin," he said.

FDR took his cigarette out of his mouth, and making a pointer of it he waved it toward Louis.

"Now, Louis," he said, "the members of my Cabinet will be members of my family as it were—my official family. They will be very close to me. I don't want anybody naming a single one of them, not even you, Louis. And," he waved his cigarette in a wide arc that took in Farley, Walker and Flynn, "that," he said with a grin, "goes for you and you and you."

Having heard of this incident from one who was with the President in Warm Springs on that trip, I checked with Mr. Walker about it and asked him how Louis reacted to this pointed suggestion.

"Well," Walker said, "I remember what my own reactions were very well. I felt that he meant what he said and I never made a recommendation to the President about a member of his Cabinet at any time."

"And Louis?" I asked.

Walker smiled. "Well," he said, "you know Louis. Louis was—" He smiled again. I understood. Louis probably skipped this advice on the theory that he *was* a member of the family so it didn't apply to him. I do not know what part he played in the Cabinet selections, if any, but I do recall his remark about one who didn't have his backing. He'd heard that Harold Ickes wanted to be Commissioner of Indian Affairs, and when FDR told him he had picked Ickes to be a member of his Cabinet, Louis dragged fiercely on his Sweet Caporal for a moment, then snorted, "Well! That's the first break the Indians have had in a hundred years!"

A few days before the inauguration, Farley, Walker, Flynn and Louis went to Washington to complete some inaugural plans. They took a drawing room and as soon as they were settled Louis hunched up in a corner, drew his feet up almost to his chin, and closed his eyes. The rest of them chatted for some time, now and then glancing at Louis to see if he was really asleep or just resting his eyes. When they addressed some remarks to him with no response, they assumed he was asleep and continued the conversation without him.

After a time Farley said he believed he'd walk back to the club car. Flynn followed Farley. The door had no sooner closed when Louis sat up with a jerk, swung his feet to the floor, opened his eyes, and jabbed his finger in the surprised Walker's chest.

"Walker," he said, "what do you want out of this?" meaning of course the Roosevelt administration.

As soon as he could recover from his surprise, Walker told him truthfully that he wanted nothing whatever. He had liked Roosevelt ever since he met him for the first time in 1920 when FDR visited Montana, Walker's home state, as a candidate for Vice-President.

"I have watched and admired him," Walker said. "He stands for the things that I believe in. That is the only reason I have done what I could for his election. It is reward enough to see him in the White House. I don't want a job of any kind."

Louis regarded him steadily for a moment, then grinned. "Walker," he said, "I'm going to pay you a compliment. I believe you." "And you know," Louis said, telling of this incident, though naturally not stressing that "fake nap" too much, "he's one of the very, very few guys I could say that to if I'd asked them a similar question and they had answered as he did."

This business of Louis' pretending to be asleep was an old trick with him. All his associates knew that he was not well, and often when they gathered for a meeting and Louis would sit down and lean back in his chair and close his eyes in an attitude of great weariness, they hesitated to disturb him and went on with the discussion, leaving him to rest. He'd wait until the meeting went

on long enough for him to get the "pitch," then he'd come surprisingly alive and take an alert part in the discussions.

"Darn his little hide," one of them said. "I wouldn't put it
past him to pull a fake heart attack, if he thought he could get the
best of us."

I don't think the little boss would have gone that far, though
there is no doubt that he used every legitimate trick to gain an
advantage over those he called the "professional politicians,"
whom he never quite trusted. He didn't think they were too honest
and once he caused a rash of editorial comment when he said so
in public. The occasion was an address which he delivered to the
students of the Columbia University School of Journalism, not
long after the 1932 election. When one of the students asked him
which field had more promise for the young generation, politics or
journalism, he said:

"You can't adopt politics as a profession and remain honest.
If you are going to make your living out of politics you can't do it
honestly. If you are dishonest in journalism, of course, you won't
succeed either."

When this story appeared in the papers somebody naturally
asked him how *he* expected to be in politics and stay honest. He
looked at the questioner in surprise. "I'm not in politics," he said.
"I'm just the handy man for Franklin Roosevelt."

Those who knew him best smiled at this "handy man" title, especially Mrs. Roosevelt. "This little man was really the biggest man
from the point of view of imagination and determination I have
ever known," she once said. "His body was weak but his mind
never stopped working for a second. He made few personal friends
and he judged most of those by their loyalty to 'The Boss' as he
often called my husband.

"He seemed to have a sixth sense," she said. "Often when I
was starting on a trip he'd take a map and point out the places I
planned to visit, and say, 'Now in this town you will find the sentiment is thus and so, or in that county you will find that the people
think a certain way on a certain subject.' He sensed the feelings
of the people better than anyone I have ever known. He had a

particular ability for analyzing people both individually and in groups, even when he didn't come in contact with them. I think it was due to his many years of newspaper training.

"He was extraordinarily wise. He was also kindly and genial, but a merciless critic of people for whom he felt any sense of responsibility. At the same time he was extraordinarily sympathetic to any real need or helplessness."

FDR used this merciless side of Louis, now and then, when he had to fire somebody in the official family. FDR hated to hurt people, especially if he had to see them suffer, and squirmed and stalled when he had to let somebody go. If, however, this same somebody was going because he had not been loyal, Louis Howe had no such qualms and took delight in delivering the unpleasant news personally. He had this task delegated to him more than once.

In spite of the talk that buzzed around headquarters in New York after election about "what Louis would do in the White House" and the rumor that FDR would make him top secretary, we could not see him in that role. We knew what Presidential secretaries had to do or thought we did: sit at a big mahogany desk, all dressed up, shaking important hands, pushing buttons and acting as a sort of ambassadorial liaison man between the President and the rest of the world. We laughed when we compared Louis' corner rathole with the exotic quarters we heard Presidential secretaries occupied in the White House. And Louis Howe a "front man" after all his years of being the "behind-the-scenes man"? Many said he wouldn't even take the job, but would demand something where he would still be inconspicuous. They were wrong, of course, for FDR wanted him to have the top secretarial job and what Franklin wanted, Louis wanted. "Louis can do that job and still work behind the scenes being the mysterious figure that he loves," FDR said with a grin. Funny thing, though, FDR took it so much for granted that Louis knew he was going to Washington as the head man that, while he talked of it to others, he forgot to mention it to Louis until it was almost time for the inauguration!

A few days before Louis left for the inauguration he was talking to Walter Trumbull, an old newspaper friend, about the terrible conditions in the country and the problems that faced Franklin in Washington. "I don't care what else Franklin says in his inaugural address," he told Trumbull, "as long as he tells the people that the only thing they have to fear is fear."

Finally, on that cold March day as Franklin Roosevelt stood high above the vast throng at the Capitol Building, there in a frock coat, striped trousers and high silk hat that almost swallowed his head was the little boss himself. With a flower in his buttonhole! It was a raw and bitter day but Louis Howe didn't mind at all. He sat there, hunched down in his seat in the official stand, his coat collar turned up about his ears, his eyes glued to the face of the man with whom he had come so far since another bitter winter in Albany twenty-two years ago. And you could almost see his slight form swell with pride as Roosevelt spoke the words that cheered and thrilled a weary nation:

"The only thing we have to fear is fear itself!"

13

The White House

WHEN those energetic Roosevelts spilled into the White House with children, grandchildren, dogs and visitors, and the office wing was overrun with the exuberant secretarial staff, old-timers thought a cyclone had struck and lit out for the storm cellars.

President Hoover, always a taciturn man, had little to say to those who worked around him and the staff took its cue from him, so that the place always wore an air of dignified, almost funereal calm. All this changed in the twinkling of an eye when the Roosevelt forces moved in. Pat McKenna, the grand old Irishman who had been the receptionist in the office wing for many years, used to shake his hoary head as we flashed by, but reserved comment until one day, after we'd been there for several months and had gotten to know Pat well, and favorably, I said to him, "Pat, tell me the truth now, what did you really think of us when we first came in here?"

"To tell ye the truth," Pat said in his rich Irish brogue, with just a suggestion of a twinkle in his eye, "I thought ye wuz crazy and I still think so!"

Pat finally accepted us completely and remained our good and indulgent friend until he passed away a few years later, but I have my doubts that some of the other old-timers ever did. There was Mr. Webster, the elderly Administrative Officer at the White

House, whose duty it was to administer the oath of office to the new people. On the day he came to Louis' office to swear us in, Huey Long had been cutting some particularly high didos on Capitol Hill (Huey was already well on his way off the Roosevelt bandwagon upon which he had climbed when it seemed expedient, for he never could play second fiddle, even to the President of the United States). As we swore to "support and defend the constitution of the United States against all enemies foreign and domestic," somebody suddenly thought of Huey and added—"and Huey Long." Mr. Webster almost dropped the Bible, and there was a loud snort from Louis' direction. Later we caught it.

"You brats have got to cut out the shenanigans," Louis growled. "You are not at 331 Madison Avenue now. You are at 1600 Pennsylvania Avenue—the White House! We must have a little dignity in this setup. Besides you might have caused that old gentleman to have a stroke."

Mr. Webster survived, however, and passed away some two years later from natural causes. Frank Sanderson, who succeeded him, a great jokester himself and one of the most lovable persons in Washington, would have been fully equal to the occasion.

It was Sanderson who told us that if we wanted to get the lowdown on who was who among the daily visitors, we should keep our ears open around the front door of the lobby where one of the Negro messengers liked to hover.

"Only yesterday," Sandy said, "when Mr. George Summerlin, Chief of Protocol of the State Department, came in, someone asked the messenger who he was.

" 'Him?' said the messenger importantly. 'Don't you know *him?* Why dat's Mr. Sumberland from over at the State Compartment. He's de Chief Portico!' "

We didn't have to ask about the callers, however, as each day a list of the President's visitors was posted in the White House Press Room and passed around to the various offices. This daily calling list, flippantly referred to as "the menu," was always eagerly scanned and, when some interesting visitor was due, we found many reasons to go through the lobby at the exact moment the distinguished personage arrived. Louis muttered about this now and then, but let us get away with it if we didn't overdo it.

Among those early distinguished visitors were two as dissimilar as you could possibly imagine. They did not come through the lobby, however, but were received at the main house, where all important heads of state are received. One was Ramsay MacDonald, Prime Minister of Great Britain, who was met at the station by Louis, representing the President. The Prime Minister, an impressive figure with a thatch of white hair blowing in the breeze, was accompanied by his daughter, Ishbel, and she and Louis struck up a quick friendship on the way from the station. He gave her much attention during her visit and delighted in showing her around the grounds and through the offices. "That's one good-looking girl with brains," he said, when we teased him about being so attentive to this visitor from foreign shores. When Ishbel went back to England she and Louis exchanged lively letters, and when Hartley went abroad that summer Louis wrote her, "My son has a cosmic urge to study sociological conditions and other things in which I know you are interested. I want him to meet some of the worthwhile leaders of thought, as he is interested in taking up literary work as a career (to my intense disgust)."

Once Louis promised to send her full details for canning salmon. "It must be terrible," he wrote, "to live in a country where the supply is so plentiful that people think of sending you nothing but a fish." Kiddingly, he wrote her that he was working hard on a reply to one of her communications, but had not finished it to his liking. "But when it arrives," he assured her solemnly, "it will be a real masterpiece and if you will save the manuscript your grandchildren will doubtless be able to dispose of it for many thousands of pounds." They shared a love for detective stories and often he signed his letters to her: "Yours for bigger and better, brighter and more interesting crimes. Louis McH. Howe."

The Ras Desta Demtu, son-in-law of Haile Selassie, Emperor

of Ethiopia, and, in his own right, the Governor of Sidamo Province, was the other State visitor in the spring of 1933. Louis let us go out to see this stranger from the dark continent as he swept up impressively in the big official limousine sent to meet him. The President, Mrs. Roosevelt, and officials of the State Department stood on the portico as he stepped from the car, a little man with a huge lion's tail waving from his turban-like headgear, his impressive uniform finished off with what looked exactly like the wrapped leggings worn by the doughboys in World War I. Since His Excellency was a bit on the bandy-legged side he was not, to say the least, an impressive figure.

A situation arose during the visit of the Ras that threw the protocol division of the State Department into confusion. An elaborate luncheon had been planned in his honor, but when the experts made a recheck of the customs of his country they found that his visit coincided with one of their most rigid fast days. The visitor could eat no meat, eggs, butter, and none of their by-products. Finally, when they boiled it down, and found that the royal visitor might have to dine on a luncheon of pickles, they called off the affair! A situation like this always tickled Louis Howe's risibilities and he passed the story around for days.

Louis, as Secretary to the President, was installed in a corner office with pale green walls and massive furniture, much too big for him, and Steve Early and Marvin McIntyre were installed in no less impressive offices, though their titles were a little different. They were Assistant Secretaries to the President. There was not much difference in Louis' salary and theirs, but making Louis chief secretary was one way the President could honor him for his long and faithful service, and Steve and Mac understood. Besides, when official callers started coming, the President knew he could not see them all and that they would feel better if they could talk to one who was designated as "top secretary," the man closest to the Presidential ear. And Louis certainly was that.

The President insisted that Louis live in the White House, and he was given the big Lincoln bedroom with its famous Lincoln bed, a connecting dressing room and private bath. When Louis looked at the big room and the big bed and compared it with his small frame, he laughed.

"Put up a bed in that little room in there," he said, indicating the dressing room, which was as big as a good-sized bedroom in a modern apartment, "so I won't rattle around like a pea in a pod." So he slept in the little corner room, which faced out on the White House front lawn and the green beauty of Lafayette Park, and used the big room as a study. Soon it began to look like any other room he ever occupied, newspapers stacked on chairs and tables, discarded envelopes and Sweet Caps all around. The servants at the White House were pained, as they surveyed this mess, but didn't dare touch anything until he said so. The big room is now used by the Presidential family as a sitting room, newly decorated during the rebuilding of the White House, and is full of dignity and charm, while the little bedroom where Louis used to curl up in a knot, amidst a shambles of papers and other odd items, is now decorated in soft colors with silken draperies, a far cry from the rough days of Louis' occupancy.

Somebody asked Louis why he didn't choose the bedroom where Andrew Jackson slept, since he and Andy were both pretty forthright characters with a lot in common.

"Mein Gawd, no!" he cried. "I'm afraid I'd see the ghost of old Andy stalking around in there at night. He might even run his horses over my bed in his ghostly battle of New Orleans and ruin my sleep."

He didn't seem to fear "Abe's ghost," or else felt that it had been properly laid before he got there.

In organizing the office force Louis placed each member of his gang where he thought we could be most useful to Franklin—and to him. His gang at this time consisted of Margaret Durand; Isabelle Walmsley, a sparkling girl with an infectious laugh who had gone to work for Miss Durand during the campaign; Lucile Flanagan, a charming and gracious woman who also had joined the Howe forces in 1932; Miss Hachmeister, Katherine C. Blackburn and myself. He also brought in Fred Pryor, an old friend from Navy days, a dignified colored man who was his special clerk and messenger.

After the President's inaugural address mail rolled into the White House in a tidal wave, and ever afterwards, when FDR took to the air and said, "My friends,"—men, women and children automatically reached for their pencils to tell their friend in Washington about their troubles. Folks who counted the daily run of letters found that FDR received more mail in his first six months in the White House than had Mr. Hoover in four years. This vast volume of mail was one of Louis' biggest headaches. He often said his favorite nightmare was one in which he was in an airplane, high up, so that the whole map of the United States was spread out beneath him, looking as it does in the school geography. "It always appears to be covered with a white blanket flowing toward one point," he said. "As the plane descends I find to my horror that the white blanket consists of letters—letters flowing from every part of the country—and their ultimate destination is the White House."

More than 6,500 letters came in daily and Louis figured out that one man with a trained eye might skim over 2,880 letters (allowing half a minute to each letter) in a twenty-four-hour period without time out for anything else, and by then there'd be a new batch of 6,500 to read. The very idea appalled Louis who didn't like to read any letter more than a paragraph long.

He sent for Rudolph Forster, Executive Clerk at the White House, who had been there since President McKinley's administration, and, with his fine mind and vast store of knowledge, was the White House's own "Ask Mr. Foster Service" with a slight difference in the spelling of the name. Louis sat down with him, and they labored long and hard over drafts of replies to be used in answering the mail not taken care of by the President or his three secretaries. Louis insisted the letter have the "Roosevelt touch," in contrast to the "Yours received and contents noted" type of reply previously used. These drafts were then sent to Charles Wagner, who presided over a staff room of some twenty-five or thirty attractive, intelligent girls, where the routine mail was answered. The incoming letters, with drafted replies "to match," funneled across my desk and that of Lucile Flanagan and it was our job to watch for any we didn't think would meet with Louis' O. K. One day he caught a draft that he didn't think quite "matched" the incoming letter. He shot it back, with the penciled notation: "This is a lousy answer." Wagner, a gentleman of great dignity, who had been at the White House since the days of William Howard Taft, was considerably upset, until we assured him that it didn't mean anything—that this was merely Louis' routine way of asking that a new draft be prepared.

Many people, in doubt about how to address the President of the United States, just saluted him in a simple, natural way, starting their letters with "Dear Mr. Roosevelt" or "Dear Friend" (incidentally, it's all right to say simply, "Dear Mr. President"). Some of the correspondents, however, gave their salutations an individual twist, and these amused Louis so much that now and then he'd have us make up a list of these for the President. This is one list, just as it was typed and sent to the President's office:

SALUTATIONS TO THE PRESIDENT

Our dear Leader:

Most honorable President of these United States of America:

Dear Buddy:

To our dear President—the greatest man in the world:

To Honorable Franklin Delano Roosevelt—President by the Grace of God and by a popular vote of the people of the United States of America:

Dear kind Friend of the People:

President of these United States—Honor, dear sir:

Our revered President, the most godlike ruler in the history of civilization:

Mr. Roosevelt, President and wife of this great nation:

My dear friend F. D. Roosevelt:

Our Darling Ruler:

Dear Humanitarian Friend of the People:

Your most Noble Majesty:

Much esteemed magistrate:

Dear Father of our Land:

Franklin Dillinger Roosevelt:

Highly esteemed Sir:

To the Honorable President and greatest living statesman:

To the best President there ever was:

My dear Noble Roosevelt:

Dear *Man:*

Your Highness, please:

Mine dearest President of the U. S. A.:

Sublime Prince of the Royal Secret:

Kind Uncle U. S.:

Your Honor, Mr. President of these United States:

My Pal:

Now and then we would cull excerpts from those letters which were particularly interesting and amusing, and send them to the President. Since people wrote to him about every subject under the sun it was only natural that now and then some pretty funny things crept in. This list was strictly for laughs:

"I am a widow. My husband deserated me!"

"We are all rotting for you one hundred percent."

"I am not an 'Economic royalist' but I wish to God I was!"

"I am dissable to work because of a doctor's examination."

"This will never reach you, as I know nobody can get a *litter* passed your secy's."

"I am under the Home Owners Loan Corp. I fell out of work and they closed on me."

"I was employed by the W. P. A. upon a circular saw."

"My husband is an unable war veteran. His composition was cut
off in 1934."

"I meant to wait to ask for your autograph till you left the White
House, but I'm afraid now you never will."

(Gentleman applying for a job): "I am hard to unsettle tem-
permentally. Perhaps this is largely because my work has
always included a lot of women handling."

"John L. Lewis is a snake from the first water."

"I am in the rears on my rent, but I can't help it."

"They say I am a drunken sod, but it is a lie!"

"My wife is a handicap and has been for 27 years."

(Woman writing just before election): "I pray every night that
you will get the chair."

"I'm asking about the old age pinching."

"I am a poor woman with good intentions. It is good to be good,
but I rather have an eye for an eye and a tooth for a tooth."

"I know that you are one of them God firing men."

"I am a lady and I have intended for a long time to write and
give myself up for some benefit."

The President enjoyed these little personal touches immensely,
and never failed to say that he only wished he had time to read
and answer every single letter himself.

On March 9, when the President called Congress into special
session to pass the Emergency Banking Act, when he closed the
banks and made other drastic moves to meet the crisis of the times,
the people, in the main, went along with him, but a few fright-
ened souls ran to Louis Howe. This was going too far, they yelped.
They didn't get far with Louis.

"Oh hell," he'd say, "any country that has for its theme song
'Who's Afraid of the Big Bad Wolf' isn't going to be too scared
by what Franklin is trying to do."

Louis told a caller an interesting story about how the President made his speech on the banking crisis (which brought an avalanche of letters) in such simple terms that any layman could understand it, whether he knew anything about economics.

"Workmen were busy tearing down the scaffolding on the South grounds of the White House after the inauguration," Louis said, "when a caller dropped in to see Franklin. The visitor brought up the subject of the banking speech. 'How,' he asked, 'did you manage to boil it down to such simple terms?'

"Franklin swung around in his chair," Louis continued, "and pointed to a workman outside who was tearing down some stands. 'See that man?' he said. 'He was out there the day I started working on my speech about the banking crisis. I decided I'd try to make a speech that the workman could understand. So you see,' he smiled, 'I really made the speech to him.'"

The office occupied by Lucile Flanagan and myself—this was before the offices were rebuilt in 1934—had big double glass doors that opened out on the colonnade that led to the White House proper. Along this walk the President came to work every morning, sailing along in his little chair, with Gus Gennerich pushing him, two or three Secret Service men fore and aft, with the head usher at the White House carrying a basket of papers the President had been working on in his bedroom. We never hit a lick until he had rounded the corner and was out of sight!

The President was always informal and gay with us, but we never quite overcame our awe of the Presidency. And though Louis had a healthy respect for the office of President, it was only natural that Franklin was just Franklin to him whether in Hyde Park, Albany or Washington. One day I suddenly came upon the President sitting in a chair on the little runway outside his office, while his valet gave him a vigorous shampoo. "Would you like a shampoo?" FDR called gaily, "I'll have McDuffie give you one as soon as he's through with me." I replied that I'd just had one, then rushed in to Louis.

"The President is out there," I said excitedly, "and just imagine, his valet is giving him a shampoo!" Louis looked up and smiled drily. "Oh yes," he said, "Franklin's hair gets dirty just like any-body's and when it does he has it washed." I felt a little silly.

Louis had his own sly way of teasing us, or, as he would have said, "taking us down a notch or two." One day, in the middle of some instructions about the day's work, he suddenly looked up and reminded me of the title he had once conferred on me as "official investigator of all new speakeasies." He asked me how many I had investigated in Washington. Some friends in Kentucky had just conferred on me several bottles of excellent Kentucky bourbon, so I told him I had not investigated any as I was running one of my own. He questioned me sharply about whether I had "the required protection" and so on and gave me quite a time of it, enjoying himself thoroughly.

I always suspected him of telling the President such office jokes and gossip, and this suspicion was well justified one evening in the White House. Marguerite "Missy" LeHand gave a little party for the girls who had come down from New York with Mr. Roose-velt and Louis. She asked us to come to the White House, for she, like Louis, lived in the White House and had a small, attrac-tive apartment on the third floor, so we expected the party to be there. However, when we arrived, the usher met us and escorted us to the second floor and down the hall toward the President's study. Missy had asked us all to wear evening clothes and now we understood! The usher opened the door and there was the President of the United States, sitting behind his big desk, mixing cocktails! He looked up with a broad grin as I walked over to speak to him.

"I hear you're an authority on liquor," he said. "Tell me—what's wrong with this rye?" I smelled it gingerly. "Well," I said, "the main thing wrong with it is that it isn't bourbon." He laughed, then reached back behind him and produced a bottle of bourbon, mixed me a highball, and when he handed it to me, I promptly spilled some.

"Now look, Kentucky," he teased, "I'm sure you have handled a highball before and I know you aren't nervous."

"Yes, I have, I am," I blurted, "but frankly, Sir, I never thought

I'd have one mixed by the President of the United States, turned bartender. It's a little upsetting." He put me at ease by whispering behind his hand that he knew the difference between good bourbon and rye, but because he had a slight sniffle Dr. McIntire had that day poked so much vile stuff up his nose he couldn't even smell!

Later, we all had dinner at the big round table in the family dining room. Lucile Flanagan, who was the bride of the party, having just been married to Ed Lewis of the well-known Lewis and Conger store in New York, had the privilege of sitting at the President's right, and Missy, acting as hostess as Mrs. Roosevelt was away, let the rest of us take turns sitting on his left. "He wants to talk to you about Kentucky," Missy whispered when it was my turn. It was then that I got an insight into FDR's remarkable memory, as well as his knowledge of my native state. He told me his father had once been president of a railroad "with Kentucky connections" (later I learned that it was the old Louisville, New Albany and Chicago road). Also, he said, his father had held wide coal interests and once took him with him to the Eastern Kentucky coal fields "long before you were born." He remembered the names of those coal counties and their county seats and reeled them off rapidly: Pikeville, Hazard, Harlan, Pineville, as I sat entranced.

Then he launched into a discussion of the political situation in my state, which was even more fascinating. This was the year that Kentucky's popular Governor A. B. "Happy" Chandler decided to run for the United States Senate against the beloved Alben W. Barkley, then Majority Leader of the Senate, and upon whom the President leaned heavily to push his legislation through on Capitol Hill. "Happy" had just been to Washington to see the President, presumably to get his blessing, and the folk down in Kentucky were consumed with curiosity about what actually took place at that meeting. Much to my surprise the President talked quite freely and told me in great detail what he said to "Happy" and what "Happy" said to him!

Finally I could not resist saying, "Mr. President, I'll bet if I went down and stood on the corner of Fourth and Walnut in Louisville, and told what you are telling me now, I'd draw the biggest crowd they ever had on that corner." (Fourth and Walnut is the site of the famous Seelbach Hotel. State Democratic Headquarters have been located in the hotel for years, and it's a political landmark.)

The President laughed heartily. "I'll bet you could," he said. "I'll just bet you could!"

However, not once did he ask me not to mention what he had told me and I didn't. I suppose he thought I had sense enough not to, or he would not have told me in the first place.

As everybody now knows, FDR took Barkley's side in that race, and even went down to the state to make speeches for him. Barkley won the nomination handily and was elected in November. "Happy" later made the Senate, but by another route.

A spot just outside our office door was the favorite resting place of Major, Mrs. Roosevelt's big police dog and, since we were scared to death of him, we were afraid to go out the door and were prisoners as he lay there basking in the sun. We appealed to Louis to do something about it. "Aw, go on and step over him," he said. "He won't bite you. He might get hydrophobia." But it turned out that we were scared with good reason.

One Saturday night Mrs. Roosevelt gave the first of her famous "Gridiron Widows" parties for the newspaperwomen and wives of newspapermen, who were not allowed to go to the famous Gridiron dinners held annually in Washington, which were strictly stag affairs. This left the newspaper gals at loose ends that night, hence Mrs. Roosevelt's parties, which became almost as well known, locally, as the dinner itself. She always had an interesting program, with amusing skits and masquerades. Louis often helped Mrs. Roosevelt plan these affairs, wrote skits and helped the girls with makeup problems. Once he made Mrs. Roosevelt up as an old apple woman, and did such a good job that not a soul had the slightest idea who she was!

On this particular Saturday night a group of us were attending another party at the Mayflower Hotel and some of the "widows" came to it after Mrs. Roosevelt's party was over. Mary Eben and Louise Hachmeister arrived all agog.

"Guess what happened at Mrs. R's party," Mary Eben said. "Major bit Hattie Caraway!"

"Major who?" shrieked a girl, who hadn't heard of the White House dog and thought some enthusiastic army major had so far forgotten himself as to take a bite out of Mrs. Hattie Caraway, the dignified lady Senator from Arkansas. Shortly after that Mrs. Roosevelt banished Major to Hyde Park, not only because of the Caraway incident but because, in one bite, he had taken the entire seat out of the gardener's pants a few days before!

The Roosevelts had bad luck with all their dogs in those days. Winks, the setter, got in the servants' dining room one morning and ate eleven breakfasts, ham and eggs and all. He survived this, strangely enough, and later died from the effects of a dogbite inflicted by a vicious canine through the bars of the high iron fence that surrounds the south grounds of the White House. Just to add to Louis' mail problems, scores of letters came in after the story of Winks' hearty breakfast hit the newspapers, from people who implored that he not be punished for this gustatory aberration.

Louis, cased in as he was in the White House where visitors usually tell you only the news they think you want to hear, soon began to feel the need of his old system of keeping up with what the editors of the country were saying, so he started what he called "The Press Intelligence Bulletin." He put Katherine Blackburn in charge and it immediately became known as "Louis Howe's Daily Bugle" and was watched for eagerly by every high government official in Washington.

Probably because Louis and his father had edited a small-town newspaper he had the greatest faith in it. When the Bronx *Home News* was so much in the public eye during the Lindbergh kidnapping case, he snorted, "Some 'smart' editor will modernize that paper now and it will fail within a year."

He had hundreds of these country newspapers combed over in

the offices of the "Bugle," which were located in the Department of Commerce Building since there wasn't room for them in the White House, and an indexed digest of articles and editorials promptly laid on his desk and the desks of other officials. If an editor out in Podunk, say, didn't like the AAA and said so, the word was passed along; if an editorialist in Kankakee growled that Roosevelt was taking too much power for himself, Louis Howe knew it, and so it went.

During the war this busy department was merged with the Office of War Information, but after the war it became a single agency again, until a Republican Congress came into power in January 1947 and put it out of business. Louis and the President supplemented their "Bugle" information by having friends throughout the country report on conditions in their respective territories. In this way they knew about what the sentiment was on any given subject, in any given section of the country, at any given time. Louis also had us culling excerpts from the letters that came across our desks, and putting a report on his desk from time to time on matters in which he was interested.

In addition, Louis was getting information by some grapevine of his own, knew what was going on in most of the government departments, and fumed and fretted when he heard of a badly organized department. He thought the Federal Emergency Relief Administration, which later became the Works Progress Administration run by Harry Hopkins, was the worst organized of the hastily formed New Deal agencies. "Hopkins has courage, he has vision and all that," he'd say, "but has he the organizing ability to keep this thing from getting out of hand? I doubt it." Next on his list of "worst organized" was the National Recovery Administration (NRA) run by General Hugh Johnson. "I'll bet you," he jibed one day at General Johnson, "that you have at least six departments under you that you don't know a damn thing about—who the heads are, what they do, and so on." General Johnson promptly took the bet but he should have known better. Louis won it, for the General found out that there were ten!

Of the Agricultural Adjustment Act administered by Henry A. Wallace, Secretary of Agriculture, his remarks were brief. "I have no comment to make on that," he said. "Wallace is crazy but he gets his way."

Many of the smart dopesters professed to believe that in working out these various New Deal reforms the President did not have the wholehearted backing of Louis Howe, that Louis went along with them for political reasons only, but that at heart he was not really a liberal. Louis just didn't talk. He was certainly no breast-beating liberal, but somehow he always seemed to be on the side of liberal causes, as witness, his admiration for Governor Hughes in his fight at Albany, his enlistment with FDR and his band of insurgents against Tammany in the Sheehan battle, his siding with the workers in the Navy Yards in their ruckuses with "the high brass," and so on. Whether all this was flaming liberalism in Louis' heart or his delight in seeing the little dog lick the big dog in a fight it would be hard to say, for Louis himself was so contradictory at times that if Freud had lived with him from the cradle to the grave he probably would have come up with the wrong answer about him. He always took the greatest delight in throwing off the track people who tried to analyze him. One time a caller, who apparently was attempting to get on his good side for some favor, went on and on about what a great man he believed Louis to be, how he knew he was the power behind the throne, the "Warwick," the "kingmaker," and so on. Suddenly Louis cut him off in the middle of a sentence.

"Oh hell," he said, "it's no trick to make a President. Give me a man who stays reasonably sober, shaves and wears a clean shirt every day and I can make him President." Needless to say the caller was horrified and we, eavesdropping in the outer office, were too, until the caller had gone and we found Louis hunched over his desk rocking back and forth with fiendish laughter.

As for the liberal tag, Louis Howe probably would have been perfectly content if you had labeled him the same kind of liberal that Franklin was. And Roosevelt's definition of a liberal was perhaps best expressed in a speech he made during the closing days of the 1932 campaign. "Civilization is a tree," he said, "which as it grows continually produces rot and deadwood. The radicals say: Cut it down! The conservatives say: Don't touch it! The liberals say: Compromise! Let's act so that we lose neither the old trunk nor the new branches!"

But Louis didn't want any kind of label, liberal or conservative. "I'm just the little guy nearest Franklin," he'd say. "The last thing in the world I want anybody to think is that I sit at his right hand and direct policies. I love to argue with him though," he'd say with a grin. "When he gets an idea I try to tear it apart. I'm the devil's own advocate, presenting every possible objection, so that if he finally decides he is right, he comes to a decision after defending it against every complaint I can make."

By June of 1933 this "little guy nearest Franklin" was telling the country about some of Franklin's policies, in an article in *The American Magazine,* called "Balanced Government, The Next Step":

> I see two great problems confronting the Administration; problems which must be met. First is the necessity of a "balanced government" and second, the further development of the Democratic party as the liberal party of the nation. What is a "balanced government" as applied to these United States? . . . In a general way a balanced government means a government of equal opportunity for everybody. A government that will act as a sort of referee and see that no foul tactics are used by those in the lead to hold back or oppress others. A government that will give full scope for natural ability and willingness to work but which will prevent the abuse of acquired or inherited power. . . . Another way in which a government, such as ours, should be balanced lies in the equal sharing in the control of the government of the three great general divisions in our modern social structure: Agriculture, Industry and what, largely, is called Finance. In such balance these forces would go forward side by side, none preying on or restricting the others. . . .
>
> It is the task of our present Administration to bring these three dominant groups into harmony.
>
> I do not profess to express the views of the President or his

conclusions, but my long association with him emboldens me to express the belief that of the two ways to bring the weak to an equality with the strong—the tearing down of the strong until they are as weak as the weakest, and the building up of the weak until they are as strong as the strongest—he will adopt the latter method.

Less than a year later, when many of the Roosevelt reforms were in the making, Louis was taking note of their progress in an article called "Life More Abundant," which he wrote for *Cosmopolitan Magazine* in April 1934:

> Gradually the crushing fear of black ruin, of anarchy, of the total destruction of all things that we have held certain in our lives, which terrified the hearts and souls of us all in those dark days of March 1933 has lifted. . . . there is growing daily a better understanding of President Roosevelt's declaration that the time has arrived to build a new kind of government founded on the doctrine of the good neighbor and not on the old cruel doctrine of "rugged individualism" and that not only had it arrived but the job was going to be done.

He went on to say that the "Square Deal," a slogan popular some years ago, was "primarily aimed at giving the citizen a chance," if he was wise enough and strong enough to accumulate at least enough material wealth to keep him a jump ahead of the sheriff, "while 'the ultimate aim of the New Deal' is the recognition that those who are regulated and governed in the interests of the common good are entitled to something far more than the mere right to struggle for existence."

He then listed some of the reforms Roosevelt was trying to put into effect—unemployment insurance, shorter working hours, a fair price for the farmer's product, regulation of fly-by-night brokers, slum clearance, and so on. He pointed out that when the difference between the two slogans was understood, it would be clearer what the Administration was aiming at and would explain the President's constant use of such phrases as "the more abundant life."

"To the President more than any man I have ever known,"

he said, "nations and governments are not things of importance, in themselves, except as the practical working out of ways in which human beings can achieve happiness and contentment as individual human beings. It is the individual which interests the President, not the machinery he has created."

Even if Louis didn't sit at Franklin's right hand and direct policies, the two of them worked closely together at all times and even had codes worked out to send each other when they were apart and had to telegraph or cable. One message caused a good laugh around Louis' office.

It was in February 1933, before we went to Washington, while FDR was on a cruise on Vincent Astor's yacht. He had been trying to persuade Senator Carter Glass of Virginia to be his Secretary of the Treasury and thought he had him sold before he sailed. However, Glass finally declined, partly because of ill health and partly, it is said, because he did not see eye to eye with Roosevelt on the gold question. His decision not to take the job was relayed to FDR at sea. Then Louis and Raymond Moley, who were working quite amicably together at this time, sat down to cudgel their brains for new names to submit to FDR for Secretary of the Treasury. They finally settled on William Woodin, the mild-mannered New York millionaire, whom Bill Lyons had almost thrown out of the Biltmore Hotel. Woodin was a liberal, an early supporter and would not offend the Wall Street crowd, but how to get the word to FDR without the news leaking out? At that time money was being contributed by the school children of the country, in a campaign started by the New York *Daily News,* to build a swimming pool for FDR in the White House. Louis had a sudden idea: "Prefer wooden to glass roof over swimming pool," he cabled FDR, who mulled over the message for quite awhile, then roared with laughter when its import sank in.

This brings to mind a little incident which illustrates how Louis' staff felt about how closely these two exchanged ideas.

Nicky Tregor, the sculptor, had come in to do a bust of the President, and when he saw Louis Howe he immediately expressed the wish to "do" him. Louis' face was really a natural for sculpture, with all the character lines, but Louis snorted that he was too busy for such foolishness. Finally he consented, provided Mr. Tregor would let him pose as he worked so that he would lose no time. This arrangement was worked out and the head begun, but Louis delayed and stalled while his half-finished head sat on the floor in Miss Durand's office, a rather macabre-looking object, as Mr. Tregor went ahead with his work on the President.

One day Nicky dashed breathlessly into the office, and rushing over to Louis' "head" began to grab handfuls of the soft clay.

"Hey!" Miss Durand said, "what are you doing? Let the little boss's head alone."

"But I need more clay immediately," Nicky pleaded, "and I have no time to go to the studio to get some. The President of the United States is waiting."

"Oh well," she shrugged, "go ahead. After all, it isn't the first time something has been transferred from the little boss's head to the big boss's. And of course," she twinkled, "vice versa."

Nicky dashed off with the clay, leaving the head looking more gruesome than ever. It was a big disappointment to us that Louis came down with an illness not long after that, and the head never was finished.

In addition to helping the President thrash out the various knotty problems that came up each day behind the scenes, Louis met many of the delegations that came to see the President.

One of these delegations almost gave us heart failure. The famous Scottsboro Case was making headlines throughout the country. Down in Alabama a Negro man, said to be the ringleader of nine Negroes charged with attacking two young white women on a freight train, was sentenced to be electrocuted. Later the sentence was voided, a new trial ordered and the trials of the other defendants in the case postponed until local feelings calmed down. This case came to be a famous *cause célèbre* and later many worthy organizations joined the fight to secure justice for the Negroes; but at this time it seemed that only the violent partisans of the accused men were active, and a huge crowd of them swarmed into Washington to demand that the President do something, and do it now.

All day long they marched around the White House carrying placards, and the number of original marchers was swelled by local sympathizers until there was an army of them. They demanded to see the President. It was a gray, dark day with bursts of rain and it was the first time we had seen mob hysteria. "The Scottsboro boys must not die! The Scottsboro boys must not die!" they shouted over and over as they circled the White House grounds, and we expected them to charge the doors at any moment.

The President and Louis were in close conference while this was going on, and finally Louis sent word that he would see some of them if they would select a delegation—he could not see them all.

Rabbit, Lucile, Isabelle and I huddled together in the outer office as this angry-looking mob filed sullenly into Louis' office, wet, disheveled, and tough-looking. They massed around the room, some in greasy sweat shirts, some in high boots, all with grim, menacing faces.

Chief Moran of the Secret Service stood in our office leaning nonchalantly against the door. "Chief," we said, "are you going to stand there and not do a thing? Suppose the little boss makes that crowd angry. They could close in on him before anybody could get here." The Chief shifted his gaze from us to a particularly rough-looking character inside, leaning against the mantel in Louis' office, chewing a wad of tobacco. He had on checked shirt, muddy boots and his hair was matted with the rain.

"See that fellow?" the Chief asked.

"Yes," we replied, "he is the worst-looking one of the lot."

The Chief smiled. "That's one of my men," he said. "One of my best agents. I have two more in there. They have been marching around the White House all day with this mob, so you just relax!"

We looked at the Chief with new respect and after that we did not worry about the little boss's safety any more. We knew the Chief would take care of it. And Louis took care of the delegation, assuring them of the President's deep interest, but that he could do nothing at this stage, and their scowls were less formidable when they went away. Later, Chief Moran presented Louis with a gold-plated badge and a pistol and said jokingly, "You can defend yourself from now on, Louis." The little boss was always very proud of these and flashed them on unsuspecting friends.

The problems of the Secret Service were many in those days, as they are all days for that matter. Once, looking out the door of our office, we saw Bob Clark of the White House detail going along the walk that led to the White House, with a lady in a pink dress. Bob held her tightly by the arm. Suddenly she broke away, struck at him with both fists and started running through the rose garden. Bob was after her like lightning, and half running along with her, half pushing her, he disappeared into the lower hallway of the White House. We rushed to Louis. He advised us not to get excited and to say nothing. The poor woman had come to Washington, he told us, and registered at one of the smart hotels with the intention of jumping out a high window. Then she had a better thought. Why not go over to the White House and jump out a window there and have better coverage in all the newspapers?

Bob was only taking her through the lower hallway of the house and out the east entrance where a car waited, which had been called when she explained her mission. She was taken to a hospital where she received good care until her people came for her.

Another delegation, which came to see the President in May 1933, was taken care of by Louis, who gave them what they afterward described as "a nice fatherly sermon." This was the first national conference of the Association of Unemployed College Alumni, representing more than thirty universities and colleges. They presented a list of demands which included requests for Federal grants to counties and other political subdivisions to be used for education. It was at this point that Louis digressed somewhat from his "fatherly attitude" to tell them very firmly that he felt that relief for the hungry should take precedence over Federal educational grants, important though he considered education to be.

Another point in their program was recognition of Soviet Russia and Louis' attitude was described as "somewhat unreceptive." He could not see, he told them, how recognition of any nation would bring back prosperity to this country. A few months later our government did recognize Soviet Russia. All in all, however, the members of the delegation felt that they had been fairly treated by Louis, even if he disagreed with them on some points. "Mr. Howe reminded us," said one delegate, "that some of the things which we are advocating, such as the public works program and the lowering of tariff barriers, are in accord with the Administration's program."

Louis' staff was present in the President's big oval office on the day he announced the recognition of Soviet Russia; staff members in those days were allowed to attend the President's press conferences and the excitement of it is still vivid in our minds. We stood in the back of the office when newsmen gathered for what we all thought was merely a routine press conference. But when a White House officer quietly stepped to the doors, closed and locked them, we knew that something tremendous was in the wind; this had never before been done. It's a good thing it was, too, for when the conference was over and the doors opened to give all newsmen the chance to get their stories on the wire simultaneously, they charged like a bunch of wild lions, almost knocking us down as we tried to escape from the mad melee that followed this announcement.

Louis did a series on radio interviews that first year with Walter Trumbull, well-known newspaperman, as the interviewer and Louis as the interviewee. These broadcasts were Trumbull's idea. A public-spirited newspaperman, Trumbull decided that it would be a real service to tell a rather bemused public in nonpartisan and nonpolitical broadcasts what these New Deal laws meant to the individual, and how they worked. That meant getting someone who could speak with authority, and Louis Howe, Trumbull knew, was the highest authority short of the President himself.

"Louis Howe always thought that what the country needed," Trumbull once said, "was a big man with plenty of ego—a leader with faith enough in America and in himself, to lead the people out of the Valley of the Jitters. Louis had no doubt who the man was. Also he had no doubt as to who was best fitted to guard and guide that man. In my opinion," Trumbull continued, "Louis Howe came near to being 'Assistant President of the United States' in those years—1933 and 1934—before his illness cut him out of the scene."

During this period on the air Louis talked on the National Recovery Act, the Federal Home Loan Bank Board, the Civil Works Administration, the Federal Security Act, etc., and he did two broadcasts on one of his favorite subjects, crime. He sent one of his crime broadcasts to the President, who was on a cruise, for his perusal. "Help! Help! Help!" he cried. "This is the damn draft and I have to give it to the press at one o'clock your time. . . . Will you be a good, kind, considerate President and glance it over before you and Joe (Davies) get on high affairs of state so that when I call I can get either a release or the changes you want me to make. Luhowe."

One broadcast was on the advantages of a motor highway connecting North and South America. Roosevelt and Howe visualized this as a project which would open up vast opportunities in the way of employment for thousands, tourist business, and new trade opportunities. There was a typical Howe touch in this broadcast, too. He warned that in Panama they would have to ferry across 12 miles of water to avoid going through the country of the San Blas Indians. "Those natives," he said, "have a marked dislike for strangers either in automobiles or out. Their aversion to visitors is as pointed as their knives and fishing spears."

In the summer of 1933, when the Economic Conference met in London and the President sent a message asking that work on stabilization plans be barred by the conference, Louis and Trumbull did a broadcast to combat criticism that Roosevelt had been the cause of "scuttling the conference."

Louis explained that the President had written the message in longhand aboard the cruiser *Indianapolis,* and that it was prompted by cablegrams from London, relayed to the cruiser, which convinced him that it was time to put the position of this country beyond question.

"It was no new decision," Louis said. "I suppose it has all been forgotten that this whole conference started in 1932 with a meeting of a commission of experts appointed by the governments of Germany, China, France, India, Italy and Japan in addition to the United States; President Hoover had sent Edmund E. Day, Director of Social Science of the Rockefeller Foundation, John H. Williams, Professor of Economics at Harvard University and Norman Davis, acting as general counselor, to this commission.

"The idea," Louis went on, "was to consider the possibilities of a general get-together meeting of all the nations to make common cause to fight against world-wide depression. The committee studied all the elements which contributed to this depression and prepared a report of some thirty-six pages which has been reprinted by the United States Department of Commerce and widely distributed in this country."

Louis' friendship with Ramsay MacDonald suffered a considerable strain when FDR and MacDonald came to the parting of the ways over certain matters on the agenda at the Conference. "Ramsay doesn't understand Franklin," Louis fumed. "He thinks Franklin is saying one thing and doing another." Franklin was rarely "wrong"—he was always "misunderstood." When Congress tangled with FDR they just didn't understand what Franklin was trying to do.

Knowing nothing of salaries paid radio personalities, Louis was horrified when he was offered what seemed to him an incredible sum to do these broadcasts—fifteen minutes on the air, once a week. He was sure it would be unethical to take it. But when he was assured that Senators and Congressmen were getting paid for addresses, and when he realized that the broadcasts would be of genuine value to the public and to Franklin, he agreed to do them.

The first thing Louis did with his earnings was to give his family a trip abroad. Then he bought a new car. Being a little man and fascinated by bigness, he picked a Lincoln convertible almost as long as a freight car, and the radio he bought for it was almost as big as a steamer trunk and was guaranteed to pick up a whisper on the moon. The only place with enough room for it was on the back seat, so that's where it went. But none of Louis' new-found wealth went for clothes. He still looked, rolling along in his fine new Lincoln, somewhat like a candidate for the relief rolls until the President and Mrs. Roosevelt saw that he bought some new raiment.

But Louis was not the only man in a high position whose clothes did not always come up to par. Some people might be horrified to learn that a former King of England came to see President Roosevelt one day wearing a hat that looked as though the cat had buried it, then scratched it up again. It was in the summertime, about five years after Edward's and Wally's world-shaking marriage. Since Edward was still a romantic figure wherever he went, the girls found chores to take them through the lobby at the time he was due. He came in, a slight, boyish, almost shy figure, and walked quickly up to the desk of Bill Simmons, the big, handsome, ex-Secret Service man from Virginia who had succeeded Pat McKenna as receptionist. Sam Jackson, the courteous colored man who was Mr. Simmons' assistant, sprang forward and took the Duke's hat, which he placed carefully on the rack that holds the visitors' hats and coats while Bill bowed the Duke into the President's office. In a flash the girls surrounded the hat and one, more daring than the rest, took it down from the rack and tried it on. It was an old-fashioned straw sailor, somewhat yellowed, with a high crown and narrow brim, a style that hadn't been seen in this country for several years.

"Why on earth," queried one of the girls in a disillusioned voice, "doesn't the Duke buy himself a new hat?"

"Why, honey chile," Bill Simmons said, "don't be silly. The man is married now and has been for five years. How can he afford a new hat?"

When we suddenly remembered that the Duke's missus had been chosen as one of the ten best-dressed women in the world for several seasons, we understood Bill's thinking.

Louis loved to kid the other secretaries, and they were kept on their toes trying to get the better of him in rebuttal. Once Marguerite LeHand sent him a hasty, penciled memo attached to a letter he had sent for the President to see. "The President," she scribbled "is to taking it up." Louis immediately sent the memo back. "Dear Missy," he said, "apropos of this memorandum would you mind sending a translation for a man without too much education as to the exact meaning of your note that 'the President is *to* taking it up.' I suppose this is some of the highbrow talk you have been hearing from the 'brain trust' lately."

Missy replied promptly. "I asked the President," she said, "to translate my note to you, as you requested. He says the following: 'The President by taking up means this—when the President dies he expects to go up, not down! When that happens he has a very large file which he is taking to Heaven with him. He will spend the next thousand (1000) years going through that file. I hope this answers your question clearly.' "

Nobody was safe from Louis' blasts of wry humor, and he often interjected them into serious matters. Once Mrs. William Brown Meloney, editor of the Sunday Magazine section of the New York *Herald Tribune,* wrote him a letter about a project she thought would interest somebody in the Administration. "At the Bellevue Psychiatry Hospital there is a great opportunity to take care of the men and women who suffer from mental diseases," she wrote. "I should give a great deal to take you through the new Bellevue Hospital. They are doing so much preventive work."

"My dear Mrs. Meloney," Louis replied, "just what is in back of your mind on the Bellevue Psychiatry Hospital? Is it that you hope when you take me through it they will find me an apt subject? It intrigues me." Mrs. Meloney took this in her stride for she and Louis had been friends for a long time. She took a great interest in Hartley and once had him appear on the youth division of the annual *Herald-Tribune* Forum. Louis' friend, Miss Ishbel MacDonald, was on the same forum, broadcasting from England, and Mrs. Franklin D. Roosevelt and many other prominent people interested in the problems of youth were also on the program. Mrs. Meloney also took Hartley to Europe with her one year, with a group of other students. Louis had great respect for her views and judgment, and she felt the same way about him.

Once a certain National Committeewoman in an Eastern state wrote to Mollie Dewson complaining that Harry Hopkins, then head of Federal Works Administration, was filling the jobs in her state with Republicans. Mollie consulted Louis who consulted an infuriated Hopkins, who insisted that the Democratic State Committee there was always inviting complaints and was dissatisfied with everything. Louis sent Hopkins' letter to Mrs. Roosevelt.

"Dear Eleanor," he said, "I have a wild desire to send Hopkins' sniffy letter to Mollie Dewson just for the fun of seeing her explode." Mrs. Roosevelt, who was very fond of Mollie and also liked a joke, advised him to send it on and see what happened. Evidently Mollie didn't explode for she is still around, and this may be her first knowledge that her two old friends conspired against her!

Louis Howe was largely responsible for that interesting innovation, The First Lady's Press Conference. No wife of the President had ever held regular conferences with the press but Mrs. Roosevelt was such a dynamic woman, with such wide interests, that the press felt that her activities would make stimulating reading. The suggestion was made to her that she hold press conferences with women reporters. She took the matter up with Louis and he readily agreed she should hold them and at regular intervals. Also, he gave her some minute pointers on what he called "loaded" questions." While he had great respect for his craft and confidence in its integrity, he knew the temptation would be great now and then for somebody to slip in a "loaded" question to the President's wife, the innocent answer to which might reveal the President's plans or other problems about which Mrs. Roosevelt would not like to be quoted. "Usually," she said later, "I was able to detect the implications of the questions and avoided any direct answer. Louis Howe had trained me well."

One day a Canadian friend sent Louis a pessimistic letter he had received from a man in the United States, who reviewed all that he thought was wrong with the country.

"Whoever wished on the President his Secretary of Labor and Secretary of Agriculture are no friends of his," one paragraph said. "He really has only one honest-to-God disinterested friend, Colonel Louis McHenry Howe. I do not except his immediate family."

Louis sent the letter to the President with this paragraph marked with red pencil. "Dear FDR," he said. "Note marked paragraph. Even the cranks are for me. I am about to order a large hat."

Louis had a hard time keeping ahead of Steve Early in the office bouts, for Steve at times was even tougher than Louis. But Steve was fair and considerate, and newsmen will tell you that in the twelve years he was press secretary to FDR they always knew where he stood. When exasperated, though, Steve could turn the air blue with explosive epithets that made Louis' "Mein Gawd!" sound like something from a ladies' pink tea. During the war Steve flew to Europe, and upon his arrival in London made a broadcast, beamed to America. The next day I asked Grace Earle, Miss Hachmeister's assistant at the White House switchboard, if she had heard Mr. Early's speech from London.

"Did he start off 'Jesus Christ on a mountaintop, hell and damnation?' " she asked.

"Why no," I said, "of course not."

She turned back to her switchboard. "It wasn't Mr. Early," she said.

Louis had to handle some difficult problems in those early days—the second Bonus March, for example. Every Democrat who remembered how the bonus marchers had been driven from

Washington at the point of bayonets in 1932, with the resultant roar from the country, shuddered when the news hit the wires that there was to be another march a few weeks after Mr. Roosevelt took office. The shudder was tempered by one laugh in our office, however. One day in the middle of April a memo came to Louis from Steve Early, which read: "The Bonus Army under Foulkrod will march on Washington on March 9, according to the United Press."

Louis sent the memo back with the terse notation, "What year?"

Hastily Steve sent another memo saying he had made a mistake and meant May 9, 1933, of course.

When the Bonus Army finally arrived in Washington the President arranged for them to be quartered in a nearby ungarrisoned army post.

"Go out and see the men at the camp," the President told Louis. "See that they have good food and shelter and above all plenty of good, hot coffee to drink. There's nothing that makes people feel as welcome as a steaming cup of coffee."

One afternoon Louis asked Mrs. Roosevelt if she would drive him out into the country. As Secretary to the President he had the use of an official car with a chauffeur, but he much preferred to have Mrs. Roosevelt do the driving, so he could talk over the happenings of the day without other ears listening in.

On this particular afternoon they drove out into Virginia for a few miles, then turned down a side road and drew up in front of a group of buildings where many men clustered around, looking curiously at the long, sleek limousine as it drew to a stop.

"Louis," said Mrs. Roosevelt in surprise, "what is this place and what are we going to do here?"

"This is where the Bonus Army is quartered," Louis answered, "and you are going in there and talk to those men, get their gripes, if any, make a tour of the camp and tell them that Franklin sent you out to see about them. Don't forget that—be sure to tell them that Franklin sent you. Inspect their quarters and get the complete story."

"But Louis," she said, "what are *you* going to do?"

"Me," he said, "I'm going to take a nap." So saying, he curled up in the corner of the car, as she stepped out and made her way into the camp.

The men received her cordially, she was supplied with some of the hot coffee, the camp commander showed her around and the camp singers entertained her with a group of songs. She had a fine time. When she went back to the car, sure enough, there Louis sat curled up in a knot, his head resting on his hand, fast asleep!

There was consternation among the Secret Service men when they heard where Mrs. Roosevelt had been. They rushed to her. "Mrs. Roosevelt," they protested, "you must not do these things. You don't know the feelings of those men—some of them might have been resentful toward the President, or you, and it could have been unpleasant. You should have had protection."

That she needed protection to mingle among these men had not occurred to Mrs. Roosevelt, but now that they'd mentioned it, she said, "Oh, but it was all right. I did have protection."

"Who?" they demanded to know. "What?"

"Why," she said with a twinkle, nodding toward Louis who'd been listening with an amused smile on his face, "that little man was with me all the time. He was so sure I'd be all right, in fact, that he stayed in the car, while I was there, and had himself a good nap."

The Secret Service men looked at Louis and blanched. If this was protection, they thought with a shiver, God help the First Lady of the land!

A little later the President himself drove out past the camp and greeted the men. Louis had a committee specially appointed to come in from the camp to see him, arranged for as many of them as possible to get jobs with the newly organized CCC, and soon they were all out of the city, and the whole incident dwindled away peaceably, in spite of all the preliminary shudders.

The CCC (Civilian Conservation Corps) was a pet project of Roosevelt's and Howe's, and the idea went back to the days when Roosevelt was Governor of New York and reforestation played a prominent part in his State Planning and Land Utilization program. He and Louis visualized a similar program for the nation, if the money and men could be found to carry it out. In FDR's message to Congress in March, he asked the establishment of the CCC "to give employment to an estimated 300,000 young men to take them off the city streets and state highways" doing "simple work . . . confining itself to forestry, the prevention of soil erosion, flood control and similar projects." The program was launched swiftly and, by July 1, these young men were in camp, working for wages, a great part of which went to support their families back home. Louis could not resist bragging a little about the program. "Franklin and I had that CCC idea for years," he'd say. "We even had maps made and pins stuck in every place where we wanted camps placed."

Robert Fechner of Massachusetts was called in to direct the CCC job. He was vice-president of the Machinists' Union, and Roosevelt and Louis, who had known him for years, felt that his appointment to head the new organization would allay the fears, expressed in some places, that "all laboring people might be put under this so-called 'regimentation' and have to work for a dollar a day from that time on!" Labor liked and trusted Fechner, who had lectured on labor questions at several colleges and had served on labor advisory committees in Massachusetts. J. J. McEntee, an old friend from the 1932 campaign days, came as Fechner's assistant.

It was no accident, perhaps, that two of these CCC camps were near Fall River, Massachusetts, and the grateful young men, working there, named one of the roads they built along the river "Louis Howe Boulevard." Mrs. Howe, who also was much interested in these camps, visited them regularly and became known affectionately to the boys as "Mother Howe."

Louis' zeal in this work brought unwittingly a barrage of criticism for one phase of the program. The Army had been called to supply the camps of the CCC boys who were in the forestry section, as the Army was the only agency that had blankets, trucks, cars, shoes, kitchen equipment, etc., needed for work in the woods.

One day a man came in with a letter of introduction to Louis from Basil O'Connor, FDR's old law partner. Louis had told Miss Durand that any time a man came in with a letter from an old friend, or a member of Congress, he would see him and for her to usher him on in. So she sent the visitor in, not bothering to send O'Connor's letter beforehand. The man was a Mr. BeVier, head of a company that manufactured toilet kits, and he wanted to sell them to the CCC for use in the forestry work. The toilet kit looked just like any other to Louis, who sent BeVier to a man in the Budget Bureau, asking him to look into the matter and if he thought the man had something worthwhile to send him to Fechner. Louis thought nothing more about the matter until a few days later, when a letter drafted for his signature came over from the Budget Bureau official, authorizing Fechner to buy the kits which cost $1.49 each. Louis, assuming that a complete investigation of the matter had been made, signed the letter, and had FDR put his own endorsement on the corner of it before sending it to Fechner.

Then a storm broke on Capitol Hill. Senator Carey, Republican of Wyoming, demanded an investigation of this "deal" as he called it, saying that similar kits could be bought for eighty-five cents. The implication, of course, was that the Presidential secretary was getting a "cut." Louis, who was away when the storm broke, rushed back and asked to be heard before the Senate Military Affairs Committee, which was doing the investigating. An attempt was made to tie him and Basil O'Connor into some kind of dark conspiracy, yet it was only after the investigation was on and Louis asked Rabbit to go into the files for the letter BeVier had brought, that he knew that Basil O'Connor had sent him. Some Republican members of the Committee, anxious to embarrass FDR, got in all the digs they could at Louis, whose only worry about the whole thing was that it might hurt Franklin.

"The transaction causes him great anxiety," said the New York

Times, "because he fears it places a blemish on the Administration and that criticism will be directed against the President. He hopes, in this testimony, to convince the public that there was nothing ulterior in the transaction."

At the conclusion of the hearings the Committee completely exonerated the little boss. "We find no evidence," the report said, "that would sustain a charge of corruption or improper motive."

To those of us who remembered the Friends-of-Roosevelt days, the idea of Louis "making a deal" was ludicrous from the beginning. More than one man came in then and endeavored to do a little slick horse trading with Louis. He'd cut them off right in the middle. "I want nothing from you," he'd say. "If you want anything from me we might as well close the conversation right now."

Louis bent so far over backward in this respect that he once offended one of his closest friends who offered, out of the fullness of her friendship, to make him a gift.

The friend was Fannie Hurst, the novelist, who met Louis for the first time when she found herself seated next to him at a luncheon at the Roosevelt town house in New York during the early days of the Roosevelt administration.

"The name of Louis Howe meant nothing to me," Miss Hurst said, "but before the luncheon was over I was struck by the arresting personality of the little man seated between Mrs. Roosevelt on his right and me on his left. We established that day the beginning of a friendship that was to ripen as the days and weeks and months went on."

Miss Hurst met Louis again on several occasions at the White House, and, as their friendship grew, Louis, who admired her brilliant intellect and her grasp of politics and world affairs, began to drop in occasionally at her home in New York, when he went there on business. On one occasion he looked so tired and ill that Miss Hurst persuaded him to have a drink of cognac before he went on to the meeting which had brought him to New York. She served the drink in a tiny ruby glass, one of a beautiful set she had picked up in Venice. Each one was a different jewel color—

amber, sapphire, emerald, etc. Louis, who loved color and beauty, was fascinated. "How Eleanor would love these," he said, holding his glass up to the light.

Impulsively Miss Hurst said, "Oh please let me give you the set and you can present it to Mrs. Roosevelt." There was a strange moment of silence before he replied, "No, no please! I never accept gifts."

Miss Hurst was stunned by his manner. "In my position I make it a rule," he added.

She did not reply and he was quick to interpret her silence. "I have offended you," he said.

She tried to treat the matter lightly, but Louis, sensitive to the core, dissected himself unmercifully.

"I am a thick-skinned boor," he said, "to inject a political philosophy into this situation. Please give me the set. I am ashamed of myself." She begged him to say no more about it, but his misery was abject.

"I don't deserve your forgiveness," he said, "but give it to me along with the set. Please."

In the end, grateful and chastened, he carried the set away.

It was to Miss Hurst that Louis Howe said, not long after this incident, "Don't look at me when I say this, or you will laugh. But at heart I am a minstrel singing outside the window of beauty." He was silent for a moment, sighed deeply, then with that flash of humor that always saved him, added, "a minstrel without even a singing voice."

"I wish," said Miss Hurst, to carry the conversation along in this lighter channel, "that you played the concertino. I love the concertino."

"Do you play one?" he asked quickly.

"No," she replied, "but someday I want to learn."

The next time Louis went to New York he called on Miss Hurst, and when he arrived, he was carrying a concertino for which he had shopped that day. The maid, who admitted him, told Miss Hurst later, "I was so afraid, when I took his hat, that Mr. Howe couldn't even walk the length of the room. He seemed so very tired and weak." And Louis Howe *was* weak, for this was near the end of his strength, but in some strange and lovely way, he seemed to feel that by bringing this gift to his friend he made up for any offense he might have caused when he first refused the gift of her beautiful glasses.

Louis' health grew more frail as the arduous days swept by, and Dr. McIntire, the President's physician, kept a careful check on him, just as he did on the President. Louis rarely traveled with the President because of his poor health, but in the summer of 1934 he surprised all the newspapermen who traveled with FDR by bobbing up in Portland, Oregon, to welcome him home from his Pacific cruise. He never left the President's side on the trip back across the country, even going with him by automobile when the party left the train at Glacier National Park, although this meant crossing the Continental Divide through Logan Pass, at a high altitude which put a terrific strain on his weak heart.

Though Louis took chances now and then with his own health, he took none with ours, and watched over us with a fatherly eye, scolding us over our late hours, and getting us promptly into Dr. McIntire's hands if we had a sniffle. Early in the spring of 1934, after a series of bouts with the flu all winter, I collapsed and had to be carted off to a hospital. When I was able to leave the hospital Louis insisted that I go to my home in Kentucky to convalesce, sent a friend along with me, engaged a stateroom for us both, and took care of all details, including the expense. He warned me to stay in Kentucky until I was entirely well, and that I'd better not try coming back sooner.

"But how will you know how I feel unless I let you know?" I asked him.

"Oh, I'll know all right," he said mysteriously. "I have my agents everywhere." Three or four times when I decided I was strong enough to return he notified me that I was not ready. I began to believe he really did have agents concealed somewhere around our place in Kentucky, when he finally decided the latter part of April that I was able to return.

It happened that the train I chose to come back on was the

"Derby Special" which left Louisville on the evening of Derby Day in Kentucky. I didn't go to the race, but knowing *him,* I went to a notary public in my home town and made an affidavit to that effect! When I presented it to him, upon my return, he cocked an eye at me and threw me a little Shakespeare. "Methinks," he said, "the lady doth protest too much." When I tried to thank him for all he had done for me he banged the desk with his fist. "Aw, cut out the butter," he growled. "You're one of my gang, aren't you? And I take care of my gang, don't I?" And that, with him, was that.

In May of that same year when Rabbit developed a hacking cough, Louis made arrangements with H. J. Anslinger, Commissioner of Narcotics, to take her along with him to Geneva, Switzerland, doing secretarial work in connection with the meeting of the Opium Advisory Committee of the League of Nations. While the United States was not a member of the League, our country was always invited to send observers to these various conferences. Louis also sent Hartley and told him to keep a sharp eye on Rabbit to see that she had enough sleep and rest. They sailed from Montreal, the delegation gave a birthday party for Rabbit on board ship, and the change, sea air and stimulating company made a great change in her health and spirits.

I bring in these remembrances only to show that this tough little man who turned such a gruff side to the world really was a softy when anything concerned "his gang" who, he knew, were loyal to Franklin and to him.

This trip of Hartley's was not solely to watch over Rabbit nor was it a free ride. He was to work for Anslinger at the Conference and thus pay his way, and he was kept busy keeping track of all the documents and acting as "runner" between the Committee headquarters and the American Consulate.

Anslinger told of an amusing incident which occurred in Paris as they were on their way back. They all had dinner at a little café one night and Rabbit, who collected odd pieces of silver, kept wishing she had a piece of the Normandy silver which adorned the table. Each member of the delegation, therefore, gallantly slipped a piece in his pocket for her. Hartley was getting pretty jumpy over all this, and finally went around to Anslinger's chair. "For God's sake, Mr. Commissioner," he said nervously, "let's quit stealing the silver. We'll all land in jail and my father will raise a row that can be heard all over Europe, because we were foolish enough to let ourselves get in such a jam." Anslinger laughed. "See that fellow in back of us with paper and pencil?" he said. "He's the fellow who makes a list of everything the souvenir hunters take from the tables. It will all be on the bill, so just relax." Hartley relaxed but, so far as I know, he never mentioned the incident to Louis when they returned home.

The day Anslinger went to the White House to make final arrangements with Louis about this trip, Louis abruptly changed the subject. "Anslinger," he said, "let me give you a piece of advice. Don't you ever send any pardon cases over here, approved, for dope peddlers. If there is one crime in the world that makes Franklin see red it is dope peddling. He has some sympathy for a man who becomes an addict and peddles in order to get it for himself, but for those slimy characters who peddle it and make addicts of other people in order to sell the stuff he has no sympathy in the world, hates them with deadly hate."

It happens that I knew this to be true for, under Louis' direction, I used to read the pardon cases and, in line with his boil-it-down program, would make a one-page brief setting forth the salient facts of the case, before turning it over to Louis. I was instructed to watch carefully for these "dope" cases and to underline the facts in red so that Franklin would be sure not to miss them when the case was passed on to him. FDR didn't believe dope peddlers ever really reformed. One former dope peddler who had been out of prison for twenty-five years was asking a pardon, so that he might have his civil rights restored. All kinds of endorsements came in for him from good citizens, the Federal Bureau of Investigation had made a thorough check of his conduct since his release, and there was nothing against him. FDR read the whole case carefully and sent it back to the Department of Justice with the notation: "Make further check." Maybe another check convinced him, but I'm not too sure.

Hartley was a student at Harvard and Louis, who was anxious for him to supplement his education with travel, arranged a few jobs for him during vacations like the one at Geneva. He always made it plain, however, that these were to be "no junkets for Louis Howe's son." If he didn't work, back he was to come by the next boat. When Secretary of State Cordell Hull went to the Seventh Pan-American Conference, held in Montevideo in the winter of 1933, he took Hartley along. Louis swelled with fatherly pride when a cablegram came in from Secretary Hull saying that Hartley would be separated from him between Buenos Aires and Santiago because he was needed on official business of the delegation. "He will accompany the official party to Santiago and join me there," Hull said. He assured Louis that Ambassador Alexander Weddell, then our Ambassador to Argentina, would keep a friendly eye on Hartley, and said, "You will be pleased, I know, to hear that he has been doing most excellent work." Louis showed the cablegram around the office, saying offhandedly that he was "glad the boy hadn't done anything to disgrace the delegation," or words to that effect, to keep from showing how proud he was. When I talked to Hartley about this trip, after I began this book, and asked him what his duties were, he said, "Office boy," and that's all I could get out of him. Just like his old man!

Because Hartley shies away from publicity as much as his father did I am sure he would not want me to mention him at all, but I know Louis Howe would have been pleased if he could have been present that April day last year when I talked to Hartley about his dad, at his home in Bayside, Long Island. Hartley, who was Commander Hartley E. Howe in World War II—and I'm sure Louis would have liked this Navy connection because of his own Navy days—is now one of the editors of *Popular Science* Magazine and has a beautiful wife and four charming children. In 1942 he married Miss Rosella Senders of Boston and the children are David, Edward, Henry and Rosemary, in that order.

Hartley and Rosella lived in Washington for a time after the war, and one evening at dinner at their home we had a lively argument about what to name the expected baby, their third child. I was insistent that, if a boy, he should be called Louis McHenry Howe, but Hartley protested.

"Father never liked his name," he said, "and I don't think he'd approve of hanging it on to another helpless infant who can't defend himself."

As a compromise they did name the baby son Henry and he was five years old when we visited them in Bayside. He was playing in the yard as we drove up to the door of the rambling old house near the bay. Hearing the voices of visitors he came running and as he rounded the corner of the house we stopped in our tracks. The youngster is the absolute image of Louis Howe as a boy. A photograph of Louis at that age is in my possession!

Much has been written about the famous White House "Brain Trust" and there has been some speculation about whether Louis Howe was a member. He would have been the first to admit that he was not, although Marguerite LeHand is my authority for the fact that it was Louis who coined the name for this mythical organization which was supposed to include Judge Samuel Rosenman, Professor Raymond Moley, Adolph Berle, Rexford Guy Tugwell, and others. Jim Kieran of the New York *Times* was the first newspaperman to use the term "Brain Trust" in print.

"The President was talking to Louis one day about a man who had been recommended to him as one who could be useful in some capacity," Miss LeHand said, "and he asked Louis to figure out where to place him."

"Oh, if you want him to be useful," Louis cracked, "why don't you use him in that 'brain trust' of yours?"

The President slapped his knee delightedly. "Brain trust!" he exclaimed. "I love it, I love it!" And soon the term became a byword in the land.

"I'm no mastermind," Louis would say when people tried to tie him in with the brain crowd. "These masterminds are usually too intellectual to convince anyone but themselves, and being so superior they never get the viewpoint of the man in the street. That's why they are usually such bad prophets. If I have any kind of knack it's a knack of sensing the other fellow's reactions—and that comes in very handy at times."

Louis' role was really best summed up by an editorial writer in New England. "Louis Howe is the most private of the President's private secretaries," he said. "Mr. Roosevelt consults brain trusters individually on matters concerning their particular activities; he sees Jim Farley on matters of broad party strategy and patronage, but he consults Louis Howe on everything."

Many believed that Louis was jealous of the members of the brain trust and there is no doubt that he kept a sharp eye on them, as he did on anybody who nudged too near Franklin. It was not that he was afraid anybody would supplant him for he knew that Franklin depended on him as he did on no other. But Louis was like a man who had helped design a great piece of architecture. He knew that the building of it took many craftsmen, but he never lost sight of the fact that *he* was the one who laid the foundation. He watched the other craftsmen just to make sure none of them grew so cocky that he began to believe he'd built the whole house by himself.

"Louis Howe," said Frank Walker, when somebody once asked him if Louis was jealous of those around the President, "could never be jealous in the sense that you are jealous lest someone supplant you. That simply could not apply to Louis for he was actually a part of Franklin Roosevelt—the two men were almost as one. Louis Howe was so completely loyal to 'his other self' that if he ever tried to keep somebody from getting too close to Franklin you can be dead sure that, for some reason of his own, he had his doubts about that person's loyalty to Franklin. Louis himself was so completely loyal that loyalty was a measuring stick by which he judged everybody. He was never actuated by a single thought except the best interest of Franklin D. Roosevelt."

Louis really felt so deeply about this that if he knew positively a man had been disloyal to Franklin his feeling of distrust often blossomed into actual hatred.

"Louis was the most intense hater I have ever known," said Mrs. Roosevelt, as we talked of Louis Howe in her Hyde Park cottage one snowy day, while Fala's grandson, Tamas McFala, frolicked in front of the glowing fireplace. "He really didn't care how people treated *him*, though. He only hated them if he thought they had done something to harm Franklin."

Once, she said, he amazed her by letting loose a blast at a man who seemed to her a harmless enough individual.

"But Louis," she said, "what did that man ever do to you to make you dislike him so?"

"Why, don't you remember," he said, harking back to an incident that had happened at least fifteen years before, "what he did to Franklin then?"

"No," she said, "but anyway that was so very, very long ago."

"That may be," he said grimly, "but I remember."

14

"Devoted Friend"

DESPITE the pains the President took to see that Louis did not overdo, and despite the care Dr. McIntire took of his health, the little boss began to fail alarmingly during his second year in the White House and by the fall of 1934 he was doing much of his work from his bedroom.

By January 1935 Louis was so ill that the President, out of deference to him, canceled the annual "Cuff Links" party, always held on FDR's birthday, January 30. In early March Louis' condition was aggravated by a severe case of bronchitis, and word came that he was in an oxygen tent. Each day Dr. McIntire told us that the little boss could not possibly get well, and we must prepare for the bad news at any moment. But even the doctor did not know the amazing vitality and will to live possessed by this frail little man. When the word went out to the country that Louis Howe was dangerously ill, letters and telegrams of sympathy poured into the White House in a steady stream, some to Louis himself, but most of them to the President. One woman wrote the President that she spent all night on her knees praying for Louis Howe's recovery. From across the sea came a personal message to Louis from the Prime Minister of Great Britain. "Ishbel and I," the cable read, "sorry to hear of your illness. Best wishes for a speedy recovery. Signed, Ramsay MacDonald."

One Friday during this tense time, as Louis gasped for breath under the oxygen tent, a special train was quietly rolled on a siding in Union Station ready to leave at any moment on a journey to Fall River, Massachusetts, with the President of the United States aboard to accompany his old friend on his last journey. No one believed that Louis Howe could possibly live more than a few hours. Cabinet members, asked to cancel all plans, packed their bags and stood by. All day the doctor and nurses watched as the feeble light of life flickered in Louis' frail breast, revived and flickered again. Servants tiptoed softly by the door with fingers to silent lips.

About five o'clock in the afternoon, Louis opened his eyes and said irritably, "Why in hell doesn't somebody give me a cigarette?"

He lived a year after that.

In fact, Louis Howe broke every rule known to Navy doctors, who admitted there was simply no case like his in the medical records. "Louis Howe is a New Deal in patients," said Earl Godwin, in his column in the Washington *Evening Star,* "and he has confounded them all."

One day shortly after the cigarette incident, Dr. McIntire came in doubled up with laughter. "Do you know what that little boss of yours has done now?" he asked. "While we were out of the room this morning he reached out under that oxygen tent for the telephone, called Harry Hopkins, and talked to him for fifteen minutes."

Somehow Louis had learned that Hopkins was having a rough time with the four-million-dollar work relief bill on Capitol Hill. Louis simply called Hopkins and told him where he thought the strategy was wrong and what he ought to do to get the bill passed. Hopkins, who, like the rest of the country, thought Louis Howe was dying, was speechless.

A certain kindly gentleman out West must have been as speechless as Hopkins when he received a reply to a telegram he sent to the President on March 15: "I am very sorry to hear on the radio this evening of the serious illness of your faithful secretary Louis McHenry Howe. Hope and pray for his recovery."

He received the following note dated March 16:

DEAR MR. ————:

The President has asked me to acknowledge the receipt of and to thank you for your telegram of March 15th.

Very sincerely yours,

LOUIS McHENRY HOWE
Secretary to the President

Louis saw a certain grim humor in the fact that people in the country thought he was dying when he felt sure he was good for awhile yet, and he asked to see some of the letters and telegrams about himself. Most of these communications were answered by Margaret Durand, but now and then Louis would dictate and sign one just to show he was still around. "Will you see to it," he said one day to one of the startled nurses, "that they don't come along and bury me while I'm taking a nap?"

Louis never came back to the office, though later on he was able to sit up part of the time and he'd wheel himself around to the President's oval study and into Mrs. Roosevelt's sitting room, in one of the President's wheel chairs which had been rigged up for him. The President went to see him every day and, finally, when he felt that Louis was well enough to be left, FDR went to Florida on a fishing trip with Vincent Astor on the Astor yacht, a trip he had deferred for weeks while Louis' life hung in the balance. The President kept in close touch with Louis' condition, however, and on March 31 wrote Mrs. Roosevelt: "Louis' improvement apparently continues and I suppose you are going ahead with the engagements, and that Grace is back with him. If he is not too 'fuzzy' give him my love and tell him I expect him to be sitting up in bed when I get back."[1]

Mrs. Howe, who had come down in January when Louis' condition first became so serious, had gone back to Fall River to arrange affairs there so that she could come down and be with Louis full time. She stayed all that spring and summer and lived in the White House; Mrs. Roosevelt had made plans to be away most of the summer, leaving only when she felt that Louis was out of

[1] Elliott Roosevelt, *F.D.R., His Personal Letters.*

immediate danger. Mrs. Howe speaks of that summer as a nightmarish one, with the heat so stifling that she moved from one bedroom to another, trying to find a cool place to lay her head. The White House was not air conditioned then, as it is today. Louis would hardly let Mrs. Howe out of his sight, insisted that she read to him constantly and, all in all, was pretty trying at times. One day she read to him all day—history, the classics, a few of his favorite "whodunits." He lay hunched up in bed, his eyes closed, drinking it all in until, as evening fell, she closed the book and said that would be all for the day. His eyes fluttered open and he looked at her reproachfully.

"What's the matter, my dear?" he said. "Don't you *like* to read to me?" Mrs. Howe, who by this time was so tired she could scarcely speak, had no answer. "If he hadn't been a sick man," she said ruefully, "I'd have taken that book and whacked him over the head with it!"

Louis saw a few close friends during this period, though mostly he was incommunicado except to Mrs. Howe and Rabbit. He spent a lot of time reading the papers, when his eyes would permit, playing solitaire and betting on the races. One day Frank Walker dropped by to see him and was asked to wait in the Lincoln Room for a little while.

Louis was spending several hours each day under the oxygen tent at that time and Walker could hear a murmur of voices as he waited in the big outside room. Knowing that Louis took the telephone under the tent now and then to talk to important officials he felt sure, as the minutes passed, that Louis had no less than the Secretary of State on the phone, conferring on matters of world importance. As he had to catch a train he began to glance at his watch and calculate whether he could wait until this important business was over.

When at least fifteen minutes had passed and his train time approached, Walker stepped to the door and told Miss Durand, who was in the room with Louis, that he had to go.

"Oh, it's all right now," she said. "Come right on in."

Walker went hastily in. There was a rustle from inside the

oxygen tent, then Louis peered out. Scattered all around him were racing forms and sheets of paper adorned with columns of his unreadable figures.

"You know," Louis said, "I just got a hot tip from Cary Grayson on a horse, but dammit, I've been stung by some of Cary's hot tips before so I got Rabbit to get me the dope sheets and let me figure out the nag's background before I risked a bet." He grinned. "Pretty good nag," he said, "so I'm placing a sizable bet. Now what's on your mind?"

Walker was so annoyed that he almost *told* Louis what was on his mind, but he restrained himself, made polite inquiries about Louis' health, then rushed away to catch his train.

On days when Louis felt particularly bad he was so irritable that, as Margaret Durand put it, "there was no living with the man." On one of these days he almost scared the wits out of poor McDuffie, the President's valet. McDuffie had come into the sick room feeling pretty important. He had a message for the little man from the President of the United States. He delivered it; then stood by, courteously waiting for an answer. Louis suddenly looked up at him and barked, "You go back and tell the President I said to go to hell!"

McDuffie was a rich mahogany color, but this almost reduced him to chalk. He fled from the room and rushed to Lizzie, his wife, who was a maid at the White House.

"What will I do?" he wailed. "I jest simply can't go in there and tell the President that. It's awful."

Lizzie, an amiable and easy-going soul, clucked reassuringly. "Don't worry about it," she said. "I'll tell him myself." She marched into the President's room.

"Mr. President," she said, "Mr. Howe said for McDuffie to tell you that that was a hell of a message you sent him."

The President leaned back in his chair and waggled his finger at her.

"Now Lizzie," he said, "don't try to clean it up. You know very well that Louis said for me to go to hell, didn't he?"

When Lizzie admitted that this was true, FDR laughed heartily and was still chuckling when she went to tell the trembling Mc-Duffie that he could relax, the worst was over.

Finally, when remodeling in the White House made it necessary to cut off the water and electricity, Louis had to be moved to the Naval Hospital. Mrs. Roosevelt took him down in the White House limousine and saw that he was comfortable. Then the President phoned him.

"How is it, Louis?" he wanted to know.

"Oh, all right, I guess," Louis replied, "but I miss all those buttons I could push at the White House and have people come running from all directions." He'd only been in the hospital a few days when something came up which, he decided, required his personal touch. He never let go, even in the sickroom. Now one of his pet projects was threatened and he had to "get in and pitch." This was the Alaska Resettlement project, which was part of the nation-wide program to restore self-sufficiency to families who had become desperate. Emergency Relief Administrations were formed in many states and drew their funds from the Federal Emergency Relief Administration. In the fall of 1934 Alaska was added to the program and the Matanuska Valley Colony there was patterned after the program in the various states. The whole project had to be planned and started between the fall of 1934 and May 1935, too short a time for such a complex undertaking, and it was now floundering badly. A strong hand was needed, but it was hard to get a man with the right administrative ability to go to Alaska and stay any length of time. Suddenly Louis thought of his old friend, S. R. Fuller, Jr., from his Navy days, a man of great administrative ability, who was now head of North American Rayon Corporation. Louis grabbed the phone. "Fuller," he said, "we've got a mess up in Alaska and you're just the man to straighten it out. You've got to start right away."

"Whoa, Louis," said the astonished Fuller, "back up. What's this all about?"

Louis patiently explained the problem at length, then asked Fuller when he could leave.

"But Louis," wailed Fuller, who had been trying all through

this conversation to break in and say no, "I'm catching a boat for Europe for my own company today!"

"To hell with that," said Louis promptly. "Franklin needs you and I need you. You've got to go."

Louis' argument was so convincing that Fuller finally canceled his trip to Europe and went to Alaska instead, thus earning Louis Howe's undying gratitude.

Another idea that Louis had, while he lay there cut off to all appearances from the outside world, concerned the next world war. World War II was then four years away from the European shores and over six years away from ours, but that little bell which seemed to ring in Louis' mind when he peered into the future and saw something that might affect Franklin or the country began to jangle insistently. Mussolini had arrogantly marched into Ethiopia. There was much talk, here and abroad, as to what steps should be taken against the arch dictator by the free nations, but to Louis Howe the duty of the democracies was plain. He reached for the telephone.

"Franklin," he said, "what are you going to do about Mussolini?"

The President, anxious to keep all such worries away from Louis, told him that he must not bother with the problem.

"But Franklin," persisted Louis impatiently, "can't you see that that strutting fake Caesar is starting another world war? You must do something about it, and do it now."

Nothing the President could say seemed to calm Louis down, and Louis brooded on the problem and talked to the doctors and nurses about it. Sometimes he'd call the White House after the President had retired and, unable to get him on the phone, he'd talk to the night operator on the switchboard.

"I could follow him as far as A, B, and C," the operator said, "but he had a profound grasp of the subject though most of it was over my head. I couldn't take it all in, but it was certainly as clear as daylight to him. He was truly an amazing little man and all of us had the greatest respect for him.

"Once," the operator said, "the President was being urged to
O. K. a certain project and was about to do so, but Mr. Howe
didn't think he should. The President was down South at the time.
Mr. Howe telephoned to the telegraph room one evening from the
hospital, and dictated such a convincing message to the President
giving the reasons why he should not, that he immediately turned
down the project."

Mussolini was not the only menace to Franklin that Louis saw
as he lay in his hospital bed, listened to the radio and fretted about
being out of things. Huey Long and Father Coughlin were two
he was watching closely, and phone calls and memos rolled to the
President's desk as Louis worried about what these two were saying and doing. As early as February he had sent a memo to FDR,
with a letter which had come to his hand. "Here is a letter," he
said, "from the president of a Montana bank, who, of all people,
has been 'converted' by Huey Long. It is symptoms like this which
I think we should watch very carefully."

Huey Long, on the Senate floor and elsewhere, was filling the
air with his lurid cries that "the rich earn more and the common
people less." His battle cry of "Every man a King" was making
headlines and his "Share the Wealth" clubs mushroomed throughout the country. He had broken completely with Roosevelt by this
time, and announced that he would "fight the Administration to
a finish unless it showed some results in redistributing the wealth."
"He is a worse dictator than Mussolini," muttered Louis Howe
angrily.

Father Coughlin was the Royal Oak, Michigan, radio priest
who was going after "the Morgans," the "kept press," "the inter-
national bankers," "the Baruchs," "the Warburgs," and bitterly
attacking FDR as the "defender of the privileged." Louis was
getting regular reports on Coughlin's activities from Hall Roosevelt, Mrs. Roosevelt's brother, who lived in Detroit, and Louis
saw that these reports, newspaper clippings, and everything else
he could get on Coughlin reached FDR's hands with the warning
that "somebody had better keep an eye on this fanatic and do

something about him" before harm was done to the President's program.

General Hugh Johnson was another who gave Louis trouble. The fiery General had also broken with the Administration and was writing a newspaper column, attacking not only Roosevelt but practically all the members of his Cabinet. Bernard Baruch, as an old friend of Johnson's, had brought him into the Roosevelt circle. Baruch phoned the White House and dictated a long memorandum to Rabbit to take to Louis in the hospital. The gist of the message was that Johnson had told Baruch he had "explained several things to Louis Howe's satisfaction." But Louis Howe, not satisfied at all, was working on a scheme to answer Johnson, and Baruch knew it. He advised against this procedure and told Louis that it would only make the General madder, and thus prolong the controversy. Baruch and Louis had several phone conversations about Johnson and finally agreed that there was nothing to be done about "Old Iron Pants," who continued to sputter in print, contributing greatly to Louis' high blood pressure and irritability.

Louis demonstrated by all this activity that though he was lying in a hospital bed, he was still the Number One White House Secretary. He never let anybody else forget it, either. Let somebody call up and tell the nurse that he would "drop around and see Louis" sometime that day. That somebody would be pretty sure to receive a call shortly after, saying that "Mr. Howe would be glad to receive him at, say, four o'clock that afternoon." There was no venom in this; Louis simply knew that since he was away from the scene, those around the President might get in the habit of dismissing him and his influence entirely. He just wanted to remind them that he remained "the little man who was there."

Knowing Louis' love for the dramatic, FDR often staged an entrance for his benefit when he paid a visit to the hospital. FDR would have Gus wheel him in with a flourish, his cigarette tilted at a jaunty angle, and would greet Louis with some cheerful, humorous remark.

"Louis," he'd say, "you've just got to get back to the White

House and get in on the show. Know what I did at the press conference this afternoon? I gave 'em a complete definition of the New Deal."

"Oh, really," Louis would say, catching the mood, "all in one afternoon?" Then they'd be off! Dr. McIntire, Dr. Duncan and the nurse would stand by, enjoying the banter, while other nurses gathered in the hall, their starched uniforms rustling as they found errands to take them past the door for a peek at the little man's famous visitor.

Sometimes the President would bring somebody with him to cheer Louis a bit. One day FDR came in with Felix Frankfurter, associate justice of the Supreme Court of the United States.

"Louis," he said, with mock gravity, "Felix and I were discussing your case on the way down. We've decided that it's unconstitutional. We're going to do something about it as soon as Felix can go more fully into the law on the subject."

Cynics on Capitol Hill and elsewhere were having a field day over Louis Howe's absence from the White House. The "honeymoon" which had carried Franklin Roosevelt triumphantly through his first and second years was beginning to show signs of waning early in 1935, when Louis first came down with his illness, and the Republicans were filling the air with brickbats. Even those Democrats who had decried "Louis Howe's influence over the President" now began to miss him and phoned often to ask about his health. Their solicitude about Louis recalls a funny story. During the last month of the campaign of 1932 Louis was in Hyde Park one weekend, working long hours with FDR on some knotty campaign problems; becoming tired, he went into the sitting room where Mrs. Roosevelt sat knitting, and stretched out on the couch to rest. A certain western United States Senator, whose predilection for imbibing was well known, had come up that weekend for a conference with FDR. He arrived about this time and walked into the sitting room where Mrs. Roosevelt sat, her knitting needles clicking, while Louis dozed on a couch by the window. The Senator, who could hardly navigate, made a low, courtly bow to Mrs. Roosevelt, then looked at Louis who, as always, was breathing hard, his face pale with weariness. The Senator pointed his finger at him.

"Louis," he said, "Louis, my good fren', you look terrible. Trouble with you, Louis, is you work too hard. Worries me, worries all your fren's. You must take it easy. Can't afford to lose you. Valu'ble man. I tell you what," he said, as he lurched toward the startled Louis, who by now was sitting up looking at him with a calculating eye as he approached, "tell you what. My shoulders are broad, you can lean on me, Louis. Jus' lean on me." So saying, he leaned his "broad shoulder" toward his fren', lost his footing and fell headlong across Louis' slight form, almost mashing the breath out of him.

Many newspapers in 1935 also took up the cry about Louis' absence from the scene of action, and blamed nearly everything that went wrong on the fact that Louis Howe, with his wise counsel, was not there to advise the President. "Roosevelt had better get his political brains out from under that oxygen tent," one newspaper said.

It is fortunate these remarks never reached Louis' ears. He knew his influence with the President was great, but the idea that Franklin was such a nincompoop he could not function alone, if he had to, would have made him mad enough to punch the cynics in the nose.

Mrs. Roosevelt was one who knew that the President was severely handicapped without Louis' counsel in those days and the days that followed. Two years after Louis' death, when FDR attempted to "purge" certain Senators who had fought his program, Mrs. Roosevelt said, "If there were political mistakes in this campaign some of them, I think, might have been avoided if Louis Howe had been alive. After Louis Howe's death Franklin never had a political adviser who argued with him, when he really disagreed, and yet still gave him unquestioned loyalty. . . .

"Harry Hopkins," she said, "gave his opinions honestly but . . . he tried in indirect ways to make Franklin do what he thought he should do. Frequently he thought it expedient to agree with

Franklin, regardless of his own opinion. This was not really so valuable a service as forcing him, as Louis Howe did, to hear unpleasant arguments. . . .

"Jim Farley argued with Franklin but never very effectively, because his reasons were based on political practicality. . . ."[2]

Once a visitor, who had heard much of Louis' love and loyalty to the President, asked Mrs. Roosevelt this question:

"It is generally known, of course, that Louis Howe lives only for Franklin Roosevelt. But, tell me, is all this love and loyalty going one way? How does the President feel about Louis? Does he appreciate this unusual little man who has devoted his life to him?"

"Why, of course," said Mrs. Roosevelt in some surprise, "the devotion between them is entirely mutual. But Franklin makes no more expression of it than Louis does and you know Louis— you'd almost think he dislikes Franklin the way he talks to him at times. As a matter of fact, Franklin is not one to express his feelings very much, either, in praise or blame. I think it is a form of shyness, really. He knows how deep is his devotion to those around him and he takes for granted that they feel the same way about him. He really doesn't talk much about it. He is even more reticent when it comes to criticizing people. I think it is pretty well known that he cannot bear to dismiss people who have proved unsatisfactory. It's because he is simply incapable of hurting anybody's feelings. I don't mean by that that Franklin cannot get angry—he does, but it is soon over. But he will go to almost any length to keep from hurting those around him.

"I remember the time," she said, "after we went to the White House, when, for various reasons, we had to let Franklin's valet go. And who did that unpleasant job? Why, I did! When I told Franklin that we simply had to let him go he looked at me with the most pitiful expression.

" 'I know, I know,' he said, 'but you know I'm leaving on a trip next week. Can't we wait awhile, just sort of postpone it until after

[2] Eleanor Roosevelt, *This I Remember* (New York: Harper and Brothers, 1949).

I'm gone?' And postpone it we did, thus sparing Franklin the pain of giving the valet the bad tidings himself.

"But going back to Louis. I didn't like him at all at first. In fact it was only after Franklin was stricken and Louis gave up everything to come and stay by his side that I came to appreciate him. So one day I went to Franklin and, almost humbly, told him I'd have to take back a great many things I'd said and thought about Louis in the past.

"Franklin looked at me and a great smile lighted his face. 'I knew, darling,' he said gently, 'that some day you would come to appreciate how fine Louis really is.'"

And while Louis Howe made little outward show of the way he felt about Franklin Roosevelt, he revealed his feelings to a friend, shortly before he passed away. "I have been as close to Franklin Roosevelt as a valet," he said, "and he is still a hero to me."

Missing those push buttons, and irked when a call to the President after office hours was delayed at the Navy Department's switchboard, Louis decided he'd have a private phone installed by his bedside, with a direct wire to the White House so he could call at any hour. The doctors took a pale view of this, as they wanted to keep him quiet at all times. So they delayed arrangements for a while. But the longer the delay the more determined Louis was to get that phone. He gave Rabbit and Hackie some bad moments about it. "I'll just tell Franklin," he said. "He'll get it for me." What they knew, but he didn't, was that Franklin already knew all about it and was conspiring with the doctors to keep Louis from getting his phone!

Louis finally became so insistent that the President, to get the girls off the hook, wrote him a letter in longhand and sent it by special messenger:

Dear Louis:

I fear the change in telephone hours is impossible. Two weeks ago I told the Cabinet and heads of agencies that as soon as Congress adjourned they were to rest and not do any work after 4:30

P.M. I am not talking to any of them after that hour. So we must be consistent and confine all our calls to working hours.

Will be up this P.M. or tomorrow.

Affectionately,

F. D. R.

The President went to the hospital the next afternoon and he knew Louis would be waiting for him, after that letter. "I'm going to pull a fast one on Louis," he said to Gus Gennerich. "I'll go right in and start talking about something else and keep him interested till time to leave, and he won't get a chance to jump on me about that phone."

While in the hospital, Louis had started growing a Vandyke beard, something he had always wanted to do in imitation of his father. So as soon as the President arrived he started on that beard.

"Louis," he chortled, "you look just like a goat. Doesn't he, Gus? Baa-baa-baa," he went on, in imitation of a goat, while Louis grinned. Then FDR started talking of this and that, keeping Louis interested until it was time to go. He said goodbye and took his leave, talking all the way to the door. As Gus wheeled him down the hall he looked up and winked. "It worked! It worked!" he said. "Louis didn't remember that telephone in time."

But FDR should have known that Louis would get that phone, eventually, though he had to make a slight concession. He didn't get the twenty-four-hour connection he had demanded. Hackie and her staff still had cold sweats when they pictured Mr. Howe calling in the middle of the night demanding to speak to Franklin. Who was to decide what was important enough to wake the President of the United States!

Shortly afterward, at one of the family picnics at Hyde Park, the President, who was holding his usual court on the lawn in a high-backed chair, called Hackie over and whispered behind his hand, "Hackie, you had quite a time with Louis about that telephone, didn't you?"

"Yes," said Hackie, a little flustered, "I did, and I didn't quite know what to do. You see, you are the President, but Mr. Howe is my boss, so I was sort of caught in the middle." The President roared with laughter, then suddenly sobered.

"I see your dilemma," he said. "I wanted Louis to get through to me when it was important, but a lot of things seem very, very important to him there in the hospital and when he gets an idea he wants to get it to me right away. But he gets at least twenty ideas a day! Even so, Hackie," he said, his voice full of affection, "you and I both know that some of them are darned good, even if Louis is a sick man."

While in the hospital Louis interested himself in the affairs of his nurse and attendants, just as he did in those of his gang in the office. When one of the sailors who attended him confided that his mother in Pennsylvania faced an operation and he might have to make a hurried trip there, Louis grabbed the phone and called the President. "The President is busy, Mr. Howe," said Hackie. "Is it important?" "You're damned right it's important," he said. "Get him on the phone right away." When he got the Presidential ear he asked authority to get a White House car and chauffeur to take his young friend to Pennsylvania, in case he had to rush off in a hurry. The President gave him the required authority and, as it turned out, the boy didn't have to go; but he was pleased, although somewhat embarrassed, to think his problem had gone all the way up to the President of the United States.

One of the sailors who read to Louis became a proud papa and named the baby "Howe," much to Louis' delight, and he kept members of the staff busy wrapping up presents for the new arrival. Friends were always sending flowers and potted plants to him and he designated one of his attendants "Keeper of the Sacred Plants," giving him a commission, blue ribbon and all, with an impressive little ceremony in his room.

We kept in close touch with Louis through Rabbit's visits, for he could not see us all. We gave her the title of "Official Ambassador to the little boss" and gathered eagerly around when she came back from the sickroom to hear the latest news of his health and pranks. Mrs. Roosevelt visited him often, and the President made it a point to go at least once a week so that Louis still felt he was part of the stirring events at the White House.

As the year 1936 loomed Louis began to fret about the speech Franklin must deliver to Congress in January on the state of the union. This was election year and the President was facing a fight in Congress on his legislative program. Louis decided the time had come for another bold Roosevelt stroke. He called Rabbit to the hospital and dictated a long letter to the President and said to him in essence: "Franklin, get in there and fight. Give them the old 'Roosevelt Dutch' in this speech. Remind them of the conditions in the country when you took over. Tell them what you have done. Ask them if the country is not infinitely better off than when you came on the scene. Give them a résumé of the laws passed for the benefit of the people. You have a lot to brag about, nothing to apologize for. Let 'em have it. They'll lap it up!"

And they did, too, for FDR took Louis' advice and gave them a fighting speech that had them on their feet yelling. Lying there on his side, his ear to the radio, listening to this roar of approval, Louis Howe smiled. He was content.

Nineteen thirty-six! Election year! The smell of sawdust began to penetrate the old war horse's nostrils. There in the hospital he dreamed up a program, which he thought would fit in with Franklin's ideas, for use in the campaign. He called this new brain child the "Good Neighbor League." This was not the "Good Neighbor Policy," later inaugurated by FDR, but something Louis conceived that would play up Franklin's sympathy for racial and minority groups. He worked out all the details and called in a man to administer it, but there was something still lacking. Money.

Louis' thoughts then turned to his old friend, "Barney" Baruch, who never came to Washington without paying him a visit. Before Baruch left for the sickroom, however, he was usually admonished by some member of the White House secretariat, "You'll probably find that Louis is fretting about some scheme he has in mind for the campaign, but the President wants him to rest and be quiet, so don't encourage him for he'll get all stirred up and that is bad for him. Just listen sympathetically, and that's all."

But Barney Baruch knew that such activity was mental therapy for Louis and, surreptitiously, egged him on. When Louis told him about his "Good Neighbor League" Baruch told him he thought it a grand idea and, without hesitation, advanced the money. The League later was incorporated into the Democratic party organization and played an important part in winning the 1936 election.

After Louis died Mrs. Roosevelt called Baruch at "Hobcaw," his home in South Carolina, where he was vacationing, to thank him for helping Louis form his Good Neighbor League. "You were wiser than the rest of us," she said. "You knew that it was medicine, food and drink to Louis to know that he was still in there fighting, doing something for Franklin. Those of us who loved Louis will never forget your kindness to him."

How Louis Howe longed to be able to take an active part in this campaign only those close to him knew. He never really discarded the idea that he might—just possibly might—be in New York when the time came, directing the show as he had always done. We gasped when Rabbit came in from the hospital to report that the little boss said he thought he'd save his strength until the campaign was under way, then have himself moved to New York, to the Biltmore Hotel, and direct the campaign from his bed in the hotel room!

Louis called his friend, S. R. Fuller, now back from Alaska, and told him his plans.

"Fuller," he said, "I want you to go with me to New York and help me run the campaign to elect Franklin this year."

Astonished, Fuller protested. "Louis," he said, "I went to Alaska for you and I'd do most anything for you, and Heaven knows I want to see the President re-elected, but let's be reasonable. I'm a businessman. I do not know one single thing about politics."

"Fuller, stop talking nonsense," Louis snapped. "I didn't ask you if you knew anything about politics. I asked you to help *me*.

And I'll guarantee one thing, my friend. When *I* get through with you you'll damned well know something about politics. So, stand by. I'll call you when I'm ready."

Louis had been thinking seriously about the campaign as early as October 1935. This fact emerged when the resourceful Bess Furman of the Associated Press, to the admiration and dismay of her colleagues, went to the hospital to interview the President's Number One Secretary when most of the newspaper fraternity had ticked him off as a dead man. Louis was dressed for the occasion in gay striped pajamas and, when Miss Furman walked in, immediately began to grumble about being kept in bed.

"You know," he said slyly, "the trouble with them is that they're afraid if I start I can't stop, so they keep my clothes off me to keep me pinned down."

Then he began to speak eagerly about the forthcoming campaign and how he thought it should be conducted. "There are possibilities, you know," he said, "that this campaign may develop into an effort on the part of the Democrats to catch liberal Republicans, and an effort on the part of the Republicans to catch the conservative-thinking Democrats.

"Do you remember the story of the two castles?" he asked. "They were rival strongholds and equally well manned. The lord of one of them had the bright idea to sneak over and take the other by surprise. So he and his troops took a hidden path in the night. To his great surprise and joy he found the gates open and not a darned soldier there! But just then a courier came dashing up to tell him that the other outfit had taken his castle, sneaking over in the night, so they just swapped citadels.

"We'll be swapping, too," he said, "liberals and conservatives. All the old issues have fallen down, prohibition is out of the way, thank Heaven, tariff has simmered down to a compromise, both parties taking about the same attitude. States' rights—the Republicans are trying to steal our clothes on that issue.

"Those Republicans," he laughed, "they are entirely too eager. They are premature. They are declaiming and ululating and boiling over and getting all 'het up' months and months in advance of the season. The actors strut and rave, but the audience is cooler than a cucumber. The Republicans remind me of the boy who buys a giant firecracker three days before the Fourth of July and then, on the night of the third, simply can't stand it any longer and gets up and fires it off.

"Isn't it true that the great mass of people have taken an interest in government such as they never had before?" he asked. "And isn't it far more generally realized that so far as restricting liberties is concerned, the personal liberties of our citizens had been taken away at every turn? If we take away from the strong man the right to hit the little man over the head with a club, is that too great a curtailment of liberty? The Government does not owe a living to any man, but it does owe him a right to make his living. We must assure the little man the right not to be clubbed.

"Go back through the President's speeches," he concluded, "and you will see that he has preached a new doctrine in the relation of a government to its people. Fifty years from now you will find it in the history books. Look it up. I will not be here."

Louis conferred frequently with Jim Farley early in 1936, for Farley, naturally, was also thinking in terms of the campaign since he was Chairman of the Democratic National Committee.

Louis had made up his mind, he told Farley, that the newly formed American Liberty League, staffed with men who had nothing in common with Franklin, in spite of its high-sounding title, would try to undercut Franklin in every way, as they had huge amounts of money and a big publicity campaign. They wouldn't dare try to block Franklin's nomination, he said, but he was afraid that Jouett Shouse, president of the League, would try to shape the Democratic platform to conform with the League's ideas. Shouse might be able to achieve this goal by getting his own men on the Resolutions Committee, since he knew so many Democrats over the country through his former association with the Democratic National Committee. Farley assured Louis that this situation was being watched carefully, but Louis fretted just the same. He had been one of those who listened to the speech Al Smith made at the big white-tie-and-tails dinner the League held in Washington in January, when the former liberal governor blasted Franklin Roosevelt and the very policies he himself once had stood for. His speech only confirmed Louis' low opinion of Smith, whom he had never trusted in anything after Smith broke with Franklin Roosevelt.

Louis' next move was to send for Katherine Blackburn. "Casey," he said, "you went through the 1932 campaign to elect Franklin and helped me set up the Research and Library Division. Get all that material together and go over it for me and we'll draw up a set of plans to use in the campaign this year. Get some new stuff to fit the changing times and put it all before me. Rabbit will give you what you need from my office. I'll go over it all and bring it up to date for this year's campaign."

Louis was impatient that he could not get up and do these things himself, but Miss Blackburn knew what he wanted and produced it. He sat up, spread the material out on his hospital bed, grabbed for a Sweet Caporal and pencil, and had the time of his life going over all the charts and other material she had worked out. When he had finished he lay back on his pillow with a sigh of content, satisfied that he had a complete blueprint of plans to elect Franklin Roosevelt for the second time.

Louis Howe did not live until November and those blueprints were never used, but when it is remembered that FDR carried every state in the Union but two that year, one has the strange feeling that, as expressed by Heywood Broun, "surely Louis Howe was leaning over the gold bar of the Kingdom on election day."

One of the last things Louis planned was a motion picture treatment of the Constitution, to bring home to the citizens the blessings they enjoyed under its banner. The picture was to be used in connection with the 160th anniversary of the signing of the Declaration of Independence and Louis felt it could be made somewhat "New Dealish" in its theme.

"The Liberty Leaguers mouth their platitudes about this great document as though they'd staked out a claim to it," he fumed. He would counteract these platitudes with something more dramatic. But time was running out on him.

And Louis Howe realized it, too, though to Franklin and his family he said nothing. But not long before he died he talked to John Keller, the young man who always read to him in the hospital, about the campaign and how he'd love to be there to run it.

"But you *will* be there," Keller said. "They can't run it without you."

Louis turned and looked at him, as he lay hunched up in bed, his breathing, as always, coming hard.

"No," he said simply, "I will not be there. Franklin is on his own now."

In that simple statement, with its finality and its resignation, Louis Howe summed up for himself and for the world what he had always known in his heart. That he had been more to Franklin Roosevelt than had any other man and that, with his passing, Franklin, at long last, would be going alone.

One of the last visitors to see Louis in the hospital was his good friend, Fannie Hurst. As she walked from the gate to the building, along the path from the hospital came Franklin Roosevelt in his wheel chair. He stopped for a moment to chat.

"Louis is not doing too well," he said gravely. "Try to cheer him up and stay with him as long as you can. I feel that his time is all too short. Talk to him, do what you can to bolster his spirits."

When Miss Hurst was shown into the room, Louis raised himself on one elbow to greet her, and she could still see traces of elation on his face from the President's visit. He asked her to sit down, then began to talk about how wonderful Eleanor and Franklin had always been to him. About Mrs. Roosevelt's daily visits to him in his sickroom at the White House. About the President's constant and devoted attention. Wheezing away, he still was the little king maker as he told her, in retrospective mood, many off-the-record stories of affairs of state, and lived over again his early days and experiences with Franklin and his family.

"In my many talks with Louis Howe," Miss Hurst said, "he seldom touched on his life before he met Franklin Roosevelt. It seemed to have little meaning for him."

He talked until the shadows of evening fell and the nurse came to the door and indicated by a nod of her head that it was time for the visitor to go. As Miss Hurst leaned over to take his hand he looked at her long and intently, and she knew that her face revealed her fear that this would be their last talk together, for she was unable to hide her sadness.

There were a few tragic times during these last days, however, when Louis saw no one for he knew nothing at all. He would lapse into a deep coma, sometimes for hours, and at other times, equally as tragic, his mind would still be functioning, but the wisdom and judgment that had directed that fine mind would be asleep. It was then that he gave the doctors, his friends and the President some anxious times, indeed. He would call the White House, and sometimes people he knew in the various government departments, and ask that things be done which, in the main, were impossible. The President let it be known, however, that no matter what Louis Howe said, nor how unusual his requests during these lapses, he must be treated with the greatest courtesy and respect. And if it became necessary to countermand any of his orders, that was done by the President himself. When these periods were over, Louis' mind was as razor-sharp as ever and he went right ahead as before. Seemingly he never realized these attacks had struck him, for more than once he picked up the phone and called the President and resumed, with clarity and keenness, a conversation he had begun perhaps two days before.

The last time I saw the little boss was when Mrs. Howe took me to see him during his last days. He lay there, a slight, wasted form, his knees drawn up to his stomach, his head resting on his hand. In addition to his Vandyke beard he had also grown a mustache, an odd and unfamiliar object on his furrowed face. He opened his eyes and a smile flickered briefly as I attempted to crack a joke.

"I hardly knew you, Boss," I said, "behind all that foliage."

He chuckled softly, then said weakly, "How have you been?" I knew that he was really a sick man when he did not add "behaving yourself," which was the way he usually greeted me. I told him to hurry back to the office before things got out of hand, but my throat had a choking feeling as I went out of the room. I knew in my heart that I would never see him again.

On the night of April 18, 1936, on a wave of laughter that swept out of the Willard Hotel where Franklin Roosevelt was wowing them with an off-the-record speech at the annual Gridiron Dinner, Louis Howe gently slept away. The President received the news as he entered the White House after the dinner, and went immediately to his study, canceled all engagements for the next week, and ordered that the flag on the White House be lowered to half mast.

And, among the Roosevelt personal papers at Hyde Park, reposes today this touching little memo, addressed to Mrs. Roosevelt: "I suggest the following to be put on Louis' tombstone: 'Devoted friend, adviser and associate of the President.' F.D.R."

At Louis Howe's state funeral in the East Room of the White House, Cabinet members, ambassadors, the great names of the nation were there. Except for the presence of Franklin, Louis Howe would have cared nothing for the awesome grandeur of this ceremony. "A lot of tommyrot," he would have said.

The President, his face pale and grave, sat with bowed head, never taking his eyes from the bronze casket as the solemn funeral service was intoned for the most faithful friend he had ever known. And when Louis Howe was laid to rest the next day at Fall River, while a cold April wind rustled through the trees, Franklin Roosevelt was there to say his last farewell.

Before the funeral, in the East room, those in Louis' office were allowed to go over and see him before the casket was closed. Flowers reached almost to the ceiling and candles shone softly on the polished floor as we tiptoed in and gazed down on him for the last time. His new mustache was neatly trimmed, his tie in place, a single orchid from Rabbit lay in his hand.

But I never like to dwell on the way he looked in his last illness, of his wasted body, the unfamiliar beard, the closed eyes and mute lips. Rather, I like to think of him at his desk, untidy and scowling over his papers, or walking along the rose-bordered path that led to his office in the White House, his head bent in thought, his mind busy with things to do for Franklin.

On such a day I looked out the door of my office and saw the little boss on his way to work. It was summer and it was hot. He wore no coat and his usual loose-fitting, baggy pants were held up by the inevitable suspenders. His high collar smothered his infinitesimal tie. A belt cut him almost in two in the middle. On his head reposed a little white hat—God knows where he got it—something on the order of a sailor's cap, with a roll around the edges. The contrast between his lined and leathery face and the snow-white hat was startling.

I called to Lucile Flanagan. "Look," I said, "will you please look at the little boss!"

She looked up, and burst into laughter. Then suddenly her eyes misted.

"God bless him," she said.

No, his exterior was not impressive, but to us it didn't matter because we knew what was beneath. And "God bless him" was the way we always felt about him.

INDEX

302

About the Author

LELA STILES was born in Cecilia, Kentucky, and started on an early career in journalism as a feature writer and columnist. She has worked for such papers as the Louisville *Courier Journal,* Cincinnati *Enquirer,* and Denver *Post.* In 1928, in search of stories for her columns, she took a job with the Democratic National Committee in New York during the Al Smith campaign, and worked with Louis Howe for the first time. From that time on, until his death in 1936, she was Howe's constant assistant. After Roosevelt's election Miss Stiles went to the White House with Howe and, after his death, stayed on the White House staff during the administrations of Presidents Roosevelt and Truman. She resigned a similar post under President Eisenhower to accept a position with the Democratic National Committee in Washington.